The Trunk Murderess: Winnie Ruth Judd

The Trunk Murderess: Winnie Ruth Judd

The Truth About an American Crime Legend
Revealed at Last

Jana Bommersbach

Poisoned Pen Press

Copyright © 1992, 2003 by Jana Bommersbach

First Trade Paperback Edition 2003

10 9 8 7 6 5 4 3

Library of Congress Catalog Card Number: 2003102489

ISBN: 978-1-59058-064-6   Trade Paperback

Poisoned Pen Press
6962 E. First Ave. Ste. 103
Scottsdale, AZ 85251
www.poisonedpenpress.com
info@poisonedpenpress.com

Printed in the United States of America

To the special people who shaped my life
and taught me that truth must always be the goal:
my grandmothers, Rose Portner Bommersbach
and the late Magdalena Mary Schlener Peterschick;
my grandfather, the late Leo Bommersbach;
and my wonderful parents, Rudy and Willie Bommersbach.

Introduction

October 16, 1931, was a bloody Friday night in Phoenix, Arizona.

In a quiet neighborhood of this quiet small town, nineteen-year-old pharmacy assistant Jack West lay in wait for two hours until his sweetheart came home from a secret date with a new beau. When eighteen-year-old Pearl Mills answered his insistent knocking on her front door, he chased her into her bedroom and stabbed her to death. Then he turned the knife on himself, inflicting a superficial wound.

Just a few blocks away in a simple duplex, twenty-six-year-old medical secretary Winnie Ruth Judd was spending the night, as she often did, with her two best girlfriends. The state of Arizona would charge that on this night, she was there to murder—to eliminate her "competition" for a married man all three women adored. She supposedly waited until her friends were asleep and then shot them to death in their beds. But the world wouldn't know about the deaths of twenty-four-year-old Hedvig "Sammy" Samuelson and thirty-two-year-old Agnes Anne LeRoi for three days. Not until the horrifying discovery that their bodies—Sammy's cut into pieces—had been stuffed into steamer trunks and shipped as Winnie Ruth Judd's baggage on the train to Los Angeles.

Jack West spent two weeks in the headlines and twenty-three months in prison repaying society before he blended into obscurity.

Winnie Ruth Judd became a household name across America as Arizona made her pay with one of the longest sentences this country has ever seen: thirty-eight years, eleven months, and twenty-two days.

This is her story.

Years before the country ever started wondering what happened to Amelia Earhart, it thought it knew everything that happened to Winnie Ruth Judd. Papers from coast to coast covered the gruesome story with the same prominence they gave to the sentencing of "Scarface" Al Capone and the rise of a young man in Germany named Adolf Hitler. Not since Lizzie Borden had a single name conjured up so much horror.

"The Trunk Murderess."

"The Tiger Woman."

"The Blond Butcher."

That's how the press labeled her in the thirties, when she was first convicted and sentenced to hang, and then declared insane and saved from the gallows by only seventy-two hours. That's what they called her in the forties and fifties and sixties as she escaped with great regularity—first to the horror and then the amusement of the country—from the asylum that was her prison. That's what they called her in 1971 when she was finally paroled, a sixty-six-year-old woman judged safe for society. That's what they still call her today, a woman nearing ninety who is trying to live out her life quietly.

An open-and-shut case. So everyone thinks. Just as everyone thinks they know the awful things Winnie Ruth Judd did during the bedtime hours of that Friday night in 1931.

They said she was a cold-blooded killer.

They said she hacked up her best friend.

They said she was insane.

They said she acted alone.

Yet to this day—now sixty years after the fact—questions remain about just how guilty Winnie Ruth Judd was. Or exactly what she was guilty of doing. Or if she could have possibly done the deed by herself. Or if she ever was insane.

Whispers have persisted all these years that the Winnie Ruth Judd case was really Phoenix's dirty secret.

A fresh investigation finds the rumors are true. It finds the story of Winnie Ruth Judd is really two stories: the one that history records, and what really happened.

But it's not just the story of a puzzling crime that still fascinates. Or of extreme punishment. Or, as this investigation reveals, of some of the most bizarre twists ever seen in a murder case. It's the story of a backwater town that would become one of America's major cities. It's the story of a moment in time—with its social taboos, its hysterical conventionality, and its concentrated political power—when this strange story could be orchestrated.

I first heard about Winnie Ruth Judd when I moved to Arizona in 1972 to work for the *Arizona Republic*, the state's largest and then most politically powerful newspaper. Arizona history is filled with colorful characters that are part of American folklore—Geronimo, Cochise, Wyatt Earp, Father Kino, Zane Grey. In a morbid way, Winnie Ruth Judd was one of them. She belonged to that tiny sorority of women judged so heinous society said they deserved the ultimate punishment. In Arizona, she was only the third woman on the roster. The first, Dolores Moore, had been executed in 1865; the second, Eva Dugan, was hanged in 1930—beheaded actually, in a botched execution that led Arizona to abandon the noose for the gas chamber. It wasn't until 1991 that the state added another woman to the exclusive group, sentencing to death Debra Jean Milke for having her four-year-old son killed on his way to see Santa Claus. The picture is similar across the nation: less than thirty-five women sit on death row today.

But the very first story I heard about Winnie Ruth Judd wasn't about her heinous crime, it was about how she was framed.

Sensational cases have a way of taking on their own lore, especially juicy cases that hark back to a time when the social code was so strict women didn't leave the house without wearing gloves and today's thriving cities were just wide spots along bad roads. It's far easier to imagine something sinister was at work than to believe a young beauty would hack up a rival.

Besides, this case was crammed with social taboos: a totally unacceptable love affair, the threat of deadly and incurable syphilis, snide rumors of lesbianism, outright declarations that these were "party girls"—the nice term used in the thirties for prostitutes. Add to that the widespread allegations that one of Phoenix's most prominent businessmen was knee-deep in the crime—allegations widely reported in out-of-state newspapers, excused and dismissed by the press at home. Mix in the mysterious shadow of William Randolph Hearst, the most powerful newspaper publisher for the day, and the intervention of First Lady Eleanor Roosevelt.

The Winnie Ruth Judd case was not just another murder mystery. It was a slice of Arizona and America at a most vulnerable moment: exactly two years after the stock market crash that ushered in the Great Depression, twelve years into the disastrous ban on "spirits" known as Prohibition, and a time when media excess would be forever defined and remain a constant embarrassment for every journalist who came after.

In the twenty years I've lived in Phoenix, I have never heard a single person say Winnie Ruth Judd got what she deserved. Instead, I've heard: "She was covering up for somebody important"; "It was a powerful man who really was responsible, but you know how women were treated in the thirties"; "If the truth of this ever came out, it would ruin a lot of good ole boys." Every time her name came up, it was inevitably coupled with the question "Do you think she really did it?"

How could so many suppositions and questions still remain when the media had for so long presented this as a black-and-white case? Historical articles in Arizona journals recount the grisly crime and leave no doubt about what happened. Newspaper libraries from Los Angeles to New York maintain thick files that painstakingly provide every bloody detail. Modern books on sensational crimes invariably include a chapter on the horrible "trunk murderess." Even the few sympathetic articles hold sympathy for her only because she was a minister's daughter who went wrong.

So why did so many people in Phoenix act as though the city was hiding its dirty linen behind her skirts?

In 1987, I decided to find out. By then I was an investigative reporter and editor for *New Times of Phoenix*, one of the nation's largest weekly newspapers. I'd spent years probing the political scene of Phoenix, so I knew how raw the politics of this town could be. I'd worked on a special project that reinvestigated the 1976 assassination of reporter Don Bolles— blown up at noon in a downtown parking lot by a car bomb—so I knew how the most outrageous of crimes could go unpunished in Arizona. I'd exposed a horrible cover-up of the death of a boy in the county jail, so I knew how "official" records could be distorted. If all these things happened in modern times, with a host of media eyes to inspect them, imagine what sins could have been committed in the old days, when one publisher dominated the communications system of this little town and police reporters were notorious for acting more like cops than journalists.

I'd already read several articles and books about the Winnie Ruth Judd case, and even with their "she's guilty as hell" tone, things didn't fit. This, coupled with all the stories I'd heard, made it obvious that the case needed a new look. If half the rumors were true, I thought, it would make a great story.

A journalist needs a "news peg" to justify a story, and the obvious peg here would be to finally get Winnie Ruth Judd to break her silence and talk. It would prove to be the hardest part of the entire investigation.

From just preliminary information, I knew Winnie Ruth Judd now called herself Marian Lane, was in her early eighties, and lived somewhere in California. If this case was ever to be reinvestigated, it had to be soon, while she and some of the other principals were still alive.

Her last Phoenix attorney, Larry Debus, wasn't at all encouraging at first. He insisted she would never sit for an interview, just as she had refused all requests from journalists since he and famed California attorney Melvin Belli had gotten her paroled in 1971. Besides, she had no love for the media, Debus added. "She just wants to be left alone," he told me. "She's afraid if she talks, they'll come after her again because her parole specified she was never to tell her story."

That's the point, I stressed. She's never talked. She didn't testify at her trial, and by the time she tried to speak, they said she was insane and who'd listen to a crazy lady? She's stayed silent all these years, and if the curiosity about this case is ever to be satisfied, she has to talk. Debus, who owed me a favor for some forgotten reason, agreed to try because her case had always troubled him. "She was the victim of small-town politics and a justice system that wasn't just," he said. "She deserved to be punished for the right crime. She wasn't." It took three years before he was finally able to convince her to meet with me.

By the time I flew to Stockton, California, to visit her in February of 1990, I knew the rumors about her case held far more fact than fancy. I'd already started plowing through the boxes of files kept under seal by the Arizona Archives on the fourth floor of the state capitol building in Phoenix. I'd already interviewed people involved in the case who shed new light on what really happened. I'd already heard again and again an outpouring of sympathy for this woman who had been portrayed to the world as a murdering witch.

But as I sat in the comfortable living room of her apartment, I thought I had to be talking to the wrong person. The bright California morning had become an overcast afternoon before this grand-motherly woman ever mentioned the name of Winnie Ruth Judd. All that day, I was sure somehow lines had gotten crossed and my trip was a waste. This lady before me couldn't be the awful "trunk murderess."

It wouldn't be the last time everything seemed out of kilter as I reinvestigated one of the nation's most enduring and salacious murders. More than once along the way, the most outlandish allegation turned out to be true. I soon found I couldn't discount anything. And I discovered that, like all legends, Winnie Ruth Judd was wrongly credited with many sins. "She went around chopping up people, didn't she?" a Phoenix city council member asked me. "She went on a killing spree, right?" another friend offered, suggesting Phoenix had in Winnie Ruth Judd its own version of Bonnie and Clyde. One after another, middle-aged friends who grew up in Phoenix recounted how their parents had frightened them with threats that if they didn't behave, "Winnie Ruth Judd will get you." They remembered that when she escaped from the asylum—a total of seven times—they'd been kept indoors for fear of encountering the "crazy killer." Children even had a jump rope rhyme about their fear. Most of the words are long forgotten, but somewhere in the ditty, they sang, "...and she'll chop you up to pieces."

In May 1990, I wrote a two-part series on my investigation for *New Times*. The series unleashed a flood of new information. Dozens of calls brought fresh leads and new people who'd been involved, revealing amazing pieces of the story.

Fortunately, Arizona archivists and librarians, recognizing the historical significance of this case, have carefully preserved enormous amounts of information. But they went far behind that, searching on their own for obscure sources that yielded unimagined treasures. Thousands of original documents—from personal letters and telegrams to internal memos and reports—were preserved under seal at the State Archives Office. During my research, archivists uncovered a long-forgotten box of files from a rural county that contained, to our astonishment and joy, a 1932 transcript of Winnie Ruth Judd telling the whole story to the county sheriff. This never-before-seen document provided minute details of both that deadly October night and its gruesome aftermath.

At the Maricopa County Court Records Office, the evidence box on the case still includes the actual bullets that killed Anne LeRoi and Sammy Samuelson. All the original police reports are still there, including interviews with potential witnesses who were ignored as the case went to trial. At the Pinal County Historical Society are records of Winnie Ruth Judd's life at the state prison in Florence, Arizona, and of the insanity hearing that saved her from the gallows.

Even more telling are the vivid memories. I interviewed over one hundred people, including the last living juror at her murder trial and the last living member of the grand jury that sought mercy for her. Neither had ever spoken to a reporter about the case before. I found the last woman to see the victims alive. I found the woman who was run out of Phoenix because she "talked too much" to the police about the prominent men who had befriended Winnie and the victims. I found people who'd heard the most remarkable things over the years and were anxious to talk to someone who would listen and believe. Family members of major players in the case were generous in sharing their memorabilia, including vast amounts of information that never showed up in any official file.

I took much of the information to experts for help. Hugh Ennis, a retired Phoenix police captain with thirty years' experience, helped me review the police reports for what they did and, suspiciously, did not show. One of the nation's most respected forensic experts, Dr. Heinz Karnitschnig, reviewed the autopsy reports and pictures—pictures never seen by the public because they were too gory even for the press of the thirties. A former chief justice of the Arizona Supreme Court, Jack D. H. Hays, reviewed the trial transcripts and appeals.

And I talked at length with Winnie Ruth Judd, getting not only the first interview in twenty years but the most complete interview she has ever given. She graciously insisted I stay with her at her apartment in early 1990. I stayed for three days, and we talked all day and twice long into the night. She shared with me secrets she'd never told anyone, memories she preferred to forget. Later, we had dozens of phone conversations. We talked until she begged that she couldn't bear to talk anymore.

Then there are the people who even now—sixty years later—still won't discuss what they know. Former Arizona governor Rose Mofford, whose fifty-year tenure in Arizona politics has left her extremely well connected, said "no way" would she discuss the case, even though she has known Winnie Ruth Judd since the 1940s. Former U.S. senator Barry Goldwater refused repeated requests for an interview, relaying the message, "You tell that girl to leave that alone."

What could be so awful so long after the fact that it must still be shielded?

That's what this book is all about.

Winnie Ruth Judd speaks at length—finally. So do the official records. So do all the people involved in the case. So do the massive newspaper files from across the country. So do the bits and shreds of evidence pieced together from thousands of sources—some never uncovered before. They are all quoted directly or used to reconstruct dialogue and scenes.

The story they tell shows history was wrong about Winnie Ruth Judd.

Chapter 1
The Last Train to Los Angeles

It was such an ordinary Sunday in Phoenix, Arizona.

October 18, 1931.

The mere 48,000 residents who called Phoenix home were cashing in on a beautiful eighty-nine-degree day. October had always been, always would be, the favorite month in this desert "oasis." It meant the end of the four-month inferno of summer, with its persistent hundred-degree days and, even more intolerable, its three-digit nights. Ahead were eight months of glorious comfort—some of the nicest weather the country offered. The payback, as everyone always thought of it. No matter how bad the summers got—and with the invention of air-conditioning still a decade off, they were god-awful—at least you were assured a beautiful winter. There wouldn't be a single hundred-degree day this October. None at all until the following June.

Most of the country soon would be fending off snow and freezing temperatures, but that kind of winter never came here. And that, everyone knew, was something to sell. For a decade the Chamber of Commerce had been marketing days like this to the country: "Phoenix, where summer winters," one slogan went. It was working. While the rest of the nation would forever remember 1929 as the year the stock market crashed, Phoenix would best remember it as the first year tourism meant $10 million for its economy.

Many were getting rich on tourism, though nobody had gotten rich when Phoenix sold its weather to health seekers, especially those with tuberculosis. "Lungers," they were commonly called. The ill still came, but as one local writer put it, "There is no rule against regaining one's health here, but it is not in the best taste to discuss it." The favorite winter visitors were "the elderly gentlemen who like to play golf all year around and the ladies of all ages who like to applaud them." Most rewarding were the tourists who came for winter and decided to put down roots. Chicago's chewing gum magnate William Wrigley, Jr., had already invested $2 million building the Arizona Biltmore Hotel six miles out of town, a gem that would attract movie stars and kings. Wrigley liked Arizona so much he built the most lavish home in the state on a hill next to the hotel, known to this day as the Wrigley Mansion.

The kind of wealth Wrigley represented was new to Phoenix, but then, everything here was new. Arizona itself was the newest state, becoming the forty-eighth on Valentine's Day in 1912. Phoenix had emerged as the state's largest city only at the end of the First World War, in 1919. Now, barely twelve years later, people were already starting to talk of Phoenix as a "metropolitan city." Not everyone was happy with the changes. One local columnist offered little sympathy for those who weren't keeping up: "The oldtimer, pushed to the wall, looks on rather bewildered and not a little hurt. Once a year, on Pioneer Day, he parades down the street and sees on either side the outside faces watching him— gaping faces from Oklahoma, amused faces from Michigan, smug faces from Kansas, bored faces from New York. No doubt he feels embarrassed."

There's a cockiness in being the biggest, even if you're the biggest in a small pond, and Phoenix was polishing the attitude. As local historian Margaret Finnerty says today,

"Phoenix was just a little farm town then, but people here were convinced it was the center of the earth." It was best to ignore the fact that Phoenix still had more blacksmiths than architects; people preferred to boast that there were already 130 doctors and 172 lawyers.

A total of 48,118 residents doesn't sound like much—especially when Phoenix today has nearly a million and has been the largest city in the Southwest since the 1960s. The best businessmen in 1931 could do was brag that it was "the largest city between El Paso and Los Angeles." They never mentioned that El Paso was over twice its size and L.A. out-populated it by four times. What was important was that if you were going from one of those large cities to the other, both the road and the railroad took you through Phoenix. As the state's largest newspaper proudly gushed, about 2,000 new residents had moved here in just the last twelve months, which "unmistakably shows that Phoenix continues to make that steady progress which has characterized its growth from a frontier community to the capital of a great island empire."

Hyperbole aside, Phoenix was doing quite fine, even if the Great Depression had slowed things down.

Phoenix measured progress by what you could see on the surface: how many miles of paved roads, how many square miles within the city limits, how many "skyscrapers"—defined here as anything over four stories. Eighty-six miles of paved roads sounds skimpy, but it was three and a half times more than this town claimed just a decade earlier. In all, the city covered just over six square miles—neatly compact, with a trolley line that could take you almost anywhere you wanted to go. Those who had bothered to count—and undoubtedly the Chamber officials already had—knew this city could cover a total of 500 square miles if it wanted. Nobody ever dreamed it would get that big in six decades, but it was nice to know there was lots of empty desert out there if millions ever came.

The skyline represented the city's greatest pride. All the great cities had skylines. New York had just built the world's tallest structure, the Empire State Building, at an astonishing one floor per day. Nobody in Phoenix could even imagine a building 102 stories tall, but they were just as excited at their own emerging profile. Already seven buildings of over four stories graced the city, including the sixteen-story Westward Ho Hotel, which would remain the tallest until 1959. There had been parties and hoopla when each new building opened.

But if you asked most residents on this October Sunday in 1931 how they would describe their community, they'd have agreed with Chamber of Commerce promotions that Phoenix was "a city of homes, schools, and churches." It wasn't just a selling point, it was the city's priority list. And nobody apologized that all three were segregated by race.

Life revolved around family and home and a strict moral code that said a man was required to be faithful and productive for his family, a woman was to raise her children to be God-fearing and successful, and the kids were to stay out of trouble. Divorce was the most horrible admission that somebody wasn't following the script and "playing around" was scandalous. "I remember the old-timers telling us boys that if we were ever caught with a woman, we were to tell the judge she was having a fit and we were holding her down—we were told never to admit to anything," says Tom Chauncey, who was an eighteen-year-old boy this Sunday but would go on to become one of the city's most prominent businessmen.

Historians recall the time as being very socially stratified, very conservative, very uptight about propriety. On the surface, everything seemed to fit those requirements. Phoenicians found it both necessary and easy to ignore the ugly underbelly of their town, pretending there was no prostitution when it was a thriving cottage industry, pretending there was no political corruption when it was rampant, pretending men never strayed and women never wandered when it was an infamous tradition.

It wasn't hard to project a public face of strict morals when your scanty town could crow it had eighty churches. And as on all Sundays, they were filled this day. Episcopalians and Presbyterians were the "best" churches in town, counting most of the city's leading families as members. Anglo Catholics went to St. Mary's in the heart of downtown, which one day would be designated a Minor Basilica by Pope John Paul II. Mexican Catholics, tired of being relegated to the basement of St. Mary's, had recently built their own impressive church. There was one synagogue. The black Baptist churches were all in South Phoenix, the poor side of town.

From eight in the morning until eight at night, these places of worship were filled with parishioners thanking the Lord the depression hadn't hit here as hard as elsewhere.

Phoenix would feel the depression less than most American cities, would recover far quicker. The vast majority hadn't invested in the stock market—"speculation" was still considered a dirty word in these conservative parts—and the crash was so inconsequential to this community the local papers gave it little attention. Those with jobs were careful to keep them. There wouldn't be any raises; there'd be lots of pay cuts. But if belts were tightened, you could make out. Some found the imposed austerity good for the soul. As one local observer put it at the time, "Everybody has 'shortened sail,' in good nautical fashion, to meet the gale and as it lessens it won't hurt us to find ourselves wasting less, expecting less, needing less."

By October 1931, Phoenix was learning it couldn't just take care of its own and ignore the economic disaster that had hit so hard almost everywhere else. Many of these churches had already started relief funds and services for the thousands of "transients and hoboes" who came to Phoenix, hoping at the best for work, at the least for relief from winter cold. Some were Arizona copper miners thrown out of work when the state's chief export became worthless. Others came from across the nation. Local public and private welfare funds would be exhausted by 1932 and proud, independent Arizona would be forced to turn to the federal government for help.

But on this Sunday, that thought was still considered "socialistic." Arizona didn't like federal intervention and it didn't like outsiders. Its Community Chest leader had said just the week before that he didn't mind taking care of Phoenicians down on their luck, but "it is not within the province of the Community Chest to attempt to provide for the shiftless and unwanted from other states." Governor George W. P. Hunt would soon issue the same warning as the state's official stance on charity.

For outsiders looking in, Phoenix lived up to its "oasis" PR. Although it sat in the Sonoran desert, it was green and lush. Cottonwood trees were so thick on some streets they almost formed a wall. Elm trees created a green canopy over Central Avenue, the major north-south thoroughfare. Towering palms gave a tropical look. Rose gardens were found everywhere, mostly for personal satisfaction, although the Chamber of Commerce had once launched a campaign to challenge Pasadena, California, as the rose capital of the country. A network of water canals laid out centuries earlier by Indians who mysteriously vanished were still the basic network for delivering water throughout the area. That they doubled as swimming holes for youngsters was an added benefit. There was only one genuine Victorian home in the entire town, but many that were considered grand.

Most Anglo families lived in single-family detached houses with generous front and back yards. The crowded tenements of the East were unknown here; so were the cookie-cutter subdivisions that would one day dominate Phoenix. Stucco over brick was the favorite building material, and most houses would be considered "custom-made" by today's standards. Many had hardwood floors; almost all had fireplaces;

a few even had basements, although that would never catch on. Almost everyone had a front porch, or at least a sleeping porch, where the night breezes provided relief from the summer heat.

On this typical Sunday, families gathered for a large dinner after church and then spent part of the afternoon reading the thickest paper of the week. The *Arizona Republic*, billing itself as "the State's Greatest Newspaper," was reporting that "Scarface" Al Capone had been convicted on five counts of tax evasion in Chicago. As the paper had been noting all week, Thomas Edison's health continued to fail and now doctors in West Orange, New Jersey, were saying the eighty-four-year-old inventor could die at any moment. Wire service photos showed Helen Keller visiting blind World War I veterans in France. President Herbert Hoover was bragging that he practiced the cost cutting he preached: The White House executive offices had spent only $113,694 in the first quarter of the fiscal year, down over $68,000 from the comparable quarter in 1930.

Closer to home, a front-page story reported that nineteen-year-old Jack West had been charged with murder for the slaying of his girlfriend on Friday night when she returned from a date with a new suitor. It was big news because, as Phoenix always prided itself, murder wasn't an ordinary thing here.

West was in the hospital recovering from the flesh wounds he'd inflicted on himself after killing eighteen-year-old Pearl Mills. The paper reported he had already confessed to county attorney Lloyd J. Andrews, admitting he was jealous because Miss Mills had thwarted his offers of marriage and had started dating someone new.

West recounted how he'd stalked her house on Thursday night and confronted her and the new beau when they returned from a dance. Then Friday night, he hid next to her house for two hours, waiting for her to come home. He chased her into her bedroom and fatally stabbed her once in the neck before turning the knife on himself.

West acknowledged he had been drinking heavily, first wood alcohol and then gin—both long outlawed by Prohibition.

The Jack West case was clearly premeditated, first-degree murder, the county attorney was saying, and the boy could expect to spend eight to ten years behind bars.

One of the most popular columns of the Sunday paper— "Little Stories of Phoenix Daily Life"—kept readers informed of who was going where and doing what. This day, the column was filled with reports of local businessmen heading north for the annual hunting season that had begun Friday morning—limit: one deer, one bear, two turkeys. And they learned that yet another bootlegger had been caught illegally "manufacturing intoxicating liquor."

Arizona had no more luck than the rest of the nation in enforcing the twelve-year-old ban on "demon rum," and although it officially supported the restrictions of the Eighteenth Amendment, liquor was both plentiful and common. Few here would mourn the repeal that was just two years away.

The downtown Fox Theater was advertising one of the first movies ever made in Arizona, *The Cisco Kid*, while over at the Orpheum Theater, twenty-four-year-old Barbara Stanwyck was starring in a forgettable movie entitled *Illicit*. The new Nash—"One car today has everything"—was offered by Miller Bros. Motors at from $795 to $2,025. "Correct hat styles for miss and matron" were on sale for $1.94. Men's dress shoes sold for $3.95. A five-pound ham cost 85¢. Cabbage was 4¢ a pound.

But this was no ordinary day for Winnie Ruth McKinnell Judd.

The twenty-six-year-old daughter of a minister didn't spend her morning at the Free Methodist Church, as she had done every Sunday of her life growing up in Darlington, Indiana. Actually, her church attendance had been spotty since she'd left home seven years earlier, the bride of a seemingly successful doctor twenty-two years her senior. But she didn't admit that in the long letters she regularly wrote home to her parents, who were finally thinking of retirement. It wasn't the only omission. Her letters were always cheery, always filled with promise that the setbacks would be overcome.

Dr. William C. Judd hadn't turned out to be the kind of provider his wife and her family had every right to expect. Forget the image of a nice family doctor who settled into a community, supplying his wife with a home and respectability. Dr. Judd instead found work as the doctor for American mining interests in Mexico, working for little money and whatever accommodations the firm provided. He changed locations often, never held any post for long. Eventually even these second-rate jobs disappeared for him. Ruth was skilled at explaining it all away without once letting on to the parents she adored that her husband couldn't keep a position because he was addicted to narcotics. It wasn't hard to make them believe the tough times were just what everyone else was experiencing in this depression. Most of the time, she believed it herself.

For now, Winnie Ruth was taking care of herself. Like so many others, she sought out Phoenix because its dry air promised relief from the tuberculosis that had long made her weak and sick. She arrived from Mexico in 1930, without her husband, without knowing a soul, without the skills to earn much of a living. Her major assets were her looks and her "sweet disposition," as many remembered. She bore a striking resemblance to the Hollywood star of the day Norma Shearer, and given other circumstances, could have taken on the look of glamour. But she never earned enough to acquire that look. Her only coat had shrunk in a cleaning, so she wore it around her shoulders like a cape. The one luxury she allowed herself was to have her long hair cut into the bob that was so fashionable.

Fortunately, she had found a six-day-a-week job at Phoenix's first private medical clinic, the Grunow Clinic. It paid seventy-five dollars a month. Sunday was her one day off, but it was not unusual for her to spend at least part of the day working at home. She was a medical secretary primarily responsible for typing up reports on exams for the doctors. She'd fibbed when she claimed to be proficient in typing and had quickly enrolled in a night class to develop the skill. The doctors had been patient with her, but she knew she had to get her accuracy and speed up to keep the job she so desperately needed. The pay was actually quite good for an unskilled woman those days. If she was careful, it paid her rent and food and left a little to slip her husband. She just had to keep going until he landed a job. He had been in California the last couple of months pursuing some promising prospects. Any day now…

Most Sundays found her doing the kind of things all working women did on their day off—washing clothes, cleaning her small apartment on Brill Street. The Sundays she enjoyed most included dinner with her best friends, Anne LeRoi and "Sammy" Samuelson, who lived a trolley ride away. They would pool their resources for something special— chicken was a favorite—and Anne would cook. Then they'd huddle around the radio, letting themselves be scared by the Sherlock Holmes mysteries that were such a favorite throughout the country.

But Winnie Ruth Judd did none of those things this Sunday. This day, she was busy packing—had been up all night packing. And now she had to find help. She went to her nice landlords, who lived across the alley from her apartment.

Violet Grimm knew something was wrong the minute she laid eyes on her tenant. "Ruthie," as almost everyone called Winifred Ruth Judd, looked tired. She seemed pre-occupied and nervous. Her hand was bandaged with a towel. "I burned it ironing," Ruth explained. Mrs. Grimm fussed at her that it should be covered with a salve and bandaged properly. Ruth insisted it was all right the way it was. But could she use the phone? And could Mr. Grimm help her with her luggage?

Howard Grimm was reading his Sunday paper when his wife interrupted to say she'd volunteered him and their son for an errand. Mrs. Judd was taking the night train to Los Angeles to see her husband, and she needed help carting her trunks. She'd even offered a dollar and a half to pay the men for their trouble.

As Grimm would later testify, he didn't mind lending a hand because he felt kindly toward the young beauty who rented one of the apartments he'd designed and built a couple years earlier. She was such a nice young woman. She was clean, she didn't have loud parties, she paid her rent—sometimes a little at a time, but all forty-five dollars was always paid in full by month's end. Mrs. Judd had even gotten friendly with his children, especially thirteen-year-old Rita. When the girl was having trouble with her Spanish classes, Mrs. Judd had helped, surprisingly conversant in the language. And when the girl balked at her piano lessons, Mrs. Judd had taught her the simple "Black Hawk Waltz" to keep her interested.

Grimm really knew just a little about Mrs. Judd, but everything he knew convinced him she could use any help. He hadn't been impressed with Dr. Judd, who had spent a few months with his wife in Phoenix before going off again to look for work. Grimm never could understand what this pretty young woman saw in the plain, older man. He suspected the good doctor liked either his booze or his dope too much, but that really wasn't his concern. Ruthie had no such vices, as far as he could tell. Her biggest problem, Grimm thought, was being in the unenviable position of a woman on her own in the roughest of economic times. Even when his contracting business had ground to a halt, Grimm was still able to make enough so his Violet didn't have to work. It was a measure of a good man to provide for his family. Dr. Judd didn't measure up.

Besides, there was a practical reason for offering Mrs. Judd a helping hand. She was such a slip of a thing—carrying just 110 pounds on her five-foot-five-inch frame—that Grimm thought it was obvious she'd need assistance moving anything heavy and bulky.

Like everyone else who encountered Winnie Ruth Judd that day—like everyone who'd seen her since Friday night—Howard and Violet Grimm would never forget the details.

As Violet Grimm would later tell reporters, Ruth Judd came to her house twice that Sunday to use the phone. Mrs. Grimm was busy clearing off the Sunday dishes and didn't hear the local number Ruth Judd gave the operator. But she did hear the young woman asking someone to lend her five dollars.

Grimm would remember that instead of her usual cheery, pleasant self, Mrs. Judd seemed nervous and preoccupied. He'd testify that he tried to show her the drawings he'd just completed for a new building, but she paid so little attention he gave up.

The train to Los Angeles was leaving at eight p.m. so Grimm planned to collect Mrs. Judd and her luggage around six-thirty. But when he told his son, Kenneth, of the plan, he found it wouldn't work. Kenneth had a youth meeting at church beginning at five p.m. The teenager ran across the alley to inquire if Mrs. Judd could be ready earlier. She said she could.

Ruth Judd was dressed in a simple brown suit and a plain hat when the men arrived; she carried a black coat over her arm. She pointed them toward the bedroom, where they found two trunks. Grimm recalled grunting as he tried to lift the big black trunk. Mrs. Judd apologized for its weight, explaining that it contained her husband's medical books and he'd need them in California if he got the job that looked so promising. As Grimm testified, it took the strength of both men to carry the trunk to their touring car outside. They tied it to the running board on the passenger side. Kenneth managed the smaller trunk himself, wedging it between the front and back seats. Winnie Ruth carried out a battered suitcase and a hatbox. She sat in the front seat as Grimm drove. Kenneth sat in the back.

It took only a few minutes to drive the fifteen blocks to the new block-long depot at Fourth Avenue and Jackson. As Ruth got out of the car, she fished in her purse for the promised payment. She handed Grimm a dollar bill, but apologized that she didn't have the right change to give him the fifty cents. "I'll have to get change to pay you the rest," she told him, as she hurried into the depot to buy her ticket. But she quickly returned. "Would it be all right if I paid you when I get back on Wednesday or Thursday?" she asked. "I'm short of funds and have to ask you for the dollar back." Mr. Grimm said that would be fine.

Beverley Stallings was working the 3:30 to 11:30 p.m. shift in the baggage room of Union Station when the Grimms' car pulled up in front. Stallings and Kenneth unlashed the large packer trunk. Kenneth managed the smaller steam trunk alone while Stallings started the paperwork. The larger trunk measured 40 by 24 by 36 and weighed 235 pounds. The smaller measured 15 by 18 by 36 and weighed 90 pounds. The trunks were 175 pounds overweight for standard luggage. His weight chart showed the owner would have to pay $4.48 extra. Stallings gave the carbon-copied paperwork to fellow baggageman Avis Boutchee. Boutchee collected the extra charges from the young woman who'd arrived with the trunks and asked for her signature; he noticed that her left hand was completely covered with a bandage. He attached the top copy of each claim check to its trunk and gave her the yellow copy. Only later did he look to see what name she signed. It was B. J. McKinnell. He had no way of knowing that was the name of Winnie Ruth Judd's younger brother.

Head porter John Washington noticed the attractive woman sitting alone in the station when he arrived for work at five p.m. that day. It seemed strange someone would be there so early. The Tucson train wasn't due until seven-thirty and the Los Angeles train didn't arrive until nearly eight. The depot was almost empty, so every now and then he found his eyes returning to the woman. As he would later testify, she seemed so nervous, so "suspicious-looking." Occasionally she'd get up and walk around, but he remembered she always kept her carry-on luggage in sight. The hatbox looked pretty new, Washington thought, but the brown leather suitcase had certainly seen better days. Washington even approached the woman once, asking if she was going to Tucson. She told him she was waiting for the L.A. train. He would testify he thought her voice was trembling.

By the time the *Golden State Limited* pulled into the station at 7:55, Beverley Stallings had already taken his half-hour supper break. He helped the baggage boys load the trunks—along with a few other pieces of luggage from the other local passenger—onto the train. As always, Stallings was in a hurry because the train stopped here for just fifteen minutes. But even in his haste, he noticed something leaking from the big packer trunk. He thought it smelled like medicine. Meanwhile, porter Washington made a point of helping the nervous young woman onto the train with her carry-on pieces. The seat she'd bought was in the rear of the chair car, third from the right. She'd be sitting up all night, Washington thought, but then he hadn't expected she could afford a berth. Nor did he expect much of a tip.

"Will you take pennies?" she asked timidly as she held out five of them, along with some other coins. "Yes ma'am," he told her, tipping his hat as he left.

H. J. Mapes was the baggageman on the train that night, managing the duties between El Paso and Los Angeles. He'd handled thousands of trunks and suitcases in his twenty-three years with Southern Pacific, but he knew right away something was wrong with the large black trunk the Phoenix crew hoisted into his baggage car. At first he was most aware of the offensive odor. But after the train got underway, he had time to inspect. He was sure it was leaking blood. The odor seemed to grow as the train crossed the Arizona desert. And the leaking never stopped.

As soon as he unloaded his car at the station in Los Angeles the next morning around 7:45, he notified district baggage agent Arthur V. Anderson that they had a problem. "I think we've got some contraband deer out here," Mapes reported.

Anderson immediately went out on the platform, where the trunks now sat on a flatbed truck. Even in the open air, he could smell the horrible odor from twelve feet away. As he got closer, he saw what looked like blood running down the sides of the trunk. He thought Mapes was probably right. People were always trying to smuggle deer meat on the train to California. Venison was a special treat. But health officials had impressed on railroad personnel that it had to stop. Anderson tagged both trunks with a pink hold slip, signifying the luggage wasn't to be released without the approval of the front office.

Nobody noticed the young woman in the brown suit who got off the train that morning except Stella Conley, the maid in the ladies' room. The woman was carrying a hatbox and had a porter in tow carting a dilapidated brown suitcase with strap handles. They passed the storage lockers along the wall and walked directly to the ladies' room. Mrs. Conley had to step aside to let them pass. The woman instructed the porter to put the suitcase behind the rest room door, against a wall. Then she balanced her hatbox on top of it. She nodded to Stella Conley as she left the rest room and sat down on a settee in the large waiting room that dominated the depot.

Mrs. Conley didn't usually let people clutter up her rest room with their luggage. That's what the pay lockers were for. But the woman was sitting there impatiently, obviously waiting for someone, so she thought she'd let it pass.

But an hour later, when the *Sunset Limited* was called, Stella Conley walked over to the woman to see if she was taking that train. "No, I'm waiting," the woman answered, not offering any more. Mrs. Conley tried again when the 10 a.m. train was called. "Lady, are you taking this train?" she asked, and again got the same response. The maid noticed that the woman's left hand was covered with a bandage. "What happened to your hand?" she inquired. "I burned it," the woman said.

"Will those bags be all right behind the door?" the woman finally asked, and Stella Conley thought it was about time. "Can't you check them?" the maid said, a little sharply. "I haven't got the money to check them," the woman admitted. She told Mrs. Conley she was waiting for her brother, who was a junior at the University of Southern California. She'd sent him a message to meet her, but she wasn't sure he'd gotten it before he went to his morning classes. If he didn't come soon, she'd have to go out to the school to get him, and she only had enough money for a streetcar ride.

"Well, in that case, I'll try to keep an eye on the bags," Mrs. Conley allowed. She'd already guessed the woman couldn't have much. People who did never carried tattered luggage like the suitcase behind her door.

A few minutes later, the woman got up to leave. "I'm going to go get my brother, but in case he shows up here, he's tall and has reddish-blond hair," she informed Mrs. Conley. The maid didn't think that was much of a description; too many young college men could answer to it. "Who will your brother be looking for?" she asked. The woman spelled out her name: "Mrs. J-U-D-D."

"If your brother comes, shall I let him have the bags?" the maid asked.

"No, don't let anyone have the bags until I come back," Mrs. Judd instructed. The maid insisted, "When you return, please come tell me so I know the right person got the bags." Mrs. Judd promised. After she left, Mrs. Conley tried to move the suitcase farther out of the way to be sure no one filched it. It was so heavy she couldn't lift it. "No one will bother that," she thought.

By the time Stella Conley's shift was up at 3 p.m. neither Mrs. Judd nor her college brother had come to claim the bags behind the bathroom door.

George Brooker was the delivery clerk that day at L.A.'s Central Station. As he'd done every workday for the last four years, he exchanged claim checks for baggage and filled out the required paperwork. When he went to take down the numbers on the two trunks on the flatbed, he noticed an awful smell. Some kind of fluid was leaking out. There was already a spot on the concrete about the size of a dinner plate. He noted that both trunks were pink-tagged.

About noon, Brooker watched as a Ford roadster drove up and backed toward the loading dock. He didn't recognize the attractive woman who got out of the car, but the tall young man with her looked familiar. Brooker thought he might be one of the college boys who hired on temporarily over the Christmas holidays to help with the crunch of extra mail and luggage. Hours later, he'd finally put a name with the face. The college kid was Burton McKinnell—the only sibling of Winnie Ruth Judd.

The young man handed Brooker two claim tickets. Brooker immediately took them into the front office.

Baggage agent Anderson came out to personally handle the situation. "Who does this baggage belong to?" he asked.

"To me," the young woman answered.

"What's inside the trunks?"

"Just personal things, clothing."

"It must be something else," he insisted. "It wouldn't be a bottle of broken booze, I don't suppose?" he suggested with a laugh. The woman assured him it wasn't.

Anderson led the woman and her companion toward the flatbed. They were about four feet away when he asked if they couldn't smell the nauseating odor. The woman acted as though there was nothing wrong, claiming she couldn't smell a thing. Her young companion looked horrified. He could see the stain on the concrete from the leaking fluid; noticed that flies were swarming around the trunks. "Well, I can smell it," he blurted out. Anderson suggested the woman move closer to the trunks. When she was right up next to them, she admitted she did smell something.

"What could be in those trunks to cause that stink?" Anderson asked rather sharply.

"Well, I don't know," the woman calmly answered. "I can't imagine what it is."

Anderson pointed out the liquid that was still dripping. The woman turned to her companion. "What do you suppose that is?" she asked him, and the young man just stared at her. Anderson noticed nothing in the woman's behavior to make him believe she was nervous or uncomfortable. In fact, she seemed as perplexed as he was. Her young companion seemed totally befuddled by the entire scene.

"Please open the trunks, ma'am," Anderson instructed. As he would later testify, "I told her that whatever was leaking would undoubtedly damage the other contents. I didn't want her to later file a claim against the railroad for what was ruined, so we should determine the extent of the problem now."

The woman seemed hesitant and her companion jumped in with an alternative: "It might cause some embarrassment to open the trunks here. Why not come out to the house and examine the contents there?" Anderson refused. The woman opened her purse and fumbled around inside with her one good hand—Anderson now noticed that the other was bandaged—as though looking for the keys to unlock the trunks.

"My husband has the keys," she told him, and Anderson took it for a lie right away. The woman said she'd have to telephone her husband to bring the keys to the station. Anderson offered the use of his office phone. She went inside and thumbed through the L.A. phone book, claiming she didn't remember her husband's number and couldn't find it listed. "I'll have to go get my husband and bring him down here," she informed Anderson. The boy with her still looked as if he couldn't figure out what was going on, the baggage agent thought. He watched as the woman and the young man calmly walked to the car and drove away.

They never returned.

At 4:30 that afternoon, Anderson called the Los Angeles Police Department to report two suspicious trunks.

Detective Frank Ryan's normal 8 to 5 shift was nearly over when the call came in, and he hoped he could head straight home after a quick stop at the depot. He had no idea he was in for a long night. After ten years with the L.A.P.D., Lieutenant Ryan knew what blood looked like and how it smelled, and he was sure the sticky liquid oozing out of the trunk was blood. Anderson brought him a sack of passkeys and Ryan picked the lock of the big black trunk.

On the top was a piece of rug. He moved it aside and found a number of books and papers. Beneath them were pieces of women's clothing, some smeared with blood. They were piled on top of a homemade quilt. He lifted a corner of the quilt.

He was looking at the head of a woman.

As he instinctively jerked his hand away, the quilt was pulled aside. Crammed into the trunk was a dark-haired woman wearing pink pajamas. She was on her side, her head in one corner and her knees drawn up.

Lieutenant Ryan recoiled so violently the lid slammed shut with a thud. He rushed into the depot office and called precinct headquarters, requesting fingerprint men and the guys from the morgue.

As he waited for the backup, Ryan opened the smaller trunk. Several sheets of paper lay on the top, some stained with blood. A light cotton blanket was stuffed around the contents. Underneath were two bundles wrapped in women's clothing. He unwrapped the first one.

It contained a human foot and a leg from the knee down. He opened the second.

Inside was the torso of a woman from the head to the navel.

Ryan decided he'd seen enough and had better wait for the lab men. But he already knew something that made him sick.

The pieces in this trunk didn't add up to a whole body.

The trunks were put in an ambulance and taken to the morgue.

There was nobody around to alert railroad officials or the L.A.P.D. that two more bags were still stashed behind the door of the ladies' room.

Winnie Ruth Judd Speaks
—From a letter to her attorney, 1952

I was born on January 29, 1905 during a blizzard in a parsonage at Oxford, Indiana, where my father was a minister. My mother and father both had been school teachers. My mother was thirty-eight years of age when she married and I was the first of two children. Because of her age, quick medical care had to be given her, and I chilled and contracted pneumonia at birth. At age four, my weakened lungs were suspectable, and I contracted tuberculosis, which has sapped my vitality all through life. Some years I might feel fine and be doing well in school, and the next year I might run a low temperature and be so toxic from my condition that it made me feel stupid—and hindered my learning.

My brother was 19 months younger than me and we were very affectionate towards each other. My father was one of the most kindly and Godly souls. He was a Free Methodist minister and a great man in my heart and also in the heart of thousands of his parishoners. He believed that everyone had some good in him. He addressed everyone as "My good man," "my good woman." He preached love, not hell fire, from his pulpit. The world would seem brighter just to talk to him. He was an old-fashioned circuit rider.

My mother was a kindly Christian woman—a bit timid—but a hard-working person, a tidy housekeeper and always willing to make a sacrifice for her family and others who needed her services in sickness.

I usually went with my father when he filled the pulpit at his country churches. He taught me that the most important thing in life, besides believing in God, was to like people and have them to like me. This charming characteristic of his grew up with me. Only recently, a news reporter described my personality as hypnotic, because of my many friends. This is preposterous. I like everybody and want them to like me. This trait is a natural part of my personality.

When I attended school I did not fit in with modern school activities. I had never attended a circus, carnival, ball game, movie, skating rink or bowling alley; nor was I allowed to wear jewelry. My mother did not think these things were wrong, but our church did not approve of it.

We lived a simple life in a comfortable home, but I did have a repressed childhood and later a very repressed marriage.

Chapter 2
They Were the Best of Friends

Anne LeRoi was already in her pink cotton pajamas when Winnie Ruth Judd arrived.

It was about 9:30 p.m. on Friday, October 16, 1931. Anne had been wearing the pajamas all evening, during dinner and visiting and bridge. She often did for an "at home" night with the girls.

Her roommate, Hedvig "Sammy" Samuelson, was in bed. Sammy spent most of her time there, too sick and weak from TB to get around much. Her entire wardrobe, it seemed, was composed of various types of silk pajamas; they complimented her slim figure. She preferred a lounging style that was appropriate even with guests.

Everyone called them "the girls," a title they didn't mind, even though Anne was thirty-two years old and Sammy was twenty-four. In fact, they found it endearing.

Ruth let herself in the back door off the kitchen, as she always did. She knew this duplex unit on North Second Street as well as she knew the apartment she rented a few blocks away. She knew the back door would be unlocked, because it was never latched, just as she knew the front door was used only by "company." She wasn't company. She was a former roommate and still best friend. She called out a hello as she walked into the kitchen.

It seemed so natural that the three young women had become friends. All were newcomers to this small desert town. All were away from familiar surroundings and family: Anne had grown up in Oregon, Sammy in North Dakota, Ruth in Indiana. The desert, with its nonexistent winters and its exotic vegetation, seemed a strange place to these women who were all accustomed to four distinct seasons and were convinced the green they remembered wasn't duplicated here.

The bond between Anne and Sammy was already strong by the time they arrived in Phoenix together in February 1931. They'd met in Alaska, where Anne had worked as a nurse and Sammy as a teacher. The wet, cold climate of the Alaskan Territory had been disastrous for Sammy's TB; they came to Phoenix for the same reason Ruth had come a year earlier, hoping the dry desert air would give relief. Ruth had found the weather here allowed her to hold down a job and lead a basically normal life. Sammy wasn't so lucky. She would never be well enough to either work for pay or do much housework.

They were all young women on their own, sharing the strains of making it without a man in a day when having a good male provider was not only a female badge of honor but a necessity. Anne was twice divorced, Sammy had never married, and Ruth had a never-home, never-reliable husband. Both Ruth and Anne knew the responsibility of being the only breadwinner in their households, knew the poverty of women working for poor wages. Sammy had saved about $400 before she became too ill to work and lived on that, as well as Anne's generosity.

By the time the girls arrived in town, Ruth was already working as a medical secretary at the Grunow Clinic. Anne hired on immediately as the X-ray technician. She also worked six days a week, earning $125 a month—$50 more than Ruth. They started visiting during coffee breaks, going to lunch together, sharing their evenings. Ruth invited Anne and Sammy to her apartment for dinner; they invited her back. Soon they even became neighbors.

Anne and Sammy lived in a cozy duplex on the outskirts of town, just a few blocks off the trolley line. When the other half of the duplex became available in May 1931, Ruth moved in. The women became inseparable.

Ruth's husband, William Judd, became part of the scene, off and on, for several months. By all accounts, they made a friendly foursome, often having dinner together and then entertaining themselves with cards or the radio. Dr. Judd also had much in common with the girls. He and Anne had both interned at Good Samaritan Hospital in Portland, Oregon; Anne's parents lived on a farm near the Judd family's Oregon farm. Dr. Judd had two sisters who were teachers, like Sammy, and Sammy's younger brother was a doctor.

But neither Ruth nor the girls had seen Dr. Judd for the last two months as he looked for work in Los Angeles.

For all three women, this year had been an ordeal. Their hopes for a "new life" in Phoenix were constantly being dashed.

Ruth's dream that she and her husband could settle down here was thwarted by his inability to control his addiction and hold a job. Sammy wasn't making the kind of improvement the desert climate had promised. And worst of all, Anne found she, too, had contracted tuberculosis. By June, she was too sick to work and wanted to go home to her family in Portland for a few weeks' rest. But she feared she would lose her job, and didn't have the money to make the trip. Ruth pleaded with the doctors at the clinic to hold open Anne's job and give her traveling money. One of the doctors wrote out a check for a hundred dollars.

Anne's departure forced Sammy into a sanatorium, where she could get the daily care she needed. Ruth moved into the girls' half of the duplex. It was a little larger and had nicer furniture. By July, things seemed to be looking up. Anne was reporting that her health had improved so much she could return to Phoenix and her job. In preparation for her arrival, Ruth moved Sammy back into the duplex, taking over Anne's normal caretaker responsibilities until the three women were reunited in August. While waiting for Anne to get back, Ruth wrote her a friendly letter: "Sammy and I are together every day waiting for our little Anne to return to the fold. Sure, I think the three of us can get along fine until I go to the doctor [meaning until she rejoined her husband]. We talk a lot about our Anne and how she is going to behave herself when she gets back."

After Anne returned in August, the three new roommates tried to adjust to living in a one-bedroom apartment. Not only were the quarters cramped, but the women discovered they had different viewpoints on housekeeping: Anne was fastidious, Ruth careless. As one mutual friend was to recall, that domestic difference led to "petty arguments."

But housekeeping was the least of their worries as Anne tried to resume her career. At first it seemed that she wasn't going to get her job back. One doctor in particular at the clinic wasn't fond of Anne, and during her absence, he had taught a young nurse how to run the X-ray machine. As far as he was concerned, they didn't need Anne and her specialized skills anymore. Ruth would later recount how she begged the doctors to reinstate her friend. Finally, to everyone's relief, Anne was told to come back to work.

The roommates lasted only two months. In early October, Ruth moved into her own one-bedroom apartment on Brill Street. It was only a couple of blocks away from the Grunow Clinic, allowing her to walk to work rather than pay the daily fare for the ten-minute trolley ride from the duplex.

This change of residence would come back to haunt Ruth Judd.

Everyone would always remember all three women as cheerful, considerate, and pleasant. And they'd remember one other significant fact. All were beautiful.

At five feet five and 110 pounds, Ruth was the smallest. She had large blue eyes and a small bow mouth, high cheekbones and graceful, arching brows. When she smiled, her eyes lit up. Her light hair was sometimes blond, sometimes hennaed for a reddish glow, and she kept it short, in the bobbed style of the day. Although she never owned much finery, it wasn't hard to imagine her draped in furs and satin.

Sammy would have come in second in the beauty department but first on the personality scale. In spite of her illness, she had not lost her striking looks. At five feet seven inches, she was the tallest, seeming even taller because she weighed only 120 pounds. She had blue eyes and light auburn hair that she wore cropped short. News reports would describe her as "a very feminine, clinging-vine type." Maybe because she'd once been a teacher, maybe because she had little else to do every day, she kept up on the news and read voraciously. She also wrote her family often and maintained a daily diary.

It was common for Sammy to hold court when the girls entertained. And they loved to entertain. Since Sammy couldn't go out much, entertainment meant parties at their duplex. Ruth was often there, even after she moved out to her own apartment. So were other girlfriends Anne had made in town. And so were a host of gentlemen: doctors from the clinic, businessmen from both Phoenix and out of town. A favorite guest was a tall, handsome, broad-shouldered Irishman named Jack Halloran whom they'd met through Ruth. "Happy Jack," as some in the press would later call him, would arrive, not always announced, with food and booze—hang Prohibition, everyone knew it was a joke. He'd often bring his friends, other successful businessmen like him who also had families at home but wanted a night out with attractive young women. Sometimes the men brought presents.

As Sammy had written just that morning to her sister, "Yesterday we received the loveliest surprise. You know we had to give up our Philco radio when we both became ill last spring. Well, a man that we had only met the day before had a lovely Jackson Bell radio that they had been using for demonstrations, came over and presented us with this lovely $50 radio. It has eight tubes and the most wonderful tone I've ever heard. Last night I got Chicago, Cincinnati, Texas, San Fran., L.A., Mexico and Denver. Mr. Ryan is from El Paso, Texas, and we very likely won't see him again so there's no strings attached. Wasn't that a lovely thing to do. Of course, he is a man of means, but even at that, it was a lovely surprise."

Anne would have been the runner-up in this beauty contest, but that didn't mean she couldn't turn a head. She was the heftiest, at 145 pounds, but carried it well on her five-foot-six-inch frame. Although friends would recall her as a "brunette beauty," newspapers would also describe her as "mannish." She was not only the oldest but the one most capable of caring for herself. A smart woman, she realized that anyone could become a nurse but few had yet mastered the specialized training for the new diagnostic wonder of medicine: being an X-ray technician meant job security and a little better pay than the ordinary nursing crew received.

As the breadwinner in the household, Anne pretty well decided how things were done. Even if she hadn't shouldered that role, few would have questioned her authority to rule the roost. She wasn't shy about expressing exactly what she thought, and probably would have been a hit on a debate team. Her greatest worry was Sammy. She spoke constantly about her friend's health problems and fretted that the desert climate hadn't yet done much to give Sammy back her strength. At least a couple of times a week, Anne would pick up some little trinket at the drugstore she thought Sammy would like.

She showed this gentleness almost exclusively to Sammy. To all others, she was the woman in charge. If anyone was the camp director of these three friends, it was Anne.

With their good looks and wit and charm, one would have expected all of them to find good husbands and join the ranks of housewives. That's certainly how Winnie Ruth McKinnell herself had expected to end up.

She was an eighteen-year-old assistant in an Indiana psychiatric hospital in 1923 when she was smitten by the forty-one-year-old doctor who headed one of the units. They would purposely run into each other in the cafeteria and share an iced watermelon, she remembered years later. Dr. William C. Judd finally asked her out for dinner that August. She very much wanted to go, but the same night, she was scheduled to deliver a speech about missionary work at her father's church. She could go to dinner afterward, she suggested, if the doctor would accompany her to church first. He agreed. She'd later recount with gleeful embarrassment how she looked "right from the country" that evening because she wore everything new she owned; a black satin dress, tan shoes, a lavender hat. They dated exclusively and constantly until her father married them in his Free Methodist Church on April 18, 1924.

Ruth left home for the first time that same night on a honeymoon trip that would mark her first train ride, her first sight of New Orleans, her first stay in a hotel, her first visit to Mexico. She still recalls it with the gentleness reserved for only the sweetest of memories.

Dr. Judd took his bride to Vanegas, Mexico, where he'd landed a job as doctor for the crew at an American-owned silver mine. As Ruth wrote her family en route, "We are eating in the queerest Mexican restaurants. I'm trying to learn Spanish. The Mexicans are very nice and polite.... Doctor and I are going to go broke if we don't quit meeting poor, blind and crippled beggars. I hate to look at the poor things. We have given them a few cents apiece...I am well and happy."

The three years in Mexico would turn out to be the only happiness the couple ever shared. Ruth even realized her greatest dream. She became pregnant. But the weather in that section of Mexico had flared her tuberculosis. Dr. Judd knew she was too weak to carry and deliver a child. As he'd expected, she lost the baby. A second pregnancy a year later ended the same way.

By the end of 1927, Ruth was so sick her husband sent her to a sanatorium in LaVina, California, hoping the treatments would check her TB. She got well enough in a few months to rejoin him at his new post in Dolores, Mexico. But that climate didn't agree with her either, and in late 1928, she went back to the States for more treatment. She tried Mexico once more, joining her husband in 1929 at yet another job, with the St. Lois Mining Company in Tyoltita, north and east of Mazatlán. That climate, however, proved still worse for her illness, and by early 1930, she was hoping to be restored to health in Phoenix. Dr. Judd promised to join her, assuring her he could find a job in a town so in need of doctors. But he never did.

Ruth Judd had a ready excuse for her husband's addiction: He'd been given an overdose of morphine for a wound while serving in the Army during the First World War. Whether that story was true is not known, but by the time she came to Phoenix in June of 1930, Ruth Judd was well aware her promising doctor husband had a drug problem that constantly threatened their livelihood.

In Phoenix, she first found work with the prominent Leigh Ford family, caring for the invalid wife and watching the children. It was room and board and eighty dollars a month. Ruth was just the kind of clean, gentle, churchgoing, no-trouble young woman the Fords needed, they would later explain. She met their friends and neighbors, and it was there she got to know the Jack Halloran family, who lived next door.

Halloran was forty-four years old and one of the town's success stories. Someone would later describe him as "about as prominent a man as you'd find in Phoenix in those days." When anyone in Phoenix named the movers and shakers, Jack Halloran's name was on the list. He and his wife and three children lived in the silk-stocking section of town. If you wanted a political favor, Jack Halloran knew who to ask. People remember him as a take-charge kind of guy whose laugh could fill a room.

The relationship he and Ruth Judd developed would be the most catastrophic either of them ever had.

The promise of a $125-a-week job lured Ruth Judd away from the Ford family. But she didn't know the job was patronage. On the day of the next election, the new guy fired her. Luckily, she was soon able to hire on at the new Grunow Clinic, founded by a Chicago millionaire who wintered in Phoenix. He built it in honor of his daughter, who died before her illness could be properly diagnosed.

Ruth was as situated as she'd ever be by the time her husband finally joined her in January 1931. By then he'd lost another job in Mexico and had checked himself into a veterans hospital for treatment of his addiction. He'd spent five months in the hospital immediately before coming to Phoenix. But he never stayed with Ruth long. Striking out at a job in Phoenix, he tried other spots in Arizona, then Mexico again, but still found nothing. Prospects in California—the last real hope for the couple—dimmed each day.

Although to this day Winnie Ruth Judd talks at length about her love for her husband, letters written in 1931 show she wasn't wearing any rose-colored glasses about their situation. She confided the most to her brother, Burton McKinnell, in Los Angeles. On August 8, she wrote him a long letter about her husband's job search, admitting, "Doctor and I have a scrap every few days." She made it clear she wasn't making a move until she was sure he was firmly situated: "I will stay here until he makes enough to take care of me. I don't want to give up my job and then be broke again. I am all alone. I wish that mama could come out now. I have a little house and am all alone. Why don't you come over next weekend? Hike over and visit me. We can talk over how and when we can get mama out here."

At this point, Ruth apparently didn't know how much her parents knew about her troubles. While her letters to them had always remained upbeat—minimizing the difficulties and putting a happy face on her husband's prospects—Burton had been more honest. He had apparently relayed to their parents what was really going on, and the elder McKinnells were obviously worried. When the police later searched his apartment, they found a September 28 letter to Burton from his parents. It read in part: "Now tell us why Ruth sent for you. All about it. We will write and ask her too…Is Doctor Judd at [his sister's] yet? Or at Ruth's. You see by her letter he was to see you Sunday, the twentieth. What for, Burton? Is he trying to give Ruth trouble? Has he left her?"

But to her husband, Ruth wrote letters about her undying love and continually begged him to return to Phoenix—job or not. As she had just written him, "It is much cooler here now. Come home soon. It isn't a pretty home, doctor, but again, we ain't got barrels of money, maybe we are all ragged and funny, but we will travel along, singing a song 'Side by Side,' because we love each other."

Anne LeRoi hadn't had much better luck. She'd married first in 1925 while still in nurse's training in Oregon, keeping her nuptials to William Mason a secret so she wouldn't be expelled. The hospital found out anyway and she was asked to leave. The marriage lasted eighteen months. As Mason later explained, "We did not quarrel, but it was a case of incompatibility and we agreed to a settlement and divorce." After the divorce, Mason said he insisted Anne reenter nursing school. "We saw each other occasionally and were friendly. She was a fine little girl, very sweet, very pretty, very romantically inclined. She was exceedingly bright and of an outstanding personality."

Little is known of her second marriage, to LeRoi Smith, except it didn't last. Anne kept his first name as her new last name when she moved to Alaska. Mason said he saw her once after that, when she passed through Seattle where he was working. "She had a girl with her whom she was taking to Arizona from Alaska," he remembered. "I presume this was Miss Samuelson. Since then I have heard but little of her." Anne was currently engaged to be married to a man in Oregon, but that seemed iffy. She had confided to a friend recently that she didn't like to talk about marriage plans because it "upset Sammy." Friends would recall how "very, very devoted" Anne was to Sammy. Doctors at the Grunow Clinic were convinced Anne and Sammy were lesbian lovers.

Anne was surprised to see Ruth walk in the back door the evening of Friday, October 16. Twice that day during work, Anne had begged Ruth to come over for supper. Another friend, Evelyn Nace, was coming by and the four women could play bridge. Anne had tried everything, including a recitation of the menu: there were leftover pork chops in the fridge, supplied the night before by the nice young doctor who was planning to rent the other half of the duplex; creamed salmon; canned corn, scalloped potatoes, and a salad.

Ruth had begged off both times. "I'm behind on typing my medical histories and I've got to take the work home," she explained. That was partially true. The other part was that she expected to spend the night with her clandestine boyfriend, Jack Halloran. The girls, of course, knew "Happy Jack," although Ruth hoped they didn't know everything. She hoped they didn't realize her "friendship" with Jack had been a love affair for the last ten months, that she wanted to get pregnant by Halloran, and how he'd pledged to her that regardless of his other flirtations, she was the one he wanted.

Ruth was well aware that Halloran and his business friends spent considerable time at the duplex with the girls. While she roomed with them, she had come to realize he was responsible for more than just bringing the bootleg liquor or an occasional gift. She realized Halloran frequently slipped them considerable sums of money. She'd watched him flirt shamelessly with both Anne and Sammy. She was jealous of them and knew they were jealous of her.

But Jack hadn't shown up for their date that night, and Ruth got miffed, deciding she wouldn't be home if he finally came over. She took the ten-minute trolley ride out to see her best friends.

Evelyn Nace can still envision that night when she shared dinner and bridge with Anne and Sammy. Miss Nace was also employed by the Grunow Clinic, where she had developed a casual friendship with Ruth and Anne. She had never met Sammy until that evening. She remembers she accepted Anne's invitation because one of the clinic's doctors had suggested she befriend these newcomers to Phoenix.

Anne put dinner on the table, but didn't eat because she was feeling ill, Evelyn recalls; Evelyn and Sammy ate while Anne sipped tea. Evelyn remembers Sammy sat at the table to eat but felt too weak to sit up for bridge, so the three women moved into the bedroom. There was just enough room between the two single beds to set up a card table. They played bridge for about forty minutes. Anne won. There was the usual talk and gossip: Sammy reported the doctor who might move next door was "a tall and homely chap but an interesting talker and unmarried." The party broke up about 9:30 p.m. Both Anne and Sammy walked Evelyn to the door and waved goodbye.

Ruth arrived just minutes after Evelyn left, covering her earlier excuse by saying she had gotten her work done more quickly than she'd expected. She should stay the night, her former roommates suggested. It was already late and the trolley line would be closing down soon. Saturday was a workday for both Anne and Ruth, so they should start thinking about getting some sleep. Besides, they had a big day ahead of them—they were all going to look at the house Ruth hoped would be their new home.

For months Ruth had been working with a realtor to find a large house to buy. Her parents were thinking of retiring and had suggested they could move to Phoenix to be near their only daughter. They'd sell their house in Indiana and use the money for the down payment.

Ruth and Anne and Sammy had come up with a subplot to this plan: If the house had a section with a private entrance and a few generous rooms, the girls would move in too. The house payments would be covered by the rents paid by Ruth and Anne—hopefully, less than either was currently paying. Ruth was especially anxious for the deal to go through. She missed her parents desperately and, just as much, missed the security they provided. The realtor had told her only yesterday that he'd found a house he thought would be perfect. Ruth had asked to borrow his car so she and the girls could inspect it Saturday after work. Anne would have to drive because Ruth was a lousy driver. The realtor had told her he didn't like loaning out his automobile, and Ruth said she'd find other transportation.

Yes, Ruth should stay the night and sleep on the pullout couch in the living room as she often did. Anne loaned her a pair of pink dotted pajamas with a ruffle around the neck. Ruth changed. Then they all clustered for a talk in the little bedroom.

That's how this unremarkable Friday night began for the three women. Getting together as they'd done hundreds of times. It was a common scene of sharing and at-home entertainment played out throughout this small town in the midst of the depression. There was nothing to suggest this night would be any different.

By the time it was over, Anne LeRoi and Hedvig Samuelson would be dead, each with a bullet wound in the head.

Anne's body would be stuffed in the bottom of the big steamer trunk.

Sammy's body would be cut into four pieces.

And Winnie Ruth Judd would be on the run.

> *Winnie Ruth Judd Speaks*
> *—From a personal letter, 1952*

On October 15, 1931, I was merely an insignificant young woman. I worked in an office as many other young women did. I lived in a world wherein it was necessary for me to work or starve. There is no particular significance in this fact. Many other women who were sick, like myself, worked at various jobs to earn their living, never earning a dishonest dollar in their lives.

I had never been in trouble of any kind. But just a few days later the whole world was talking about me. Who was I? What was I like? These questions and this interest on the part of the public gave certain members of the press a golden opportunity. The answers they gave were so sensational that the public still wanted to know more about me.

The press had never seen or met me but they called me "Tiger Woman!" "Wolf Woman!" "Velvet Tigress!" "Butcher!"

Was this justice? Did not these names and sensational stories condemn me before I ever came to trial? Regardless of personal opinion toward me, is this not true? Many stories filled with distorted facts and lies have been written about me. Can a human being turn "wolf woman" or into a "mad monster" overnight? I had never been even remotely in any kind of trouble. I had always lived a Christian life and I am still a Christian.

    I have always contended my innocence of murder.

Chapter 3
The Dragnet

"Two Women's Bodies Shipped Here in Trunks by Fiendish
Killer" —*Los Angeles Times*, October 20, 1931
"Trunk Murderess of N.D. Teacher, Companion Eludes
Coast Dragnet"—*Fargo Forum*, October 20, 1931
"Mad Woman Hunted in California as Trunk Slayer"
—*New York American*, October 21, 1931
"Mind Inflamed by Drugs Blamed in Trunk Murder"
—*Phoenix Gazette*, October 21, 1931
"'Hungry for Love,' Her Notes to Mate Show"
—*Los Angeles Examiner*, October 22, 1931

The first time the American public ever heard the name
Winnie Ruth Judd, it was repulsed. People had to search
back to 1892 to find another name that inspired such disgust,
and papers then were too genteel to print the gory details of
the Lizzie Borden case. There would be no reprieve from
the horror this time.

Newspapers throughout the nation heralded the discovery
at the Los Angeles train depot with such vivid descriptions
readers were instantly sickened.

This wasn't just a murder but a double murder.

It wasn't just a double murder, it was a double murder
coupled with mutilation.

And this most unspeakable of crimes was committed not by some raging animal of a man but by a member of the weaker sex.

Nobody even blinked when the papers from coast to coast used the word "fiend." Only a fiend could do this.

With the disgust was a tinge of fear: the mysterious woman from Phoenix had vanished into the busy Los Angeles streets and was still at large. Who knew how dangerous she was or if she would kill again?

Before the Tuesday morning papers could hit the streets, law enforcement officials had launched a dragnet that would become the largest manhunt in the history of the West. It would last until Friday afternoon, when a weak, hysterical Winnie Ruth Judd finally gave herself up. By then hundreds of officers in California and Arizona had done little else but search for her. They had detained and questioned nine blond women who appeared to match her description, each one of them turned in by a panicky public. They had grilled her husband and brother for hours. They had interviewed her neighbors back in Phoenix, everyone she worked with, and anyone even remotely touched by the case. They had probed into her personal life and the lives of the victims. And they'd fed it all to eager reporters who regurgitated it to a now obsessed public.

Readers that first shocking day could never have imagined that for the next forty years—through Pearl Harbor, three wars, *Sputnik*, John Kennedy's assassination, the moon landing—they would still be habitually reading about this horrible woman from Phoenix who traveled with such awful luggage.

Newspapers were the main lifeline to the story that hit the nation's gut. Radio was just beginning to find its voice in news coverage, and television was still to come, so people relied on the written word. And nobody could get enough. Few crimes have ever seen the barrage of coverage that was devoted to the Winnie Ruth Judd case; few criminals have so instantly become a household word across America. Historians say the overwhelming public fascination was a mixture of disgust and morbid glee. "The Winnie Ruth Judd case took people's minds off the Depression," Arizona historian James E. Cook later wrote.

It was the perfect kind of crime and she the perfect kind of criminal for the lust that so defined the press of the 1930s. Journalists still study this era as the best example of "media excess." Newspapers didn't just report what was going on—couching, as they do today, criminal charges in such protective words as "allegedly"; demanding, as they do today, multiple sources to verify information. Newspapers were judge and jury: trying, convicting, and hanging within their pages. They did it in a style that was unreserved and blunt—a style these same newspapers decry today as "supermarket sleaze," having long ago forgotten that this reckless manner was standard fare in their own pages in the thirties.

Many commentators looking back on the era say the press was most out of control reporting the 1932 kidnapping of Charles Lindbergh's twenty-month-old son. History now shows that the accused kidnapper, Bruno Hauptmann, could not get a fair trial because of the incendiary press coverage. (His widow is still trying to prove her husband was executed in 1936 for a crime he did not commit.) But before that, the press cut its teeth on Winnie Ruth Judd.

The teeth sharpening started that very first day. Newspapers, then as now, are fixated on breaking a story—being the first to give readers the latest news, beating the competition. Pity the poor reporter who misses a juicy story while covering boring City Hall. Speed becomes all-important: gathering as much information as quickly as possible and writing it in time to meet the next deadline. In that haste, mistakes are often made—a common complaint today as six decades ago—but the fear of first-day mistakes never overrides the fear of being scooped. Scooping your rivals is seen not only as a duty but as a badge of honor. Reporters please their editors and keep their jobs by uncovering the latest scandal; they're unemployed if they don't. When everyone is covering the same story, readers might not know or care which paper got the story first, but editors surely do.

The scooping battle is most intense in cities where papers have different owners and are truly competitive for the revenue from advertising and copy sales. Los Angeles and New York were prime examples in 1931. The battle was so fierce in Los Angeles that at one point, teams of reporters from the competing morning papers almost came to blows over Winnie Ruth Judd. But even in cities like Phoenix, where both papers were under one ownership, the individual reporting staffs tried to outdo each other.

And outdo each other they did that first day. Reporters were able to gather an amazing amount of information very quickly, and editors readily shelved other stories to free up enormous space to cover every word. One of the first things they did was give her a label.

"Trunk Murderess,"

"Tiger Woman."

"Blond Butcher."

Winnie Ruth Judd wasn't even the first to wear the "tiger woman" name. Just two years earlier, the press had plastered that title on a female murderer who was executed in Pennsylvania. But if they weren't original, they were unrelenting.

Phoenix papers obviously were obsessed with the stunning hometown crime, reassigning virtually their entire news staffs to cover the story. Nothing less would have been expected or tolerated. As old-timers remember, nothing else seemed very important while the Winnie Ruth Judd case was unfolding. "It's all anyone in Phoenix wanted to talk about," says Jack Williams, who was a Phoenix radio reporter at the time but would go on to be mayor of the city and governor of Arizona. "But it wasn't just here. You can't even imagine what a cataclysmic effect it had on the whole country. This was the most notorious crime in the United States."

The fascination of the Los Angeles papers rivaled what was happening in Phoenix. L.A. could claim this as a "hometown" crime too, since the bodies had been discovered there. But L.A. had something Phoenix didn't. It had real competition between its individually owned newspapers. And it had one other factor that would greatly impact this case.

Los Angeles had William Randolph Hearst.

He was the fiercest, most daring, most reckless, and most powerful publisher the country would ever know. Biographies are still being written about him. Orson Welles would immortalize him in the classic movie *Citizen Kane*. He would be both admired and reviled. Hearst was to take an intense personal interest in the Winnie Ruth Judd case, providing the money for her defense, demanding that a leading California attorney head her team of lawyers, offering to pay for an appeal to the U.S. Supreme Court.

His private papers don't spell out the reason for his interest or the largesse he provided. One of his biographers says he loved a juicy fight and had a soft spot for women in trouble. To this day Winnie Ruth Judd says she doesn't understand why he did those things, but she remembers being approached twice by one of his reporters with messages that "Mr. Hearst wants to help you." She remembers her husband got testy about Hearst's offers. "I will thank Mr. Hearst to leave you alone," he told her.

In 1931, Hearst was hell-bent on making his *Los Angeles Examiner* the best, loudest, and most profitable voice in the West's most promising city. He went head-to-head with the Chandler family, who were just as intent on keeping the *Los Angeles Times* on top of the heap—which unlike Hearst's paper—would endure. As the two papers battled for dominance of the morning newspaper market, they went to elaborate lengths to ensure that they didn't lose any readers or revenue by failing to print enough about the Winnie Ruth Judd case.

Whatever queasiness a conservative "establishment" paper like the *Times* had in getting into the muck of a loathsome murder story was stifled in its quest to hold readers. The *Examiner* didn't have to overcome any qualms. This story was custom-made for Hearst's kind of newspaper. He'd built a communications empire no one would ever match by giving readers all they could stomach. His papers were never timid, never satisfied with just "official" sources, never fearful they'd gone too far. Some of the worst reporting this nation has ever seen came from Hearst papers. But so did some of the best.

At the moment Winnie Ruth Judd's name hit everyone's lips, Hearst owned a newspaper—sometimes two or three—in every major city of the country: New York, Boston, Washington, D.C., Chicago, Detroit, San Francisco, Seattle, Atlanta, Pittsburgh, Milwaukee, Baltimore. In all, about thirty papers carried his banner. But just as significantly, he owned something no one else in the country had: his own wire service. His International News Service took stories each day from his individual papers and sold them to about a thousand other papers throughout the country. Even though the Associated Press was a bigger wire service then—it supplied news to 1,305 papers—it did not have the "single voice" that was coming from Hearst's empire.

In America in 1931, there wasn't even a close second to Hearst's dominant and domineering style of journalism.

His *Examiner* quickly offered a $1,000 reward for "exclusive information" leading to the capture of Winnie Ruth Judd—as much as most Americans still collecting a paycheck could expect to earn in a year. Not to be outdone, the *Los Angeles Times* offered a $1,500 reward. It wouldn't be the last time these newspapers reached into their pockets to elicit information.

Eventually each would also publish its own version of Winnie Ruth Judd's life story—supposedly written by her, for astonishing sums. The "battle of the confessions," as they would be called in the Phoenix press, supposedly paid her thousands of dollars. Phoenix was outraged that crime could pay so well.

In Arizona, "checkbook" journalism was a filthy word. The Phoenix papers refused to offer a cent for anything. The sheriff couldn't even convince the County Board of Supervisors to cough up $250 for information on the city's most wanted fugitive.

While the *New York Times* prided itself on being a model of restraint—and stood almost alone in upholding that standard in this case—Hearst's three New York tabloids joined the feeding frenzy. The *New York Journal, New York American,* and *New York Daily Mirror* all played the story like chapters in a seamy dime novel. On their pages would be printed some of the most outlandish and absurd allegations uttered in the case.

What the nation's readers got, from the very first day, was a bizarre and deranged story. They got minute details about the lives of everyone touched by this tragedy. They read the personal letters written by the victims and the woman accused of killing them. They got pop psychology to explain the "weird" lives these people supposedly lived. And they got fistfuls of erroneous information.

By the time Winnie Ruth Judd turned herself in, the public knew all about her—her childhood, her marriage, her life in Phoenix, her secret boyfriend, the kind of hosiery she preferred. They knew she colored her hair, specialized in Mexican cooking, and had an open account at Wade's grocery store in Phoenix. They knew her family thought she was devoted to her ne'er-do-well husband, but they also knew she was having an illicit affair with Jack Halloran.

And they were certain she was guilty as hell.

The first words on the crime came from the radio on Monday night, just hours after the discovery at the depot. Stations across the country broke into their usual entertainment programs with news flashes that gave only the skimpiest of information: Bloody trunks were found in Los Angeles. The woman who had checked them in Phoenix had disappeared. In Los Angeles, the *Times* did radio one better, using its new "electronic bulletin board" to broadcast details.

By the time the morning papers became available, people were waiting to gobble up the details. And the *Times* was ready to claim its first scoop.

"FLASH: The largest crowd which has so far patronized the Times-Richfield Electric Newspaper filled all corners and sidewalks near Sixth and Hill last night to follow developments in the trunk murder case, flashed on the screen by teletype from the *Times* office in bulletin form as fast as the facts became known to the police," it bragged. "The broadcasting by this means of the car number of the suspects put thousands on the alert for this vital clew long before it had become public in any other way."

The *Times* played the crime story in its prime spot on page one—above stories on despised gangster Al Capone facing sentencing and beloved inventor Thomas Edison lying in state—calling it "one of the most brutal crimes in the criminal history of the Southwest."

"Bodies of Two Murdered Women Hid in Luggage," read the main headline, followed by the subhead, "Mysterious couple disappear after seeking grewsome death trunks sent here from Phoenix."

The story began: "Ghastly discovery of the bodies of two women, one mutilated and a section missing, crammed into a small steamer trunk and a large wardrobe trunk, was made by authorities last night as they smashed the locks of the luggage after it had been deposited at Central Station earlier in the day by a Southern Pacific passenger train from Phoenix.

"Blood issuing from the luggage brought it under suspicion immediately on its arrival at 7:45 a.m. and it was placed under surveillance—but a woman and a man who made an effort to claim the pieces about noon escaped...."

"With fiendish irony the murderer gathered up the exploded shells, one of the leaden slugs and an unexploded cartridge and dropped them into the purse of one of the women. Then he tossed the purse into the trunk with the bodies and clamped down the lids on the remains of his murderous orgy....

"Among the grewsome relics of the fiendish act was a green-handled bread knife, about ten inches long, with a cutting and a saw-tooth edge. Officers said it may have been the instrument with which the dismembering of the woman was done. Fingerprints etched in blood on the knife's blade may go far toward the identification of the killer."

Just as stunning as the words of its story were the pictures used to illustrate it. As readers digested the ugly words, they looked at the sweet faces of the victims. No newspaper could have hoped to get pictures like these in the few short hours between the discovery of the trunks and the final press deadline. They were available, the paper noted, only because the murderer had supplied them. The photos, some smeared with blood, had been thrown into the trunks on top of the bodies.

There was a picture of lovely Hedvig Samuelson, so young and vulnerable. "Smashed locks revealed the mutilated body of the woman believed to be Miss Samuelson. After being shot through the head near the right ear, in the left arm between the elbow and the shoulder and in the upper abdomen, the body had been separated between the lower abdomen and the knees—the section that is missing. It is believed possibly to be in other luggage not yet discovered...The torso, head and arms had been wrapped with rags and jammed down into the smaller trunk. Her lower limbs were thrown in the larger trunk with the body believed to be that of Mrs. LeRoi."

There were two snapshots of pretty Agnes Anne LeRoi. In one, she was posing in her nurse's uniform; in the other, she smiled warmly toward the camera, a girl who could turn any head. "The body believed to be that of Mrs. LeRoi was not mutilated, but had been jammed into the larger trunk. She had been shot once through the head."

The real scoop of the day came in the morning *Examiner*, whose reporters had gotten considerably more information out of the police than the *Times* had managed. The *Examiner* was able to name the "mysterious couple" that had sought to claim the luggage—one Winnie Ruth Judd and her younger brother, Burton McKinnell.

And the paper revealed police had finally found the missing section of Miss Samuelson's body.

It was late Monday night, October 19, when somebody noticed the old suitcase and hatbox stashed behind the door of the ladies' room in the Los Angeles depot. Considering the excitement of the bloody trunks, officials immediately called police. L.A. detective David Davidson arrived at 11:20 p.m. and rushed the baggage down to the morgue.

His written report to his captain detailed what he found: "One old tan suitcase contained the lower female torso (waist to knees) clothed in pink pajamas and wrapped in a sheet and blanket. Intestines and bladder were missing. One new appearing tan hat box contained an empty black surgeons' bag, surgical dressing, one old kit of surgeon's instruments, one .25 Colt automatic pistol Pt27573, several pieces of women's wearing apparel, 40 rounds (1 box) Winchester .25 automatic cartridges, and miscellaneous cosmetics."

But even this discovery wouldn't be the biggest bombshell in the *Examiner*'s main story that first morning. The paper was about to begin its press run when the latest, hottest piece of information was discovered. Editors quickly inserted a "bulletin" in bold type above its lead story:

"BULLETIN: At three o'clock this morning Detective Lieutenant Art Bergeron announced that B. J. McKinnell, brother of Mrs. Ruth Judd, had admitted Mrs. Judd confessed to him that she murdered the two women shipped from Phoenix in trunks, and that she had added she was 'perfectly justified.'"

The same story was carried around the nation by the International News Service, letting everyone know from the very first moment that police had fingered the most horrible kind of killer: a butcher who thought her actions could be explained away. Psychotic killers are like that, the public surmised.

"Two murdered women, the body of each crammed into a trunk, arrived in Los Angeles as baggage yesterday!" the *Examiner* told readers in its earthy style. The paper seemed to delight in detailing the contents of that baggage.

"Carefully—one at a time—both trunks were opened. In the larger one was the body of an older and larger woman. She had been shoved into the trunk and partly hidden by a mass of clothing, blankets, letters and a jumble of other material, apparently thrown hastily on top of the corpse.…

"In the body of the younger woman were three bullet wounds. One was through the left temple, one in the left breast and one in the left shoulder. Too, there was a bullet wound on the third finger of the left hand, suggesting that the girl had died while hopelessly trying to ward off her assailant.…She had been stuffed into the smaller trunk, for the body had been severed by a keen-edged instrument—cut completely into three pieces, but the portion from the waist to the knees was missing! She had been dead not more than two days, the surgeons said. …

"When the trunks had been emptied of their human contents a more thorough examination was made of the two receptacles. This is what the officers found: A diploma from the North Dakota State Normal School, Minot, N.D., issued to Hedvig Samuelson July 24, 1925; a copy of the 'Rubayiat' by Omar Khayyam and a book, 'Rainbow Weather' by Margaret Haygray; a framed motto, covered with glass, but with the text smeared by blood; many photographs, some in an envelope addressed to Hedvig Samuelson from Juneau, Alaska, May 29, 1931; many Christmas cards and a list of first names, such as a school teacher would make of her pupils; three teachers' portfolios filled with material used for teaching children in kindergarten or other primary grades; clippings, Mother Goose rhymes, simple little verses; two women's purses, one containing three .25 caliber shells, exploded, the other containing a fourth shell and a spent bullet, and a few wisps of hair sticking to the bloody glass of the obliterated motto. These hairs, should they prove not to belong to the heads of the two slain women, are considered by police as their strongest ironclad clew with which to identify the killer or killers."

Across the country, the *New York Journal* was already speculating on a motive. "The grisly butchery of the women was believed to have capped a quarrel which arose when they refused Mrs. Judd's request to kill a pet cat that had fits," the *Journal* told its readers that same morning, printing a story sent throughout the nation by the International News Service. Its sister paper, the *New York Daily Mirror*, suggested Mrs. Judd might have "fed bits of her victims to her pet cat."

When the blood and gore of the crime wasn't enough, these New York tabloids added other spices sure to get reader attention. Their pages were the first to publicly claim there was a "queer love" between the victims—a juicy smear that shocked a nation horrified by homosexuality. They twisted the most ordinary, insignificant bits of information into sleazy allegations. All three women loved "weird thrill parties, purposely subjecting their nerves to shocks and strains," the *Journal* breathlessly told readers, never explaining it had reached this contorted conclusion because the women, like many Americans, were hooked on the weekly Sherlock Holmes mystery radio show. The paper also suggested that Mrs. Judd had once tried to poison Anne LeRoi. It based the absurd allegation on a letter in which Anne jokingly complained about Ruth's bad cooking.

The *New York Times* with its typical restraint, printed a story sent over the wire by the Associated Press, editing out the sensational descriptions and characterizing the crime only as a "grim mystery." Other papers around the country ran the A.P. story without sanitizing the copy, telling readers Samuelson's body had been "hacked into pieces."

At home in Phoenix, the city's sister dailies—the *Arizona Republic* and the *Phoenix Gazette*—also did not hold back. The morning *Republic* called it "one of the cruelest yet crudest crimes in Southwest criminal annals." The afternoon *Gazette* labeled it "Phoenix' most sensational murder case." It would be forty-five years before another story got as much ink in Phoenix—1976, when *Republic* investigative reporter Don Bolles was blown up at high noon by a car bomb.

In 1931, the *Republic* had just solidified its dominance over the media in Phoenix. It had recently purchased the independent *Gazette* and had brought thousand-watt radio to Phoenix with a news and entertainment station known as KTAR, whose last three letters stood for *The Arizona Republic*. All three spoke with a politically conservative voice—the *Republic* had been named the *Arizona Republican* until November 1930. Both papers were best known, then as now, as boosters for the growth of Phoenix and protectors of their friends. Their sameness was so pervasive that in 1931 they were known derisively as "Pete and Repeat." Today they're most often called "the Repulsive and the Gazoo."

In two-inch-high letters, the *Republic* announced the crime that would forever hang over Phoenix's head: "TWO PHOENIX WOMEN SLAIN."

As was the style of the day, the main headline was followed by subheads—in this case, four—that highlighted the story.

"Bodies of victims, one dismembered, found in trunks."

"Mrs. Agnes Anne LeRoi, local x-ray technician, and Miss Hedvig Samuelson, school teacher, believed to be those brutally killed in city Friday."

"Two are held as witnesses on coast."

"Southern Pacific baggageman in Los Angeles makes gruesome discovery after man and woman call for containers; officers believe solution near."

Its stories recited the basic facts of the discovery at the depot and noted both Burton McKinnell and Dr. William C. Judd were being held for questioning. But the highlight of the *Republic*'s first-day story was the detective work its own reporters were doing.

The *Republic* had found out that neighbors saw a gray Packard in the driveway of the death bungalow for hours on Saturday afternoon—the day before the trunks were shipped to Los Angeles. The "mysterious car," as the *Republic* called it, showed up again on Monday night, not long after the trunks were discovered in Los Angeles. Police told the paper the driver made a hasty retreat when an officer guarding the house turned on a porch light. This same car, reporters would find, was seen frequently at Ruth Judd's apartment in the week before the killings.

Somehow, *Republic* reporters were never able to put a name with the car.

Police knew who owned the Packard. So did the neighbors. Out-of-state papers readily reported the identity. But at home, that information never came out. It wouldn't be the last time information widely reported across the country wasn't found in the pages of the hometown paper.

By the time the *Phoenix Gazette* was published Tuesday afternoon, it had accumulated the boldest, most complete information available on the case. This paper had the advantage of time—while morning papers were printed just after midnight, afternoon editions were printed about noon. From the depth of its coverage, it's obvious the *Gazette* had reporters working all night. Its main headline ran in two-inch-high letters in two lines above the nameplate—a spot reserved for only the most significant of news: "MRS. JUDD SOUGHT IN DOUBLE TRUNK SLAYING."

In all, the *Gazette*'s front page was dominated by nine headlines on the case. Two more pages inside the paper were devoted to various related stories. The *Gazette* was able to piece together a thorough and amazingly accurate account of Winnie Ruth Judd's activities around the time of the killings. It helped the public walk through three pivotal days in her life. Readers—especially those who knew her—scoured the stories trying to learn how this most unremarkable of women was involved in such a remarkable murder case.

They learned that Mrs. Judd, "known as a calm person who spent most of her evenings writing on a typewriter," had been hostess to three parties the week of the killings. The final party was given on Thursday night, just twenty-four hours before the girls died. It was attended by another woman and some men. Neighbors said it was "a little bit loud."

The victims themselves were also having parties that week, hosting a new doctor from the Grunow Clinic for supper on Thursday night, entertaining a clinic nurse for dinner and bridge that fateful Friday night. Nurse Evelyn Nace said both girls seemed happy and without any sense of apprehension when she left them at about 9:30 p.m.

An hour later, a neighbor, Mrs. Jennie McGrath rose from her bed when she heard three shots coming from the direction of the girls' bungalow. She said there was one shot, then a pause, followed by two more shots in quick succession. She looked out the window of her sleeping porch but saw no lights on at the bungalow. She didn't investigate further. Another neighbor, Gene Cunningham, would later recount the same experience. He said he didn't check out the sounds either, but went back to sleep.

Saturday morning, clinic secretary Mrs. Ernest Smith took a call from Ruth Judd, who said she would be arriving for work a little late. Shortly after, a woman purporting to be Anne LeRoi called to say that she wasn't coming in to work that day because she was going to Tucson for a visit. Mrs.

Smith angrily told the caller she was already late for work and Dr. Louis Baldwin would be put out with this sudden change of plans. The secretary insisted the caller relay the message directly to the doctor.

Dr. Baldwin wasn't at all happy to hear his X-ray technician was skipping work on a Saturday when he had a full load of patients. He told her that this behavior was unacceptable and he expected her to cancel her travel plans and come to work.

Mrs. Smith listened in on the call. "That wasn't Mrs. LeRoi," she said to the doctor after he hung up. "I think that was Ruth Judd."

When Ruth arrived at the clinic later that morning, Mrs. Smith confronted her with the subterfuge. She told police that Ruth denied impersonating her friend.

The suspicions raised by the call were only heightened by Ruth's appearance. Evelyn Nace remembered her as "white as a ghost and nervous." Dr. Baldwin recalled she looked untidy. Someone else thought she appeared to have been up all night.

The most shocking information came from Richard Swartz, a driver for the Lightning Delivery Company. A woman called his office Saturday night asking that a trunk be picked up at the bungalow—2929 North Second Street—and delivered to the train depot. Swartz told reporters and police he found the house dark, with the woman at the front door explaining she was leaving town and had already turned off the lights. He said he found a single trunk sitting in the living room—a trunk so heavy it required the aid of his two assistants to carry it. When he asked the woman what was in the trunk, she told him it was filled with books. Swartz warned her that a trunk that heavy couldn't be shipped as luggage. He said she hesitated for a long time and seemed confused, but then directed him to deliver her and the trunk to an apartment on Brill Street.

Swartz remembered that the woman acted as if she was in a daze. He had to ask her three times to move out of his way so he could get by her with the trunk. Then she stood like a statue in the doorway of the Brill Street apartment as he drove away. He noted that she'd twice promised him a tip but didn't give any.

"In carrying the trunk from the house the workmen left it for a short time in the doorway," the *Gazette* reported. "Last night two rings of what appeared to have been caused by blood dripping from the trunk were discovered."

Police told the press they were convinced the women had been killed in their bedroom. Both mattresses were missing. The corner of a bedroom rug had been "crudely hacked out with a pair of surgical scissors." There were splatters of blood under one bed, dotting the floor and splashing up as high as the baseboard. There was no blood on the walls of the bedroom.

Police would later find one mattress, which contained no blood spots, in a vacant lot miles from the death house; the other mattress was never found. The piece cut from the bedroom rug was found inside the bloody trunks.

At Ruth's apartment on Brill Street, police found a satchel of surgical instruments, suggesting the dismemberment of Sammy's body occurred there.

The first-day plum for the *Gazette* was an "exclusive" story written by internationally known detective W. J. Burns, who spent his winters in Phoenix. Although the story was pure speculation and was printed more as a public relations coup than as a serious news story, Burns, remarkably, was able to spotlight two points that would forever haunt the case. "I feel that the motive is the deepest mystery in the crime," he wrote, little knowing that six decades later, people would still be questioning the why of this tragedy.

"The fact that the murderer or murderers in this case sought to hide their crime by shipping the bodies to Los Angeles indicates that the mind of the criminal was inflamed,"

Burns added. "It was not at all a calm individual who killed the two women....The trunk murder case was handled very clumsily and it is quite possible that the crime was committed without much deliberation."

That point would always undercut the state's eventual declaration to the jury: that Winnie Ruth Judd was a murderer who had carefully premeditated and orchestrated the death of her best friends. The state would cling to that theory even as evidence piled up proving, if it proved anything, that there was no planning at all. But by then nobody with control over Winnie Ruth Judd's life seemed to care.

Ruth's recent move to her own apartment was cited as proof of "friction" between the women. Bits and pieces of letters written to family and friends were widely quoted to demonstrate the growing animosity that officials claimed had broken up the household.

Sammy had written to her sister on August 10: "Ruth Judd is staying with us but somehow it seems she doesn't belong here. I don't know how it will work out, but if the doctor gets a position she probably will join him. It doesn't bother me, but I don't think Anne likes it."

On September 28, Anne had written her fiancé in Oregon: "Ruth is leaving us in a few days. Dr. Judd is coming home so she will take an apartment. It really hasn't worked out so well having three of us. We are very fond of her and she is a sweet girl, but three just seems to be a wrong number when one is used to living by oneself and just one other very congenial one."

On October 2, in the last letter her parents would receive from Sammy, she wrote: "Ruth Judd, the girl that was staying with us, moved so we are alone again and we like it so much better. Three never get along very well."

One of the eighteen letters to Ruth from her husband that police found in her apartment contained this hint of trouble: "I don't want to write a letter to lie around for Sammy and Mrs. LeRoi to read," Dr. Judd wrote. "I had supposed you thought so much of those two girls that you would be perfectly happy with them, but if you are not, it puts a different face on matters. I am not at all surprised at what you tell me. I do not dare write you freely because you are so careless with letters." Dr. Judd always refused to elaborate on what the problem was between his wife and the girls, saying only that Ruth disapproved of Anne's lifestyle.

Even letters that seem benign and joking were quoted to insinuate the women were enemies. Anne wrote her brother that she'd been subjected to another of Ruth's Mexican dishes one luncheon and joked, "It almost did me in." When queried by the media, the brother said he didn't think the comment was meant seriously.

None of those missives sound very threatening; none give any hint of the horrible violence that brought them to light.

But there was one letter that police revealed to substantiate that there had been violence in the past. It was the last letter Sammy ever wrote. On the day she would die, she penned a three-page letter to her sister. It was found, waiting to be mailed, under the desk blotter in the duplex. An officer read from the letter, telling the press it said: "We are much happier by ourselves as Ruth and Anne clashed on so many things and their quarrels were sometimes violent."

That was *not* what the letter said. The handwritten letter is still preserved in the files of the Arizona Archives. It actually reads: "We are so much happier here by ourselves. Ruth and Anne clashed in many things. We get along so well but it shows there has to be a lot of tolerance which comes from love."

Young Burton McKinnell, the second half of the "mysterious couple" at the train depot, was immediately suspected as being his sister's accomplice. Police figured he either helped her plan the killings or, at the least, knew in advance she was bringing her victims to Los Angeles.

William Judd was also an instant suspect. Police surmised that perhaps the doctor had made a clandestine trip to Phoenix and aided his wife in the crime.

But it soon became clear none of that was true. Neither man had been in Phoenix for months. Both had ironclad alibis for their whereabouts the night of the killing. Both were as perplexed about Ruth's involvement as were friends in Phoenix who knew her well.

But if neither of them was involved, police were faced with a new dilemma.

Because it was absolutely clear that somebody had helped Winnie Ruth Judd.

"Phoenix officers hunt accomplice in brutal killings," read one of the *Gazette* subheadlines that first morning. "County officials flying to coast city to return dismembered bodies; warrants issued for three."

Officials in Phoenix told the *Gazette* that loading the trunks was "a feat believed beyond the unaided strength of Mrs. Judd."

County attorney Lloyd "Dogie" Andrews told the *Gazette*, "From the evidence gathered by police, Mrs. Judd's complicity is evident—we know she attempted to dispose of the bodies. It would be foolish, considering all we have learned, to go on the theory Mrs. Judd alone was responsible for the slayings. She is a woman of slight build and it would have been impossible for her alone to have handled the bodies. There is little doubt a man was involved in the packing of the bodies into the trunks." As a result, he filed a warrant charging Winnie Ruth Judd, John Doe, and Richard Roe jointly of first-degree murder in the slaying of Miss Samuelson. A second warrant charged Winnie Ruth alone with the murder of Anne LeRoi.

Police and the reading public alike found the whole scenario very befuddling: Ruth and her accomplice, for some unknown reason, killed the two girls, then tried to conceal the crime in a most absurd way. Immediately people wondered why the bodies weren't dumped in the thousands of square miles of vacant, uninviting desert that surrounded Phoenix, where coyotes and buzzards would have devoured the evidence and scattered the bones. But taking bleeding bodies on the train to California? Famed detective Burns was right, many decided that first day: nobody thought this out very carefully.

It seemed clear there was more here than a horrible murder. It seemed, from that very first day, there was a real possibility of some kind of convoluted conspiracy.

All these years later, that still remains a dominant theme in the case of Winnie Ruth Judd. It is a basic point that has kept the fascination of this case alive for so long. It has led many to believe the real story was never revealed because of *who* her accomplice was, whether he was involved in the actual killings or not. And it has convinced some—including veteran investigative reporters and a career police officer—that she probably did not kill anyone.

The Phoenix papers, however, found the evidence clear and obvious: Winnie Ruth Judd was a killer. Whoever else was involved would be ferreted out later. Police would surely discover the identity of the accomplice, or maybe accomplices. But for now, it was clear Winnie Ruth Judd should pay for this crime.

For three days, as the manhunt continued without success, the Phoenix papers reported the latest tidbits that cemented the accomplice theory. Both said police found "startling" evidence in the death house to prove complicity but never spelled out what it was. Either the police never told reporters what they'd found, or the newsmen decided to keep it a secret. Officer after officer was quoted about how they were making progress in the case, and their confidence that they would soon identify the accomplice(s).

But all of a sudden, four days into the manhunt, officials did an abrupt about-face.

Los Angeles detectives, working 500 miles away from the scene of the crime and without a single officer having come to Phoenix, told reporters they had "wholly abandoned the theory that Mrs. Judd had a male accomplice."

Phoenix police and the county attorney backtracked crazily, telling the media that regardless of their original conviction, it was no longer foolish to consider Mrs. Judd capable of doing everything all by herself. In fact, county attorney Lloyd Andrews was now declaring he found it reasonable to believe Mrs. Judd was singularly responsible for the entire crime. It was a theory he would later take to a jury.

There is no explanation in the media for this astonishing change of mind. Nobody even tried to explain away all the previous declarations. The police simply said they had been horribly wrong at the start and everyone should trust that they were right now.

It demanded a leap of faith that many couldn't muster. How could the existence of an accomplice be so clear one day and disappear the next? Those following the case closely were never convinced. Some would go to their graves believing Winnie Ruth Judd was railroaded.

◇ ◇ ◇

Regardless of what would eventually be said and reported, the stories reported the very first day were particularly significant. They gave the "first blush" of the case, both to the police and the public. They were stories unpolluted by anything except what trained police eyes could see and experienced police minds could decipher. They were stories that had no political consideration, no concern for "Whose toes are we stepping on here?" Those factors would kick in very quickly, history shows, but in the first frantic hours of discovering a horrendous double murder, they hadn't yet.

For the reading public, that first blush would forever color their impression of what had happened. As every journalist knows, nothing sticks in the reader's mind as much as the first story. For one thing, the revelation of a shocking story is guaranteed high readership. Millions of words would be written about Winnie Ruth Judd, but the few thousand that appeared that first day would be the best remembered. Wrong information, even if it was corrected later, would never really be corrected in readers' minds. It is a situation that exists as much today as it did in 1931.

From the very first day, crucial misinformation was presented as fact in the Winnie Ruth Judd case.

Take the major "scoop" of the day: Burton McKinnell admitting his sister had confessed.

McKinnell would always insist he was misquoted and never told police any such thing. He would become a champion for his sister, publishing at his own expense a twelve-page booklet that pleaded her innocence. He would move to Arizona to be at her side—as would his aged mother and father—and would become an amateur detective in trying to uncover evidence to help her. But from that first day, the public was convinced that her brother had helped seal her fate.

A few newspapers, such as the *Los Angeles Times*, later ran lengthy stories allowing McKinnell to set the record straight. But most papers treated his protests perfunctorily. Some reported McKinnell had "recanted and changed his story." Most simply said he "claimed he was misquoted."

This writer's investigation found the transcript of the police interview with McKinnell. It shows he had good reason to protest so loudly.

Burton McKinnell tells a roomful of officers that his sister showed up on campus, unannounced, about 11 a.m. Monday morning, ordering him to get his car because "'I want you to take these trunks and take them out in the ocean and sink them.'

"I asked her why such drastic measures and she told me that she didn't want me to ask any questions—that the less I knew the better off I would be and a sentence like that has a certain amount of significance, whereupon I saw if I assisted her in getting the desired trunks that there would be no dispute."

"Question by officer: Did you guess what was in the trunks?

"Answer: I didn't. I asked her what was in the trunks and she refused to answer me.

"Question: Did you keep asking her?

"Answer: I didn't because I saw the logic of it…I anticipated there was something wrong, of course, or she wouldn't want the trunks sunk at sea and to press that question in the face of that supposition, I felt that she was right—that I should not know."

McKinnell is asked what he thought when they were refused the trunks at the station.

"We left and I said, 'Ruth, what's in that trunk, a man or a woman?' And she said, 'Burton, I am not going to answer any questions' and she said, 'I can justify everything.' When she said she was justified I said, 'I am not interested in your justification and think the thing to concentrate on now is what the next step is to take' and then we were silent, the both of us for some time and then she asked me for money because she said she had to leave and I said, 'I think that is the best thing you can do' and I said, 'I wish you all the luck in the world, kid,' and she left."

Burton gave her five dollars—the only bill he had—as she stepped out of his car onto a busy L.A. street.

Again and again in the twelve-page transcript of that interview, various officers probe the same questions and Burton McKinnell always gives the same answers.

But misquoting her brother was the least of the mistakes the media made that first day.

Consider the mistake about how many bodies had been mutilated. Many papers reported that both bodies had been cut up when, in fact, it was only Sammy's body. As time went on, virtually every newspaper would write about the "butchered bodies," a mistake made so often over all these years that it became part of the folklore of the case.

But none of the mistakes made that first day in 1931 was as important as the one that would forever haunt the case.

"Grisly butchery" is how the International News Service described Sammy's condition in its initial stories. "Hacked into pieces," said the Associated Press. The words inspire an immediate visual image that defines the horror. It was the ingredient that catapulted these murders into the annals of America's Most Famous Crimes.

"That's the thing that made this case so sensational," notes attorney Larry Debus, who represented Winnie Ruth Judd in the late sixties. "If the body hadn't been cut up, this would have been just another homicide and nobody would have ever heard of Winnie Ruth Judd."

It is still the most sensational aspect of the case. And the exact description first used in 1931 is still used today. The 1986 true-crime book *Fallen Angels*, by Marvin J. Wolf and Katherine Mader, which chronicles strange murders and mysteries with a Los Angeles angle, includes a chapter called "Winnie's Bloody Trunks." Here's how the writers describe what happened: "Winnie got a surgical saw and a butcher knife. She hacked Samuelson's body into pieces...."

Only a handful of people ever saw the autopsy pictures. The county attorney who prosecuted Winnie Ruth Judd did. So did her defense attorneys. But the judge who sat at her murder trial did not. Neither did the jurors as they were deciding her fate. Newspaper readers certainly never did. These pictures were considered too awful even for the lurid press of the thirties. So the public relied on the written word. Even correct newspaper reports that the body had been "dismembered" didn't erase the hacked image. Everyone believed that if they got a glimpse of those autopsy pictures, they'd see a body chopped up into little pieces.

Autopsy pictures are never easy to look at and to this day are almost never published. They show death at its rawest, before a mortician can camouflage the damage. In modern criminal cases, these photos are sometimes submitted as evidence to give a jury the stark reality of death. They always inspire revulsion and disgust. Even hardened police officers— and certainly hardened journalists—never get blasé about them. Though it is often necessary to view them, it's not a duty approached eagerly.

Holding an envelope containing these particular autopsy pictures provokes an extra moment of hesitation. Photos of a dead body are one thing; photos of one that has been reduced to hunks of flesh are another. You unconsciously hold your breath as you open the envelope and then find yourself quickly sucking in air at the shocking images.

It's a stark room where the pictures of Hedvig Samuelson were taken, probably painted industrial gray. You can't tell because the photos were made in the only film then available for professionals and amateurs alike: black and white. At the center of the room is a flat gurney holding the corpse. The photographer shot pictures of the body from several angles, some from a distance, some close up.

But none of that is what you notice first.

First you notice that Hedvig Samuelson was not "hacked into pieces."

She was not the victim of "grisly butchery."

The very first thing you notice is that she was cut apart so precisely the coroner was able to stitch her back together.

Chapter 4
Pandemonium in Phoenix

Violet Grimm almost fainted when police told her what was inside the trunks her husband and son had taken to the depot for Ruth Judd.

Her daughter, Rita, a grandmother today, was a thirteen-year-old-girl that Monday night in 1931 when police arrived with the news.

"We were sitting at the dining room table doing our homework and Mother answered the door," Rita Grimm Esche remembers. "Two policemen were there. They asked her if Dad and Kenneth had taken the trunks, and she told them they had. My dad went to the door then and the policeman asked if he knew what was inside the trunks. 'Yes, I knew what was in them—the doctor's books,' he said. The policeman said, 'No, by the time they got to Los Angeles, blood was dripping out.' My mother said, 'Oh, they shot a deer illegally,' but the police said, 'No, it's worse than that. It's body parts.' I thought Mother was going to faint. It was pretty shocking. I remember the kids at school would tease me when the newspapers reported my dad had hauled the trunks to the station."

Howard Grimm would often tell the story of his taxi service to officials and reporters alike. "And that woman still owes me $1.50," he complained to the *Gazette*.

But what Rita remembers most, after all these years, is that she grew up believing a terrible injustice had been done to Winnie Ruth Judd. "None of us who knew her ever believed she did it," Rita Grimm Esche says in the first interview she has ever given on the case. "We knew she didn't cut the body up. She was just a telephone receptionist at the clinic, and the body was cut up by a professional. She couldn't have done that. But we didn't think she shot them either. We found it impossible to believe she could kill anyone. She was ladylike and shy."

Rita came to that conviction because of her mother, who maintained a lifelong friendship with Winnie Ruth Judd and joined a growing number of Phoenicians working behind the scenes to get her exonerated. "Mother became friendly with Ruth's mother," Rita recalls. "Ruth's mother told her that Ruth had been assured she wouldn't get the death penalty if she kept her mouth shut."

The Grimm household wasn't the only one in shock that Monday night in 1931, as the news flashes of the bloody trunks started playing on the radio. Across town, another little girl would always remember it as the most puzzling chapter in her family's history.

Edna George was twelve years old that night, the oldest of six children living "out in the boonies" on North Twenty-sixth Street, a part of Phoenix now consumed by houses and shopping centers. All these years, she's felt a need to tell someone what happened when her father came home from work. Edna George Bowman not only talks about it for the first time, she writes out a six-page letter to be sure it's down right.

"My father, Clay George, was a plumber," she explains. "He worked for Hudlow and Fleetner. They kept their shop open in the depression to keep their two people working—both their people had families to support. Daddy came home from work that night pale and nervous. He was just ashen when he came in. Mother told him there had been news flashes on the radio about two young women who had been murdered and their bodies were taken to L.A. on the train. 'That's strange,' Daddy exclaimed. 'The police told me not to talk about it!' Mother gasped, 'What do you mean?' Daddy told us he had been called to clean out the plumbing at Ruth Judd's apartment. He found bits and pieces of skin, flesh, bones, and hair in there. He said the police wrapped them up and took them away. He said he had overheard two detectives talking. They said they believed Ruth's boyfriend, Jack Halloran, had something to do with the murders."

Edna Bowman says, looking back on it, she thinks her father actually meant he'd cleaned out the drains in the bungalow at 2929 North Second Street, because "the next night we got in our Model T and Daddy drove past both places, the bungalow and Ruth Judd's apartment. Daddy seemed most interested in the bungalow where the girls were murdered.

"Strangers were milling around and going in and out of those houses. Lots of people were going through the houses. Nowadays that would never be tolerated, nor should it have been then."

She remembers when the children tried to question their father about the incident, they were hushed. Even now, as senior citizens, she and her siblings are still unsettled by how troubled their father was. "My daddy came from a long line of storytellers, but he never wanted to talk about this. I don't remember my parents discussing Daddy's involvement with the case outside of our family. My brother said Daddy was afraid, that's why he didn't talk about the story. I never thought my daddy was afraid of anything, but I think he was afraid of this. He expected to testify at Ruth Judd's murder trial. Much to his relief, he was never called. Isn't that strange?"

Stranger yet is what happened next.

There is no written police record of Clay George cleaning out any drain. Whatever flesh and bone he found was never submitted as evidence in the trial. Instead, the police declared they found no evidence in any drain—either at Ruth's apartment or in the girls' bungalow. No flesh, no bone, no hair. As proof, they released a report from a different plumber they sent to check out both drains on October 26—a week after Clay George had already recovered all the evidence.

Why would the police conceal such a significant piece of evidence? Why would they lie about what the drain revealed? Why would they admonish Clay George—a family man who desperately needed his job—to keep his mouth shut?

Perhaps it was due to what the police were already speculating. Because if Clay George heard right, they instantly suspected one of Phoenix's most successful and prominent citizens was somehow involved in a stupendous mess.

The kind of shock the Grimms and Georges were going through that night was replicated in home after home throughout town. Those who knew Ruth Judd were sure there had to be some mistake. As prominent businessman Leigh Ford—Ruth's first employer in Phoenix—told police, "If a thousand people were standing in a row and I was called upon to pick the person who might commit a crime of this kind, Ruth Judd would be the last one that I would pick."

It took only hours for people to realize this crime said some awful things about Phoenix, Arizona.

"Everyone thought this was a very nice, innocent town," remembers former governor Jack Williams. "This case was like taking the top off a nest of centipedes and here are all these slimy creatures."

Of all the people in Phoenix who lived through the case, Jack Williams has particular reason to remember it without any romanticism, any second guessing. Winnie Ruth Judd would touch his life in four ways: he was a resident of a town so tight that everyone knew everyone; he was a radio reporter who would cover the Ruth Judd case; he would be the mayor of Phoenix during some of her infamous escapes from the state hospital; he would become the governor who finally paroled her when she was an old woman.

Williams was a twenty-one-year-old radio announcer in 1931 for KOY Radio, a station that ran the same kind of programs every other station featured—music and entertainment. The only real news on radio then was presented on network-affiliated stations that ran five minutes of national news every hour. KOY wasn't affiliated with a network, it was an independent station, and its owners had yet to see any need for a local news show. The only competition was KTAR Radio, which was affiliated with NBC and owned by the *Republic*. KTAR didn't offer local news either. It felt its blurb of national news was enough.

Jack Williams and Winnie Ruth Judd brought local radio news to Phoenix. During her trial, Williams was approached by an eager young man who suggested the station "dramatize" the courtroom testimony every night. Williams, who still wishes the idea had been his own, says he hired the guy for a dollar a day to sit through the trial and then write a script each night. At midnight, the reporter, Williams, and whoever else they could grab would read the parts. Williams doesn't recall if he played the part of the judge or the prosecutor or the defense attorney, but he remembers it was a novel idea. "We ran the show late when our signal could be picked up back east, and we had a lot of listeners all over the country," he says. "This kind of thing had never been done before, so it got a lot of attention. It was really the first local radio news program Phoenix ever had."

Williams recalls there was an instant acknowledgment throughout Phoenix that Ruth Judd wasn't in it alone. And simultaneously coupled with that was speculation about who else had been involved. He remembers some men "left town," fearful they'd be drawn into the case; others were unfairly tainted by being exposed as men who had partied with the women.

As Williams looks back now, he realizes how the Winnie Ruth Judd case stripped Phoenix of its facade of innocence. He and other old-timers still shudder when the era they held so dear is unmasked by historians today.

"In this town at that time, hanky was the name and panky was the game," says Don Dedera, a longtime journalist, writer, and historian in Arizona, adding that few eras practiced the kind of hypocrisy Phoenix perfected then. It presented itself as God-fearing and morally strict, conveniently ignoring its ugly underbelly of prostitution, gambling, drug trafficking, bootlegging, political corruption, graft, payoffs, more political corruption.

The description used most often by old-timers to sum up Phoenix in those days is: "Everybody knew everybody." Dedera notes it is impossible today—when Phoenix is a major city and people don't know the family next door—to understand the significance of that description. While old-timers prefer to remember it meant the town was cozy and friendly, Dedera says it more accurately signaled, "this town was easily manipulated by a very few people."

Agreement comes from *Republic* journalist James E. Cook, who writes a twice weekly historical column on Arizona. He has written often about the "political machine" that ran Phoenix in those days. It handed out jobs at a time when jobs were scarce; it got a cut from the sin businesses it allowed to flourish; it made sure none of its friends got in serious trouble. "Looking back at that era, I can very easily get a picture of this as a small town where there's a subculture of cops, attorneys, playboys, and party girls," Cook says. "Some very powerful cops were members of this subculture. If they wanted to protect a friend, they could do it easily. This town had a booster mentality. The machine was to see that it kept growing and prospering, and everyone guarded against anything that would harm that."

It was a mood that would last for a long time in Phoenix. As former *Republic* investigative reporter Logan McKechnie puts it, "Phoenix was and continued to be until the early seventies a provincial community where influence was important. Where you could, in fact, cover things up and hide things." That wouldn't start changing until the 1970s when the *Republic* hired aggressive investigative reporters—Don Bolles and McKechnie among them—to expose the problems. "Until that time, it was influence that counted. In Winnie Ruth Judd's era, I have to believe that if you had influence, you could get anything."

Jack Williams shares a story he says pinpoints how cozy things were in the thirties: A political candidate known for his excessive drinking ended up in jail on a Friday night just before the election. The police chief called the party chairman and asked what should be done with the guy. The chairman said it would be convenient if he stayed in jail until after the polls closed Tuesday. No problem, the chief said.

If police were doing that kind of political favor to keep a drunk politician off the streets, imagine what they were capable of doing when faced with a serious problem. Cook says his historical research shows they were capable of almost anything. "If they wanted to lose evidence, they could," he says. "If they wanted to protect their friends, they could."

One of the first problems Phoenix saw was the way the Winnie Ruth Judd case was going to expose the city's venerable tradition known as the "summer bachelors."

As soon as the temperatures started hitting three digits, every businessman worthy of the title sent his wife and children away to cooler climes. That left the working men footloose and fancy-free, as they liked to say in those days. Legend has it that as one train pulled away from the station with the wife and kiddies, another brought in the "summer wives."

Those who weren't imported were local working girls like Ruth Judd, Anne LeRoi, and Hedvig Samuelson.

Most families were sent to the cool mountain community of Prescott, about a hundred miles north of Phoenix. The pattern was so defined—a convenient rail line connected the two cities—in order to allow businessmen to take the train on Friday nights to spend the weekends with their families, then return early Monday morning in time for another work week and the ladies they had waiting in the heat.

The freedom afforded the summer bachelors allowed affairs to flourish, although they were never supposed to bloom. The system seemed to have only two rules: Nobody was supposed to get caught and the girlfriends were required to disappear for the winter.

The dalliance is all the more shocking considering the social mores of the day. Former governor Jack Williams describes the standard this way: "It was a very, very strict society, but it didn't seem strict at the time. If you went back to the puritan age, a man couldn't kiss his wife on Sunday, he couldn't dance, he couldn't play cards, he couldn't drink. We'd broken a whole lot of rules by this time. Western women were rather on a pedestal—they were very special people. Men were supposed to pay great respect to them. Women weren't supposed to ever issue an oath. Men did curse, but not in the presence of ladies.

"Because of biological differences, women were doomed, if indiscreet, to have a child unexpectedly, while men were allowed a few indiscretions. But if you were ever caught, it was curtains for a career and a reputation."

For a long time Phoenix was afraid the Winnie Ruth Judd mess was going to bring the curtain down on some of the most prominent families in town.

Hearst's newspapers found all of this delicious. They quickly put Phoenix on notice that the summer habits in the desert were just the kind of information their readers loved. The first grenade was lobbed within a few days of the discovery of the bodies.

"Astonishing new secrets of the intimate diary of Agnes Anne LeRoi, 'trunk murder' victim, leaked out from two sources today and rocked Phoenix official and social circles with threatened exposure of 'playboys' who helped Miss LeRoi and her chum, Hedvig Samuelson, 'enjoy life,'" the International News Service reported.

"The diary was said to have been divided into two parts, one containing intimate details of the 'party lives' of the slain girls," the report continued. "This section of the diary is said to be in the hands of an attorney who is guarding the contents in the interest of wealthy men clients whose names may be drawn into the baffling 'all-woman triangle.'" The weird contents of the diary were discussed everywhere on the streets today and names were mentioned that adorn the social register of the capital city.

"Deputy County Attorney Harry Johnson confirmed the existence of the diary. He was asked if he had the diary or had seen it. 'I have not been able to obtain the diary,' Johnson said. Questioned as to why the diary could not be produced through an official demand, Johnson replied, 'I have been instructed by County Attorney Lloyd Andrews by telephone not to give out anything to the press.'…

"A prominent resident of Phoenix said he had seen the diary shortly after it was found in Miss LeRoi's rooms. A representative of a local organization, this resident said, had taken the diary to an office and it was locked up in a safe. Revelations of the contents of the diary, it was admitted, would wreck several prominent homes and efforts were being made to keep names in the diary from being drawn into the court records."

Those efforts were successful. There is no record that law enforcement officials ever sought to wrest the diary from the private lawyer. There is no record of a subpoena or even a police report showing the lawyer was questioned. The diary was never discussed at the trial. It is apparently lost to history.

Reports of the diary were missing from the pages of the *Arizona Republic* and the *Phoenix Gazette*: the local papers were selectively editing information on the case, even as papers from New York to California did not hesitate to name names. But in a town where everybody knew everybody, residents could readily provide names and faces for the "big men" and "playboys."

The most prominent face belonged to a movie-star-handsome Irishman with an easy, engaging smile. For a long time the *Republic* and the *Gazette* referred to him only as "Mr. X." Mr. X was really Jack Halloran—a name that would forever remain prominent in this case.

Chapter 5
"Happy Jack"

Jack Halloran was a busy man the week the girls died.

As usual, he had his lumberyard to run. He had meetings at the tony Phoenix Country Club, where he joined the town's major lawyers, politicians, and businessmen on the board of directors. The Community Chest campaign was gearing up to raise money for charity, and he was head of its industrial division. His family was back from the summer cabin in Prescott's Hassayampa Mountain Club and the kids were busy in school. He was eager for the hunting season to open Friday. His buddy Ed Ryan from El Paso was in town for a few days, and that always meant a party. And his dance card was filled with Winnie Ruth Judd.

The mental snapshot old-timers have of Jack Halloran then shows a successful businessman, a community leader, a solid family man. He served on the board of the Phoenix Chamber of Commerce. He was a grand knight of the Knights of Columbus and a president of the Southwest Golf Association. He belonged to Elks Lodge 335.

His religion was the only kink keeping him from the list of Phoenix blue bloods. His children went to Catholic schools and the family worshiped at St. Mary's. But for upstanding men like Halloran, even Phoenix was able to overcome its distrust of Catholics—although it agreed with the nation that one could never be elected president.

Halloran had a charming, salesman's personality that had served him well in both business and his private life. He first came to Phoenix in 1915 as Arizona sales manager for a California wholesale lumber company. Four years later, he bought the controlling interest in the Bennett Lumber Company, one of Phoenix's "pioneer businesses," which could trace its roots back to 1892. He renamed the firm the Halloran-Bennett Lumber Company and embarked on an ambitious expansion plan. By October 1931, the yard covered nearly two city blocks in the heart of Phoenix—a site now occupied by the county courts. He and his family lived only a dozen blocks away in a charming house built in 1920 in the Craftsman Bungalow style. It was then the best part of town. These days it's a historic section where run-down houses are being renovated.

Jack Halloran's activities that fateful week can be pieced together from police reports—some of which were uncovered during this writer's investigation—and the independent detective work done by Winnie Ruth Judd's brother and other supporters.

Halloran was busy that week organizing a big hunting party for the weekend. He intended to go to northern Arizona with a group of doctors from the Grunow Clinic and other business friends. They all wanted to bag a deer. Winnie Ruth Judd dreamed about going along too, although she knew that would endanger the secrecy of their affair. But she offered her help. There was a nurse at the clinic who came from northern Arizona and supposedly knew all the best hunting spots. Maybe she could advise Jack.

Halloran thought that was a fine idea and asked Ruth to set up a dinner with the nurse for Wednesday night. But he got drunk with friends instead, not showing up at Ruth's Brill Street apartment until about nine p.m. She wasn't pleased that he'd blown off their dinner date and sent him packing. But first he sweet-talked her into rescheduling the date for the next night.

Pretty Maude Marshall, a schoolteacher who lived in the apartment adjoining Ruth Judd's, was coming home about the time Halloran was leaving Wednesday night. As she walked by his large gray Packard, he made a flirtatious remark. She huffed off, offended by the impertinence. When she got inside, she scribbled the license plate of the car on the back of a magazine. It was a natural reaction for a woman living alone to protect herself by noting information on a pest who was bothering her. She had no way of realizing how significant her scribble would turn out to be.

Things went much better Thursday night. Halloran picked up Ruth at her apartment about seven p.m. and they drove out to fetch Lucille Moore, who had come to the "big city" to pursue her nursing career from a small farming community in the White Mountains of Arizona. Lucille was still new in town and hadn't made many friends. She had lunch with Ruth now and then during the work week, and knew Anne LeRoi only by sight.

The dinner plans were simple. Ruth had the makings of huevos rancheros at her apartment—a Mexican dish she'd learned to prepare when she lived south of the border with her husband—and Jack had a bottle of tequila. But on the drive to her apartment, Jack announced that he was stopping off first at the girls' place. Ruth protested. She had turned down an offer to join Anne and Sammy for dinner, saying she had work to do. How would it look, she protested, if they discovered her lie? Halloran insisted they stop, explaining that Ed Ryan and another friend were visiting the girls and he needed to pick them up. Ruth made him promise he wouldn't tell Anne and Sammy she was in the car and wouldn't dally. Although she wouldn't admit it to Jack, Ruth had another reason for not wanting to stop: She wasn't eager for her friends to know she had introduced Jack Halloran to *another* young, pretty woman.

Halloran parked in the driveway next to the girls' bungalow, leaving Ruth and Lucille waiting in the car. The few words spoken in the next few minutes would become the centerpiece of the prosecution's case against Winnie Ruth Judd.

As Lucille Moore later told the police, Ruth asked her, "What do you think of Jack?" Miss Moore said she answered, "I think he's nice." "He's better than that," Ruth told her. "He's perfectly grand. Anne and Sammy think so too. You know, I used to live here with Anne and Sammy, but we had a little difference and I moved away—in fact, that is what I moved over, our difference was about Jack."

To Ruth's dismay, both Anne and Sammy came out of the house. She rushed from the car and embraced them both with a hello hug, making no move to introduce them to Lucille. The girls insisted everyone stay at their place for dinner. A new doctor at the clinic, H. J. Brinkerhoff, was already inside—he'd brought pork chops for this get-acquainted celebration—and they could a make party of it. Ruth protested that dinner was already set at her apartment and they had to leave.

Jack and his friends piled into the car. During the short drive to her apartment, Ruth scolded Jack for breaking his promise. "Oh, forget it," he laughed it off.

Lucille Moore always remembered how uncomfortable she was when she discovered Ruth's husband wasn't waiting for them at the apartment. It wasn't proper, she protested quietly to Ruth, to have such a party when the man of the house wasn't home. She asked that someone drive her back to her apartment. Ruth insisted it was all innocent fun and these were just friends, and convinced Lucille to stay.

Lucille Moore never did get over her uneasy feelings that night. She had assumed that as a married woman, Ruth was true to her mate. She'd never met Halloran before, but was well aware of who he was and that he, too, had a family. It was disturbing to see the "considerable affection" between Ruth and Jack.

"During the course of the evening, Ruth kissed Jack numerous times—in fact, every time she passed him or got near him," Lucille would tell police. "Jack did not seem to be the aggressor, but he did not resist these advances." Lucille remembered that at one point, Ruth confided that "she loved Jack very much but it would never do her any good, because they were both married."

About midnight, Ruth and Halloran drove Lucille home. Lucille Moore's life would never be the same again.

It was late Friday night when Maude Marshall heard someone bring Ruth Judd home to the Brill Street complex. The schoolteacher had been out for the evening and had returned home just after midnight. She remembered noticing that Ruth's apartment—separated from hers by only a thin wall— was dark and there were no indications anyone was home. Maude Marshall immediately went to bed, but didn't sleep well. She roused about one-thirty when she heard a heavy car pulling into the driveway. It paused only briefly. Someone got out and went into Ruth's apartment as the car pulled away. Miss Marshall assumed the awful man who'd tried to flirt with her two nights earlier had dropped Ruth Judd off at home.

It would be days before this shy teacher realized her late night memory plunged her into an awful murder case. By the time she was awakened by the noises, the most gruesome aspects of the case had already been set in motion.

Police would establish that Anne and Sammy were killed about 10:30 p.m. that Friday night. Medical experts would eventually conclude that Anne's body was placed into the trunk within six hours of her death, before rigor mortis set in. They would further testify that the dismemberment of

Sammy's body occurred "within a few hours" after death, before her blood started to coagulate. Any longer, the experts said, and the coagulated blood would have remained in her body. But her autopsy showed she had been completely drained of all blood and body fluids.

The police came knocking on Miss Marshall's door after the trunks were discovered. She told them what she knew, stressing she hadn't actually seen the car Friday night, but *assumed* it was the same one as on Wednesday night. She handed over the magazine scrap with the license number she had noted. The police had no trouble tracing the owner. The car belonged to Jack Halloran.

Ruth's brother, Burton, came knocking too, because his sister had instructed him to search out Maude Marshall. In the pamphlet he later published pleading her innocence, Burton reproduced a handwritten note Ruth sent him while she was awaiting trial. The name of the man she mentions is blacked out, apparently to protect Burton from libel. Today Ruth Judd admits her brother excised Halloran's name.

The note reads: "Burton. Go see Miss Marshall at 1130 E. Brill and tell her part of this. Ask her if she saw Halloran's car at 11:30 or 1:30 or both that night....I ought to have evidence, for Halloran will have alibis, lies plenty. Love Ruth."

As imprecise as Maude Marshall was about the Friday night car, her story alerted police to a significant element of the exploding case: They knew Ruth Judd had no car; somebody was chauffeuring her around in those crucial hours after the killing.

But Miss Marshall wasn't the only one who alerted the police and sheriff's offices—both of whom were investigating the case at this point—to Halloran's possible whereabouts Friday night. There was also the story told by Dr. R. B. Raney, who lived across the street from the girls' bungalow.

When Sheriff John R. McFadden found Dr. Raney, he realized he wasn't looking for just one person, but two.

Dr. Raney told McFadden he had been out that Friday night celebrating his birthday and returned to his house about eleven p.m. He said he saw two cars parked by the bungalow. One he recalled as a large, enclosed car; he couldn't describe the other. Dr. Raney said he was called almost immediately for an emergency operation at St. Joseph's Hospital, and returned home again about one a.m. A large, enclosed car was just turning around in front of the bungalow, leaving with its headlights out, he reported.

Officials now had cars placed at both the death house and Ruth's apartment late Friday night. But they would forever keep this information secret.

What wasn't a secret was that Halloran's gray Packard was seen parked at the death house "for hours" on Saturday afternoon by several of the neighbors. These witnesses gave that information to the Phoenix press, which never identified the owner of the "mysterious car." But out-of-state papers noted the car was Jack Halloran's.

Neither Miss Marshall or Dr. Raney would ever be called to the stand. Nobody—neither prosecutors nor Ruth's defense attorneys—seemed interested in tracking Halloran's activities that Friday night.

That still angers Winnie Ruth Judd. In an exclusive three-day interview in 1990 with this writer, she stressed repeatedly that her neighbor could have helped to exonerate her. "The schoolteacher saw Jack Halloran drag me off the porch Friday night, but that never came out and she was run out of town."

Where did Halloran drag you off to? she is asked. She almost spits the answer: "To the girls' house." Then she refuses to elaborate.

But the details she cannot bring herself to utter were found in the course of this investigation—in a sixty-year-old transcript of Winnie Ruth Judd describing, in minute detail, the events of that night. She said she fled the death house and ran to her apartment on Brill Street, although a trolley driver would later testify he hauled her most of the way, dropping her off several blocks from her apartment because the line was closing down for the night and she could no longer make her usual connection. She said Halloran arrived shortly after, drunk and boisterous and unbelieving of the story she told him of the shooting. She said he drove her back to the death house and then took over. She said he dropped her off at her apartment about one-thirty a.m. To this day, she believes Maude Marshall could have verified all that.

And she has always believed Dr. Raney knew exactly whose car he passed in front of the death house twice that Friday night. She says she and Halloran were leaving the bungalow as Dr. Raney came home from the hospital. Halloran had his headlights out so as not to attract attention. He was afraid Dr. Raney had recognized his car, she says, because Raney was the doctor then treating Jack Halloran's son.

In concealing Miss Marshall's and Dr. Raney's statements the police showed that from the start, they had a very narrow interest in what happened that night. Most significantly, it did not extend to the question of who had dismembered Hedvig Samuelson's body.

And they got away with it because police in the 1930s were under no legal obligation to reveal what they uncovered in an investigation. They told the press only what they wanted to tell them. They told defense attorneys nothing at all.

Time and again, this probe shows, police would declare one thing to the press while actual witness statements showed another. Time and again, they simply "forgot" to mention what they found.

This was also an era when the principle of evidence discovery was unknown in Arizona courts—just as it still is in the federal court system and in some states. Today Arizona courts require that both prosecutors and defenders get copies of all police reports and witness statements in a case—it's considered fair play that everyone know what the police have discovered. Hiding information now is grounds for a reversal or a new trial. But back then defense attorneys were left in the dark. They had no legal right to see police reports and had to hire their own private detectives to investigate a case. Their best hope was to trick an officer on the witness stand into revealing the existence of an official report. Then they would ask the court to order him to produce a copy so it could be submitted as evidence. There was no tripping up a witness by showing he'd changed or embellished his story between his original police interview and his testimony.

Retired Phoenix police captain Hugh Ennis, who is a student of criminology, explains that officers then saw their role as proving guilt, not helping out the accused. And they were well instructed on how to make sure a slick defense attorney didn't trick them. "You'll notice that officers who testified in the Judd case never said they refreshed their memories from a police report, they always said they consulted their notes," says Ennis, who spent thirty years in law enforcement. "Lieutenant Ryan of Los Angeles [who discovered the trunks] tells the court he burned his notes. That's the way it was played for a long time. You were very careful never to admit there was a police report. I remember when the rules on discovery got strict in the sixties, and we were told we had to hand all this stuff over to the defense attorneys. The police thought it was the end of law enforcement as we knew it. We thought it was ludicrous."

Considering what officials suspected about Jack Halloran, it seems amazing they let him spell out Winnie Ruth Judd's "motive" for the killings. But that's what happened.

"The double trunk murder was fanned into being by a kiss," the *New York American* reported in a story written within the first forty-eight hours of the manhunt.

Winnie Ruth McKinnell, age seven, with her brother, Burton. (*Photo courtesy of Winnie Ruth Judd.*)

In this never-before-published portrait, a young Winnie Ruth poses with her parents and brother. The Rev. H.J. McKinnell and his wife, Carrie, never waivered in believing their daughter's innocence, and her brother, Burton, went to great lengths to expose the untold story. (*Photo courtesy of Winnie Ruth Judd.*)

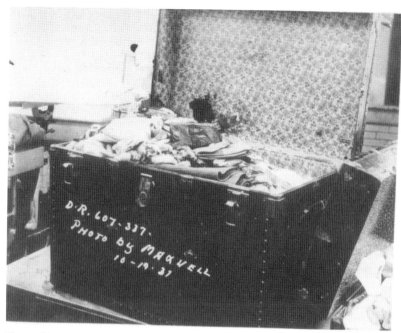

The packing trunk that carried body pieces, shot in the Los Angeles Morgue and presented as evidence in Winnie Ruth Judd's murder trial. (*Photo from the Archives of Maricopa County Superior Court, Phoenix, Arizona.*)

A part of the "drain pipe" letter Ruth Judd wrote while hiding from the law. The prosecution said it was her admission of cold-blooded murder. (*Photo from the Archives of Maricopa County Superior Court.*)

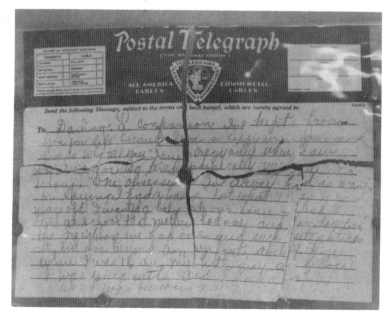

WILL JUSTICE TRIUMPH

Indictment of Halloran as Accessory May Yet Save Beauty From Gallows

By PETER LEVINS

Readers throughout the country were shocked at the unfolding drama and were anxious to see all the major players. At left: Jack Halloran, who was indicted as an "assessory to murder"; the victims posing together, Anne LeRoi and Hedvig Samuelson; "the slim blonde who may hang in Arizona," and a picture of the crowds visiting the death house.

IN THE JUDD CASE?

A county clerk showed off the trunk and valise that would be submitted into evidene in the murder trial. "Two important witnesses" were Miss Lucille Moore (in fur collar) and Miss Evelyn Nace. At top are portraits of Ruth Judd and her husband, while at the bottom is the trapdoor of the gallows at Arizona State Prison. (*Reprint from the New York Daily News, January 1, 1933.*)

The death house became a major tourist attraction as the owner of the bungalo charged curiosity seekers 10 cents. Thousands trampled through the house before police got around to gathering evidence for their murder investigation. (*Photo from the personal files of Orien Fifer Jr. and Jerry McLain, both formerly with The Arizona Republic.*)

Thousands gathered at the courthouse in Phoenix to meet the motorcade that brought Winnie Ruth Judd back from Los Angeles to face trial. The courthouse, at the southwest corner of Washington and First Avenue, has been restored to its 1930's glory. (*Photo from the personal files of Orien Fifer Jr. and Jerry McLain.*)

"It has always been my impression that Mrs. Judd put up a tremendous fight for her life," said the Los Angeles doctor who photographed these numerous bruises shortly after Winnie Ruth surrender to police. (*Photo from the Arizona Department of Library, Archives and Public Records.*)

Ruth Judd enters the Phoenix jail, flanked by jail matron Jewel Jordan and Sheriff J.R. McFadden. Both Mrs. Jordan and Sheriff McFadden pleaded for mercy for Winnie Ruth Judd. (*Photo from the personal files of Orien Fifer Jr. and Jerry McLain.*)

Ruth Judd talks with her attorneys during the murder trial, Paul Schenck (with white hair) and Herman Lewkowitz (in glasses.) Sheriff McFadden is in the background, standing by the window. (*Photo courtesy of Jerry Lewkowitz.*)

Ruth Judd and her husband, Dr. William C. Judd, during her murder trial. The young lady had every reason to believe marrying a doctor would give her a good life, but that's not how it turned out. (*Photo from the personal files of Orien Fifer Jr. and Jerry McLain.*)

Phoenix was fixated on the Judd murder trial and the courtroom was packed every day, sometimes to overflowing. Some came to support her; others to jeer. (*Photo from the personal files of Orien Fifer Jr. and Jerry McLain.*)

Winnie Ruth Judd at her murder trial in 1932, her hand still bandaged: She said her hand wound proved self-defense; prosecutors said she'd inflicted the wound on herself. (Photo courtesy of Jerry Lewkowitz.)

The courtroom in Florence was packed for Winnie Ruth Judd's insanity hearing--on the eve of her execution date--in 1933. She looked and acted "crazy as a loon." Always at her side was prison matron Ella Heath (in the white hat); her father sat nearby reading the newspaper, while her mother is at far left in the print dress. (*International News Photo courtesy of Relfe Family*.)

In the 1950s, Ruth Judd is returned to the state hospital, after one of her many escapes, by Sheriff Cal Bois. (*Photo courtesy of photographer Frank King*.)

Ruth Judd posed with her guardian, Mrs. Elizabeth Harvey (at left) in the 1940s at Arizona State Hospital. (*Photo courtesy of Winnie Ruth Judd.*)

Ruth Judd loved animals and on a happy day in prison, was captured with a black cat. (*Photo courtesy of the Relfe Family.*)

Winnie Ruth Judd in 1969, recaptured after six-and-a-half years of blissful freedom. (*Photo courtesy of Lois Boyles.*)

Ruth Judd at age seventy-seven—a free woman who no longer wanted to remember the past. She now went by the name "Marian Lane."(*Photo coutresy of Winnie Ruth Judd.*)

Ruth Judd first visited the author's home on Halloween in 1992, wearing an upside-down clown costume like one she'd made decades earlier while at the Arizona State Hospital. She delighted the neighborhood children with the strange getup, and then came in for coffee, where she autographed the book about her life. (*Photos from the author's personal files.*)

Ever got a brick for your birthday? The author gave one to Marian Lane in 1997 as the Orpheum Theater was raising money for its restoration. Marian had attended the Phoenix theater in the 1930s in happier days before she became the infamous Winnie Ruth Judd. (*Photos from the author's personal files.*)

Ruth Judd was an accomplished seamstress who made elaborate children's and doll's clothing--some of which won ribbons at the Arizona State Fair while she was incarcerated in the insane asylum. Years later, when she needed constant oxygen, she showed off her handiwork with great pride. (*Photos from the author's personal files.*)

Marian Lane and the author shared a love of Christmas and entertaining. They're shown at the author's home in 1993.

Marian Lane shows off her chocolate cake at a 92nd birthday luncheon the author gave her at the University Club in central Phoenix.(*Photos from the author's personal files.*)

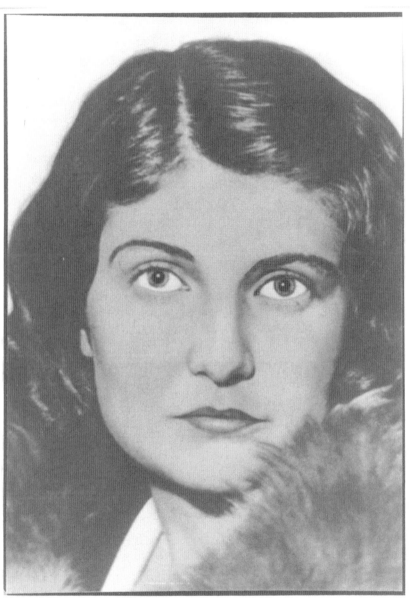

Winnie Ruth Judd was such a beauty in the 1930s, some compared her to the ranking Hollywood starlet of the day, Norma Shearer. She always loved this picture of herself. (*Photo courtesy of Winnie Ruth Judd.*)

"This sensational theory was advanced by authorities in Phoenix tonight after J. J. 'Jack' Halloran, wealthy lumberman, told a story that emphasized the jealousy motive for the killing. Halloran, forty-four and married, admitted that at a drinking party last Thursday night he had kissed Miss Samuelson. Winnie Ruth Judd…attended the party and saw the kiss. Halloran said he first went to Mrs. Judd's house and had some drinks. After that he accompanied her to the apartment of Mrs. LeRoi and Miss Samuelson."

Halloran named two eyewitnesses to the kiss, the story added: Lucille Moore, the young nurse who knew the best hunting spots in northern Arizona, and Dr. H. J. Brinkerhoff, the new doctor from the Grunow Clinic. Police told the *American* they intended to question both.

They did. They just never told anyone Halloran's story didn't check out. Instead, they told the Phoenix press it was Lucille Moore who first mentioned the "deadly kiss," making her the key witness against Winnie Ruth Judd.

The actual police interviews with Lucille Moore show the only kiss she witnessed was Ruth kissing Jack. Unlike Halloran's version of the story, she told police she never attended a party at the girls' bungalow; she'd never been inside the place. The closest she'd been was sitting in the driveway waiting for Halloran. She insisted she was driven straight home after dinner at Ruth's; they did not stop at the girls' place, as Halloran claimed.

Halloran's story further fell apart when police questioned Dr. Brinkerhoff. Being new in Phoenix, Brinkerhoff told them, he welcomed the invitation to have dinner with Anne and Sammy that Thursday. About six p.m., three men arrived who were obviously old friends of the girls. One was a man named Jack, another was a Mr. Ryan from El Paso, and Brinkerhoff never did catch the third name. He stated that Ryan brought a radio for the girls and set it up in the bedroom; Jack left, returning later to fetch the other men. After all three left, Brinkerhoff said, he had a pleasant dinner with Anne and Sammy. Mrs. Judd was mentioned in a casual way, and he remembered the girls seemed "very friendly toward her," as the police report notes. Dr. Brinkerhoff said the three of them spent the evening alone and he left them between ten-thirty and eleven p.m. He did not see any "deadly kiss."

When the specific kiss angle didn't pan out, prosecutors switched to a general jealousy theory for their motive. Ruth was insanely jealous that Halloran favored the girls over her, they said. She killed to eliminate her competition for her illicit love affair. She planned the murder for weeks, they would tell the jury. Prosecutors told the press they would show all this when Miss Moore—their "star witness"—testified at the trial.

Miss Moore later testified about the dinner party that Thursday night. She was not asked a single question about any kiss, deadly or not. Nor was she asked about the affection she had witnessed between Ruth and Jack. The most damaging thing she related was Ruth's statement that the three women had a "difference" over Halloran that led to Ruth's change of address. Winnie Ruth Judd's defense attorneys did not ask her any questions at all.

Lucille Moore's involvement had been innocent. So had Dr. Brinkerhoff's. Under normal circumstances, there was no shame in accepting dinner invitations, which is all either of them had done. But nothing was accepted as normal if it was tied to the "trunk murderess." Both would suffer just because their names were drawn into this messy case. Lucille Moore would never again nurse in the "big city," as she'd always intended, but would flee to rural Arizona, where she lives to this day. Dr. Brinkerhoff's out-of-state fiancée quickly called off their pending marriage. Years later, he married a Phoenix girl. He has since died.

◇◇◇

Jack Halloran was on the golf course the first time a reporter tried to interview him. He angrily stated he had nothing to do with the case and his only transgression had been in associating with the girls. "I am guilty of no greater fault then being indiscreet," he said. He would later issue a long statement to the Phoenix papers blasting the "sensational" coverage of the Los Angeles papers that labeled him a "millionaire playboy" and insisted on calling him "Happy Jack." He noted that his hometown papers had been far kinder, and boasted that he could handle the situation: "I'm a big Mick and I can take it."

Jack Halloran was treated very kindly by the Phoenix press. Time and again, the shreds of information police did reveal about him were found not in Phoenix but in the out-of-state newspapers. And those papers were well aware that it was more than the local press that didn't want anything negative reported on Jack Halloran. As the *Los Angeles Examiner* reported, an official in the county attorney's office balked at questions about Halloran's involvement in the case: "That's nonsense. Jack Halloran is a friend of mine. He's a fine fellow."

The quote came from the county attorney himself, Lloyd Andrews. Andrews's widow, Francie, insists to this day that they were not great buddies. "People thought that, because they both belonged to the country club and they both liked to golf," she explains. "But they were just casual acquaintances."

Casual or not, there is no paper trail on Jack Halloran. Not a single report remains from the police department or the sheriff's office on the interviews with Jack Halloran. Written reports—many are verbatim interviews, some are interview summaries dictated by detectives—were found for virtually every other individual the police questioned. But in thousands of pages of police documents, there is nothing that shows what officers asked Halloran or what he answered.

The county attorney wasn't the only man in Phoenix who called Jack Halloran a friend.

"I knew him well and never believed that he was involved," says former U.S. senator Paul Fannin. "He was very highly respected. He and his family were very embarrassed by it. He made the mistake of being associated with them—going to parties and things of that nature, but no way was he involved in any sense. He was a good friend of mine and I always respected him."

Tom Chauncey, who became one of the town's major movers and shakers, agrees. "Jack was a handsome man-about-town. He was very generous and very kind. He was terribly well liked. He had a fantastic business then. He was one of the most prosperous men in the valley. He was very prominent in social circles, as prominent as any man in Phoenix. This destroyed him. It was a terrible thing. He was ostracized. His business went to hell. I always thought he was unfairly accused. I don't think he had a damn thing to do with it."

"Jack had a great personality—everyone liked him," remembers Harold Spotts. Spotts retired recently after fifty years as business manager for the O'Malley Lumber Company, a firm that dominated the building and supply business in Arizona for five decades. "Sure he knew lots of politicians. He had business dealings with attorneys and lots of businessmen in town," Spotts says, but he notes every businessman of any prominence could make the same claim in Phoenix in those days.

Halloran had one trait Spotts always admired: "He was a great salesman." On the other hand, he continues, "Jack was well known as a playboy. He had lots of friends of the same type—they had more money than good sense."

Spotts, even at eighty, has a remarkable memory. He can recite not only the address where the killings took place, but its official legal description: Lot 2, Block 2, LaBelle Place.

He remembers this most obscure piece of information because the O'Malley company eventually owned the house, and Harold Spotts was in charge of their vast real estate holdings.

The way they got that particular house provides an intriguing look at what was going on behind the scenes in Phoenix as the Judd murder case unfolded.

"I knew the O'Malleys were concerned and wanted to talk to Jack about it," Spotts remembers. Halloran came down to the O'Malley offices for a private chat with the brothers who owned the company.

The O'Malleys had good reason for concern. At that point, they were one of Arizona's pre-eminent families. They had a growing and very profitable lumber business with dozens of subsidiaries that could supply virtually anything needed to build anything. They had absolutely no interest in jeopardizing their name or their businesses by being associated with the biggest mess the town had ever seen.

The only one who could taint them that way was Jack Halloran. Because, unknown to the public—unknown to anyone except the principals involved—the Halloran-Bennett Lumber Company was really owned by the O'Malleys. Spotts reveals that many lumberyards around the state were under the O'Malleys' ownership but carried someone else's name. "The O'Malley old-timers felt business would suffer if people thought all the yards were owned by the same company," he explains. There was nothing illegal in the scheme; it simply made it appear that a variety of independent companies were available for lumber needs.

The O'Malleys, like others in town, were not just concerned that Halloran was up to his neck in the Judd mess; they were concerned about rumors he had actually been involved in the girls' deaths, Spotts reveals. But after their closed-door tête-à-tête, they concluded Halloran wasn't a killer.

"Their opinion, as they expressed in the office, was that it was too bad Jack had been involved with the women, but

obviously he wouldn't have anything to do with murder—
he was at the wrong place at the wrong time," Spotts says.

Although Spotts maintains the O'Malleys held faith in
Halloran, he acknowledges they quickly decided to cut all
ties. They sold the lumber company everyone thought
Halloran owned.

Halloran started over again, independently buying another
lumberyard that Spotts recalls as never being very successful.

Ironically, when the O'Malleys called in their chit on
Halloran, they took over not only his lumberyard but all
the property the yard had accumulated in repayment for
bad debts.

One piece was a duplex bungalow at 2929 North Second
Street—the house where Anne LeRoi and Hedvig Samuelson
were killed.

Winnie Ruth Judd Speaks
—From a personal letter, 1952

*I can imagine the heartbreak of my brother when the
authorities and news reporters swarmed over him to ask
questions he knew nothing about or had anything to do
with. I was in such a dazed condition, yet I could imagine
my brother's torment. I must have thought only of flight
and self-preservation.*

*On Monday night, Oct. 19, I went to LaVina Sani-
tarium. I vaguely remember going to the room I had
occupied both times I was a patient there. It was occupied
so I went to the next room, which was also occupied,
then I went to a third room and it was unoccupied. I
went to bed there and I remember nothing for four days.
As impossible as it may sound, no one entered the room.
No one had stopped me when I went in. I do remember
getting up after the fourth day and brushed my hair and
tore some paper from the lining of the dresser, then I
walked out with no one giving me a second glance.*

Then I went to Pasadena where I telephoned a physician I knew at Bishop's sanitarium asking him if he would get a letter to my husband. He answered, "Oh Ruth, I can tell that you are sick. Tell me where you are so I can get you and do something for you." I then went to Los Angeles and wrote a letter and mailed it. From there I went to the Broadway department store where I had once worked.

I stood around staring at people I knew or who knew me. I was in such a stupor that I got locked in the store all night. I didn't think to change clothes, but to steal anything was the farthest from my mind.

I slept in the furniture department of that store under a rug. When I awakened the next morning, people were rushing all around me going about their business.

Later in the day I heard a woman discussing me. She was reading a newspaper and she said, "her husband wants her to call this number," and she mentioned the number. Immediately I called that number and my husband answered in Spanish and told me to meet him at the Biltmore theater.

It took me no more than ten minutes to reach the Biltmore and he had a car waiting at the back entrance of the Biltmore garage. I kept thinking "when will it end, when will it end?" When I met my husband another man was with him who said he was my attorney. We drove to a funeral parlor. My husband had promised the sheriff and prosecuting attorney that he would turn me over to them on condition that I first be put in a psychopathic hospital under observation for one month, because he thought I would be unable to tell coherently what happened.

The promises made by officials were not kept.

Chapter 6
The Surrender

Winnie Ruth Judd finally gave herself up to Los Angeles police late in the afternoon on Friday, October 23, 1931. The surrender came in the most ironic of places: a funeral home.

Officials throughout the West sighed with relief as they called off the hundreds of officers who had been fruitlessly looking for Ruth Judd. They learned, to their consternation, she had been hiding under their noses in her old haunts: the sanatorium where she'd twice been treated for her TB and the Broadway store where she once was a clerk. Dozens of people had come in contact with her—some of whom should have recognized her.

But the sight of her now made officers—and reporters—flinch.

She looked small and frail and bewildered in the newspaper photos that appeared on front pages coast to coast. Her fashionably bobbed hair needed washing. Her dress was soiled and she wore no hose. Her face was gaunt from hunger. She seemed on the verge of collapse. Her enormous eyes looked unfocused. Around her shoulders was the comforting arm of a man who looked too ordinary, too old to be this young beauty's husband.

Reporters took one look at Ruth Judd, heard the first words out of her mouth, and knew this case had taken a major turn.

"I had to shoot her, I had to shoot her," she sobbed, then hid her face in her husband's shoulder.

An attorney hired by Dr. Judd read her statement: "I had gone to the girls' home to remonstrate with Miss Samuelson for some nasty things she had said about Mrs. LeRoi. Miss Samuelson got hold of a gun and shot me in the left hand. I struggled with her and the gun fell. Mrs. LeRoi grabbed an ironing board and started to strike me over the head with it. In the struggle I got hold of the gun and Sammy got shot. Mrs. LeRoi was still coming at me with the ironing board and I had to shoot her. Then I ran from the place..."

Ruth Judd cradled the proof of this "dramatic plea of self-defense," as some papers called it: her left hand was purple and swollen, a bullet still embedded, already gangrenous.

Officials instantly realized they were now faced with a glitch to their slam-dunk case. They had a woman who admitted to being a killer but not a murderer. They had a killer whose justification would let her walk free. Because even in 1931, it was no crime to kill in self-defense.

Either her story made this bizarre case even more perplexing, or else, as authorities quickly concluded, it was "absurd."

On the surface, it was easy to dismiss the story as preposterous. People who kill in self-defense don't cut up a victim. They don't hide bodies in trunks. They don't travel hundreds of miles to dispose of corpses. They don't do any of the things the police believed Winnie Ruth Judd had done.

But to prove her story was inane, officials had to prove she couldn't have been wounded on Friday night during a melee with the girls, but shot herself later as part of the cover-up.

And that's what they did. At least, that's what they publicly revealed.

"The self-defense plea is characterized as 'inconceivable' by officers and investigators here and in Los Angeles," the *Gazette* reported the next day. "Deductions from a cursory survey of circumstantial evidence and facts [have] led to the belief that the bullet wound in Mrs. Judd's hand...was self-inflicted and probably occurred while she was unloading the death gun in her apartment at 1130 East Brill Street after the double tragedy."

Police revealed to the paper that they'd found a .25-caliber cartridge shell in her apartment, the same kind of bullet that had killed the girls.

"Persons who saw Mrs. Judd Saturday have declared her left hand was not bandaged that day," the *Gazette* reported. "Others maintain on that day her right hand was bandaged. This factor, it is believed, will be an important cog in the prosecution of Mrs. Judd."

It would become the *crucial* cog. Obviously, Mrs. Judd could not have been wounded in a fight with the two women Friday night if no one saw any sign of the wound Saturday, when she came into contact with at least a dozen people at the Grunow Clinic. And just as obviously, a wounded woman could not have packed the trunks with the heavy bodies of the victims.

Most significant, a wounded woman could not have performed the dismemberment of Sammy's body. Even prosecutors were bluntly admitting that point. "If her story of being wounded in the hand on the night of the slayings should be true, it would absolutely preclude her having disposed of the bodies without the aid of an accomplice," deputy county attorney G. A. Rodgers told *The Arizona Republic*.

But Rodgers added a quick caveat: "It is, however, inconceivable. Evidence tends to show that if she has a wound in her hand, it was self-inflicted. We have witnesses who saw her sometimes with one hand bandaged, sometimes the other, and some witnesses who saw her the morning after the slayings with neither hand bandaged."

That should have been the end of the story. Nobody knew it was a lie.

Police records uncovered in this investigation show officials well knew Winnie Ruth Judd turned up for work Saturday morning with a bandaged hand. They even had a witness who swore she had the bandage Friday night, immediately after the killings. But they hid that evidence. Their action would have a profound effect on the outcome of her case.

Grace Mitchell certainly saw Ruth Judd's bandaged left hand. So did little Stella Kerkes and her father, Mike. So did Fay Ayres. So did Emil Clemens. So did B. W. Jurgemeyer.

Grace Mitchell had an appointment to see a doctor at the Grunow Clinic that Saturday morning. "When I walked in the door, I noticed Mrs. Judd looked fearfully bad," she told police. "I noticed her eyes looked so bad. She looked in pain to me. She looked distressed, but she also looked like she was suffering."

Ruth Judd got up from her desk in the reception room and took Mrs. Mitchell into an examining room to be weighed. "I never noticed until she went to take me to the weighing room. I asked her what was the matter with her hand and she said, 'I burned it,'" Mrs. Mitchell recounted. "It was the left hand. I said, when the murder came out, that she was in physical misery. I told my husband I wagered she had been shot."

Mike Kerkes and his daughter Stella had driven to Phoenix that morning from their home in Wickenberg, a small rural community fifty-eight miles northwest of Phoenix. They were already in the waiting room when Ruth Judd arrived. "She come in the door with her left hand bandaged and she sat down," Mike Kerkes told the county attorney's investigator. "I looked up and talked to her. I knew her for some time, and I asked what is the matter and she said, 'Burned it up on the stove last night.'"

Stella Kerkes remembered Mrs. Judd was "pale and she seemed like she was restless or something." She recalled clearly the "pretty big bandage" Ruth had on her left hand. "I noticed it but I did not say anything and Daddy noticed it and he asked what is the matter with it, and she said, 'Oh, just burned it.'"

Faye Ayres was a secretary at the clinic. "I saw her go out the front door with a bandage on her left hand. I know it was her left hand," she told authorities. Emil Clemens, a handyman at the clinic, also distinctly remembered seeing Ruth Judd that Saturday with a bandage on her hand, but he couldn't recall which hand.

In contrast—contrary to their bold assertions to the media—authorities had found only one person who swore that both her hands were fine Saturday morning: young Dr. Brinker-hoff, who had shared one of the last meals with the girls and whom Halloran tried to use as an alibi for the "deadly kiss" motive. And only one person who thought he'd seen her *right* hand bandaged: Dr. Henry L. Franklin. He told officials, "As well as I can remember, it was her right hand."

Considering how the evidence was stacking up in Ruth Judd's favor, it's no wonder officials suppressed the statements of B. W. Jurgemeyer.

Jurgemeyer was driving the Indian School trolley line the week the girls were killed. He was working the Tuesday through Saturday night shift, starting at four p.m. and ending when the line closed down about midnight. In two separate interviews with county investigators, Jurgemeyer swore he remembered Mrs. Judd getting on his trolley that weekend. He said he couldn't remember if it was Friday night or Saturday night, but he was sure it was only one of those evenings. He recognized her because "she often rode my car."

About nine-thirty p.m. one of those nights, he said, he picked her up where he usually did on Third Street—a point eight blocks west of her apartment. She had a transfer voucher from the trolley that connected her to his route. Then about two hours later, she boarded the trolley again, going in the opposite direction. He placed the time at eleven-thirty because he clearly remembered her asking for her usual transfer. He was about to give her one, when he realized the other line was no longer running because it was nearly quitting time.

Prosecutors had Jurgemeyer testify to this round trip at Ruth Judd's murder trial. Here was the trolley conductor, they told the jury, who hauled her to and from her murderous crime.

And that's where their questioning ended. That's all they wanted this witness for—to show Ruth Judd's trip to the deadly encounter.

Prosecutors never asked Jurgemeyer if he noticed anything unusual about Ruth Judd on that return trip—minutes after she had supposedly committed two murders. They never asked because they didn't want him to repeat what he'd twice told officials: "Her left hand was completely wrapped. I noticed it before she got on the car." Jurgemeyer also remembered she had to use her right hand to put her token in the farebox.

Winnie Ruth Judd's defense attorneys never asked Jurgemeyer a single question at the murder trial because they had no idea the trolley driver had given the police such an explosive piece of evidence.

The prosecutors must have breathed a sigh of relief when Jurgemeyer got off the stand. Witnesses are always instructed to answer only those questions posed—not to offer more. But there is always the fear a witness will get chatty. If B. W. Jurgemeyer had blurted out his eyewitness account of Ruth Judd's left-hand injury—seen just minutes after the killings— the state's case would have been seriously damaged. This was their own witness. He could have blown the prosecution out of the water.

There's a fascinating irony here. This probe found that the scene Jurgemeyer witnessed so clearly had to have taken place on Saturday night—not that fateful Friday night. As she would admit months later to Sheriff McFadden, Ruth Judd took the trolley out to the girls' bungalow Friday night, but in her fright after the deadly fight, ran home to her own apartment. She also admitted, however, she did make a round trip on the trolley Saturday night. She told the sheriff she had noticed blood dripping on the porch as deliverymen removed the trunk from the bungalow to deliver it to her apartment. After the deliverymen left the Brill Street address, she said, she took the trolley back to the bungalow to hose the blood off the porch. On her return trip, she asked the driver for a transfer, but he told her it was too late to catch another trolley.

The prosecutors never realized their mistake. In their minds, they had an eyewitness who had seen an injured left hand immediately after the killings, and they couldn't let that get out.

The depth of their deceit was discovered during this investigation. By the time Ruth Judd stood trial for murder, officials were not only convinced she was telling the truth about her hand wound, they knew which doctor at the Grunow Clinic had "offered to dress the hand" on Saturday morning—the hand they told the world was not wounded at all.

Within the thousands of pages of witness statements is this intriguing exchange:

"Grunow Clinic Doctor David Davis: I saw her that morning but I paid no attention [to whether her hand was wounded].

"Question by state-hired psychiatrist Dr. Joseph Catton: Someone offered to dress it.

"Interjection by deputy county attorney Robert McMurchie: Yes, some surgeon up there.

"Dr. Davis: I think it was Dr. Franklin."

A few sentences later, McMurchie interjects again: "I think it was Dr. Franklin who offered to dress the hand."

There is a possibility Ruth Judd shot herself in her own apartment after the killings. She ended up with the gun at her place, so she had the opportunity. But if she did, it would have had to be done in the wee hours of that Saturday, before she showed up for work at the Grunow Clinic at 9 a.m. And if she did, wouldn't someone have heard a gunshot—especially adjoining neighbor Maude Mitchell. If the sound of a car entering the driveway could awaken Miss Mitchell, the retort of a handgun certainly would have aroused her. But Miss Mitchell heard no gunshot. Nor did anyone else in the complex. If police had found anyone who heard a shot, they would have used that information to bolster their case. And then they would have had no reason to hide those who saw the left-hand wound Saturday morning.

Knowing all this, the coverup is particularly insidious. And it was taken to ridiculous lengths.

To strengthen their public statements that Ruth Judd was lying about her wound, they trotted out the testimony of Howard Grimm and his son, Kenneth, who had hauled the trunks to the depot late Sunday afternoon. The *Republic* called their testimony "particularly strong" to destroy Ruth Judd's story.

The Grimms both insisted it was her *right* hand that was bandaged when they dropped her off at the train depot. Howard Grimm would eventually get on the witness stand and swear that to the jury.

No one apparently recognized that either the Grimms were seeing wrong or the prosecution was lying to the jury. Because they couldn't play it both ways: They couldn't tell the jury the cartridge they found in her apartment proved she'd shot herself in the left hand before leaving for Los Angeles, and also give credence to the Grimm declarations that *after she left the apartment for the last time*, the wrong hand was wounded.

Ruth Judd had the .25-caliber gun in her hand luggage when she boarded the train. The only way the Grimms could have been correct was if she had been faking a wound when she left Phoenix, and shot herself on the train. But officials never argued that. They already had plenty of eyewitnesses squirreled away who had convinced them that couldn't be true.

It certainly didn't help this masterful—if illogical—obfuscation that Sheriff John McFadden wasn't playing along. While the rest of officialdom pretended Ruth Judd could not have suffered a wound Friday night, McFadden told the Associated Press he was sure she had. As the AP reported, he surmised from his reading of the evidence that the wound had occurred when a bullet passed through Sammy and lodged in Ruth's left hand. He wasn't convinced she'd been shot first by Sammy, he told the press. Months later, when he did become convinced, nobody bothered to report the sheriff's words.

By the time the case went to trial, Ruth Judd's defense attorneys had independently found some of the people at the clinic who testified to her left-hand wound. But the defense attorneys made only the feeblest attempt to drive this point home to the jury. And the prosecutors countered with their contradicting witnesses. The entire discussion was reduced to nothing more than "did, did not" confusion.

By then it was an irrelevant question anyway: Ruth Judd's attorneys weren't arguing she'd killed in self-defense. Instead, they told the jury she killed because she was insane.

How different would their defense have been if they had known about the the trolley driver, or been privy to the entire list of people who unequivocally saw the left-hand wound?

"When police look at a body of evidence, they look at the reliability of witnesses, they look for independent corroboration," explains Hugh Ennis, the veteran officer who has long studied this case. "There was nothing to discredit the witnesses who saw her left hand bandaged. There was nothing to suggest they'd concocted their stories. The weight of the evidence shows she was wounded Friday night, and police knew that."

By the time doctors in Los Angeles treated Ruth Judd's wounded left hand, gangrene had already set in. They put her under sedation to remove the bullet, as reporters from the *Los Angeles Times* recorded her subconscious mumbling: "I had to fight 'em! I had—to—fight—'em! Pinching my finger—living through court—somebody—court."

The bullet in her hand wasn't the only injury doctors found. As the *New York Times* reported, there were "innumerable bruises all over her body." Ruth told the doctors she had gotten the bruises during the fight, as she rolled around the kitchen floor fighting off Sammy and trying to ward off the "braining" Anne was delivering with the ironing board.

Dr. Grace Line Homman examined Ruth Judd that first day at the request of defense attorneys. She also took dozens of photographs. They show Ruth draped in a bedsheet. Large bruises—some looking like pinches, others like blows—are evident on both arms, both legs, and her back.

In a letter Dr. Homman later wrote to Arizona officials, she stressed she was not paid a fee for her services, so her observations were made as a trained physician, not a hired gun.

"I have a complete record of my examination with a detailed report of the many bruises," she wrote. "Because of them, it has always been my impression that Mrs. Judd put up a tremendous fight for her life."

Winnie Ruth Judd Speaks
—From a personal letter, 1952

I had not eaten for a week and felt no hunger. Pictures taken of my body in jail showed that I had 147 bruises. I can't remember how long I was at the jail, but finally I was taken to the Georgia Street Receiving Hospital. I was given gas and hypos while the bullet was being removed from my hand.

It must have been midnight when a nurse brought a piece of paper to sign. It read: I authorize this. I refused to sign it. The nurse left and presently came back. Down at the end of the ward I saw several men. The nurse pointed out one of them as my attorney, who said I must sign it.

I had never been in jail before. I had never been in trouble. I had never had to have an attorney before. My husband had taken care of practically all business. I did not know what to do except sign it. Then the next morning my husband fired Judge Russill, my attorney, from the case, for giving a story about me—supposedly what I had told him—to newspapers, which I had not written or read.

Sometime the next day a man, whom I later learned was a Mr. Rockland, a staff reporter for the William Randolph Hearst newspaper, came to my bed with a long envelope. In it was several $1,000 bills and he said, "When you are asked who your attorney is, say Schenck." Where that money went and who took it, I never knew. Everything happening then was vague.

Just then, several men came to my bed and one of them asked, "Mrs. Judd, who is your attorney?" I did only what I was told to do ever since the first shock of the tragedy. I said "Schenck." Judge Russill shook his fists and swore vengeance and said, "Little lady, this is the sorriest thing you have ever done." He probably thought I was firing him and making him ridiculed. I did not even know what was going on.

I've been told that Judge Russill feels very badly, since he asked my brother and a minister who have gone to see him if I was the one who fired him from the case. The answer is no. I neither hired or fired him, I only did what I was told to do.

In the trial, [they said] I supposedly carried the dead weight of Sammy and Anne into the bedroom. I could not have done this even with two good hands. Evidence at the trial showed that the trunks had been moved after the bodies had been placed in them, but there were no scratches to show I had moved them and I certainly could not lift them. Four persons gave testimony that the trunks were lifted and not dragged.

At this time I was very ill, weighing only 103 pounds. Sammy was 126 and Anne, 135 pounds. I probably could not have wrested the gun from Sammy if I had not fallen on her from the impact of the blow on my head with an ironing board by Anne.

I was not present when dismemberment, and the bodies placed in the trunks, took place. However, I admit this was a ghastly deed. I've asked God many times to forgive me for the part I played in transporting the trunks to Los Angeles, but I was sick, wounded and suffering from shock.

If I committed a crime it was for not giving myself up to the police, since I had fought for my life.

There have been many statements I supposedly made such as I shot myself in the hand trying to commit suicide and that I made a confession to murder. If I did make such statements, I have no knowledge of them.

I am confessing to shooting Sammy and Anne but never will I confess to murder—only self defense.

Chapter 7
The Battle of the Confessions

Ruth Judd was not in custody twenty-four hours before two Los Angeles papers started printing "exclusive confessions" they said she had written for them. The papers reportedly paid her anywhere from $5,000 to $15,000. Either one was a fortune.

She wasn't in custody thirty-six hours before the script she was following started to disintegrate.

She wasn't in custody forty-eight hours before the plumber at the Broadway department store in L.A. found a torn, water-soaked letter she wrote while in hiding. The "drainpipe letter" to her husband would seal her fate.

The *Los Angeles Times* called its exclusive "My Story," and claimed it was written in Ruth Judd's own hand. It ran a by-line that was supposedly her signature. The *Examiner*'s contribution was called "My Own Story in My Own Words," which she supposedly dictated but did not write.

Although each version includes a recitation of her life, neither one sounds as if it came from her mouth. The wording doesn't resemble the speech patterns she shows in her letters and in the histories she later dictated. The words don't sound like those of a woman who is frightened or mortified by the crime she is accused of committing. They sound, in fact, chatty—as though Ruth Judd had curled up with two different reporters from two different papers and, over tea, spilled her guts. For a woman who would label the press "a bunch of morbids" and maintain a lifelong distrust of the media, that seems a most remarkable beginning.

She also makes some astonishing admissions, if indeed she authored these exclusives. The *Times* ran a story claiming Ruth Judd said this:

"It has been charged that I had an accomplice either before, during or after the actual tragedy. This is not true. I alone shot and killed both these women, who were once my friends. I did it in self-defense to save my own life, and for no other reason. I alone disposed of the bodies. I had no help of any kind from anyone...Sunday morning I dragged Sammy to the bathroom and in the bathtub I severed her body, placing parts in the trunks and my suitcase."

Even in Phoenix, where officials were cocky about how they had nabbed a killer, many didn't believe the "exclusives" were authentic. But it would not be until 1933—long after Ruth Judd was convicted—that anyone tried to determine their validity. On March 23, 1933, Arizona attorney general Arthur LaPrade sent a telegram to Ralph W. Trueblood, managing editor of the *Los Angeles Times*: "Dr. Judd testifies that *Times* story was dictated by him to your Mr. Hotchkiss, that Hotchkiss wrote the story on the typewriter as Dr. Judd dictated, Hotchkiss using his own judgment as to literary form and phraseology. Wire me collect any explanation that you can give on this subject matter."

Trueblood wired back almost immediately: "Doctor Judd's story was dictated to Kenneth O'Hara, rewrite man *LA Times* with Carlton Williams and Albert Nathan, reporters, present. O'Hara writing directly on typewriter. Phraseology and literary form chosen by O'Hara but the facts contained in story were given by Judd. Judd also read all proofs before story was printed and corroborated same by checking with his wife in county jail. She signed the proofs signifying them to be correct."

Today Winnie Ruth Judd still shudders when those newspaper "confessions" are mentioned. "I never wrote a story for any newspaper," she insists. "I never sold a story to any newspaper." It is gently suggested that perhaps her money-strapped husband had supplied the information and collected the fee. "I don't know what he did," she says, making it clear she no longer has any interest in knowing. But the so-called confessions—and the rich sums they supposedly garnered—would always haunt her.

All of this money-for-crime didn't sit well in Phoenix, where Winnie Ruth Judd's fate would eventually be decided. It tasted sour to Phoenix reporters and readers alike. The hometown papers made no attempt to hide their disgust at the "battle of confessions" going on in Los Angeles. The *Gazette* reported that "purchasing agents" from the *Times* had been sent to the county jail hospital to offer Mrs. Judd "the biggest price ever paid to a criminal in Los Angeles for his or her 'own story,' regardless of who wrote it."

The *Times* reporters were met by newsmen from the *Examiner*, who claimed they had already secured exclusive rights. "Notes were passed to Mrs. Judd as fist fights impended," the *Gazette* reported. "She would sell her 'own story' a second time if Dr. Judd would consent, but Dr. Judd had disappeared; he was 'hidden' in the office of the [*Examiner*] dictating the second installment of his 'own story.' The baffled purchasing agents cursed and threatened. At an early hour today no armistice had been signed. Two representatives of each paper sat in opposite corners of the turnkey's room, glaring and smoking innumerable cigarettes, hoping to prevent skullduggery by the other."

Several of these stories were submitted to the jury, which was asked to accept them at face value: to believe that Ruth Judd—in a moment of conscience or an act of greed—blithely told the world she alone was responsible for every single aspect of this horrible crime.

Besides the prosecutors, it was hard to find anyone in Phoenix who bought it. Instead, most reached the conclusion Winnie Ruth Judd was covering up for someone. There had been too many hints published, even in the local press. There was too much gossip on the street. There were too many people who had seen something and were only too happy to talk about it.

For many women in Phoenix, especially, she was beginning to look less like a murderess and more like a romantic heroine who was protecting her man. Some of these women would jam the courtroom each day of her trial, whispering encouraging words to the star of the show.

But it would be a long time before the public knew that even the jury was certain Winnie Ruth did not bear the guilt alone.

What the public suspected, Phoenix law enforcement officials knew. Their investigation had proved beyond any doubt that Ruth Judd could not have carried off the murder scenario by herself.

Their reports—all kept secret from the press and the public—showed they knew she was physically incapable of handling the trunks.

They knew Jack Halloran's car had been seen at Ruth's apartment and the death house both the night of the killings and the day after.

They knew her story of her wounded left hand was true.

They knew there was physical evidence inside the death house to indicate the presence of an accomplice.

They knew Sammy hadn't been "hacked up," as the public believed, but precisely cut apart with a skill Ruth Judd didn't possess.

And they knew Ruth Judd was such a bad liar she even got the time and place of the dismemberment wrong. The official autopsy reports that were eventually presented to the jury specify the dismemberment happened "within hours" of death on Friday night—not on Sunday morning, which is what Ruth Judd's newspaper "confession" claimed. And that time frame means the dismemberment took place *inside* the death house, long before the trunk was moved to Ruth's apartment.

But officials owned up to none of those things. Publicly, they said the "confessions" were proof positive that Ruth Judd alone should pay for the crime of murder.

This investigation learned that Ruth Judd—in those crucial hours after surrendering—was covering up for the two men in her life she professed to love equally: her husband and Jack Halloran.

In Ruth Judd's mind, psychologists would soon discover, the deaths of her friends were "my tragedy," while her affair with Halloran was "my one sin." As a minister's daughter who had been taught that fidelity was the cornerstone of marriage, she saw her sin as the more important of the two.

The tragedy was unavoidable because she had been attacked first, she maintained—and repeats to this day.

The affair with Halloran was both avoidable and unacceptable. It was wrong in the eyes of God and society. And she knew that knowledge of the affair would devastate her husband. Despite all they had been through in their topsy-turvy marriage, the one thing each felt certain of was the other's fidelity. "I was never jealous of my husband because I knew he was true to me," Ruth would tell psychologists. She had been a virgin on her wedding day and had sworn—in front of her officiating father and all her relatives—that she would hold herself to this one man.

And she had, until Christmas Eve of 1930. That was when Jack Halloran came calling. While any decent family man spent that evening at home with his wife and children, Jack instead showed up on her doorstep, finding the timing perfect to "comfort" the lonely young beauty.

Dr. Judd was in the hospital that Christmas, his narcotics use again out of control. He hadn't even sent Ruth a Christmas card. She was broke. She had just moved to Phoenix and had few friends. And this time of year that she'd always loved was turning into a painful symbol of the way her life was falling apart. As she would later explain, Halloran came by the apartment that night. He was handsome and charming and loving. She slept with him, discovering a passion she had never known with her husband. She fell helplessly in love.

As their affair bloomed over the following months, Ruth well knew she was not the only woman in Jack's life. "I have known that he has gone with other women, although he has denied it to me," she would tell the psychologists. "I have been happy and able to get along because I knew that he really loved me more than anybody else, and I was getting the most of him. I know, because I was getting the most of his time."

Ruth tried to reconcile the conflict of her two men, she explained, because she never stopped loving her husband, even as she was spending every available minute with Halloran—she would eventually admit she'd been with him ten of the fourteen days before the killings. "I believe you can love two people at one time," she declared.

It was with these two men that Ruth Judd still hoped to realize her most precious dream. Since her teens, she had been obsessed with becoming a mother. She once claimed that a neighbor boy had impregnated her, although the boy had never touched her. Twice pregnant by her husband while they lived in Mexico, she had lost the baby both times because of her poor health. Even so, Dr. Judd would remember how Ruth sometimes pretended she had actually given birth—greeting him at the end of the day with stories about the baby's activities, the cute things he did. He recalled her fretting for days over what to name the phantom baby. Her favorite choices were Moses, Caesar, or Napoleon. Dr. Judd said at first he thought she was kidding, but eventually realized that in her mind, she really did have a child.

This investigation has found that 30 days before the killings, Ruth Judd again thought she was pregnant. This time, the father was Jack Halloran. Doctors at the Grunow Clinic admitted to police, in a report that remained secret, that Ruth had been given a pregnancy test, but it proved negative. They said that, to protect her, they had listed the test under her maiden name. Ruth would say she thought she had miscarried again. She would eventually tell psychologists she had hemorrhaged for twelve days, with the bleeding ending about a week before the killings.

In her dazed, terrified state since the killings, Ruth Judd had to contend not only with the deaths of her friends, but with her need to protect these two men—one from his role in the tragic events, the other from the knowledge that his wife was unfaithful.

Years later, she would admit that the script was laid out for her before she ever boarded the train in Phoenix: She would protect Halloran by taking all the blame. With his role camouflaged, her husband wouldn't learn about the affair. In exchange, Halloran would work behind the scenes to ensure that officials treated her kindly.

By the time she gave herself up, Ruth Judd had convinced herself that she could pull it off. But within hours, she watched the whole script begin to fall apart.

Journalists were camped out on whatever doorstep she happened to be behind—at the funeral parlor where she surrendered, at the hospital where the bullet was removed from her hand, at the jail cell where she was kept for two weeks until she was extradited to Arizona. They threw questions at her constantly. She quickly learned how to clam up. To most of the inquiries, she either remained mute or simply said, "I refuse to answer that."

But she flared angrily when a Phoenix reporter told her he was bringing a message from "a wealthy man in Phoenix." According to the account of the incident in the Phoenix *Gazette*, the reporter told her: "He asked me to tell you he wanted you to clear him in connection with that visit you made with him to the home of the girls the night before they were killed."

Ruth Judd shot back, "He couldn't have sent that message. He knows all about it."

"Remembering that her attorneys had warned her not to talk at all, Mrs. Judd refused to comment further," the *Gazette* reported. "She was asked if she meant the man knew all about the visit to the girls or if she meant that he knew about the circumstances of the slayings. 'I won't answer any more questions,' she said to all queries."

Nowhere in the *Gazette* that day, which ran a total of ten stories on the case, is the man named.

No one ever realized that this message from Phoenix plunged Ruth Judd into new depths of terror. She knew it came from her beloved Jack. But why would he send a reporter? Was something going wrong? Could he really be trying to "clear" himself? She didn't want to face the doubts that began swirling in her mind.

Eventually, she tearfully confessed her "sin" to her husband. She tried to make it sound as meaningless as she could—of course, she never mentioned the phantom pregnancy—but Dr. Judd understood what had happened. He told her he could forgive her and he would stand by her. And however else William Judd may have failed his wife during their marriage, this time he kept his word.

To the rest of the family, Ruth would forever deny that Jack was any more than a friend. Her brother, Burton, either believed her or decided the "good wife" image would arouse more sympathy for his sister than the truth. In his fund-raising pamphlet, he steadfastly presents Ruth as a faithful wife preyed upon by her friend Jack.

Burton writes that even though Ruth had growing suspicions that Halloran was covering his own backside, she clung to the story she was supposed to tell. He says she gave him specific instructions: "The first thing Ruth wanted me to do when I arrived in Phoenix was to go and see Halloran and tell him that she hadn't talked, and to find out what he was going to do." Burton says Halloran refused to speak with him.

Any doubts about Halloran's charm—or his ability as a salesman—are dispelled by the seesaw ride he took Ruth Judd on for the next few months. She believed Halloran would stand by her. Then she thought he had deserted her. Then she was convinced he would never let her hang.

This jostling is most dramatically revealed in the psychiatric reports done on Winnie Ruth Judd by Dr. Joseph Catton, who was working for the prosecution. He first interviewed her on November 27, 1931.

"She showed scorn for Jack Halloran, stating that he was acting as do the rest of men," Dr. Catton reported to the court. "He had forsaken her. He would not raise a finger to help her, even though she may be hanged."

His report included this exchange:

"Dr. Catton: Would there have been any Ruth Judd case without Halloran?

"Ruth: No.

"Dr. Catton: Could Halloran help you if he wanted to?

"Ruth: He certainly could.

"Dr. Catton: Why don't you tell the complete story?

"Ruth: Because I can't see where it would do me any good and it would make trouble for others.

"Dr. Catton: Possibly it would do you some good.

"Ruth: My husband is telling me that every time he sees me and urging me to tell everything, and so is my attorney, Mr. Lewkowitz—but (tears in her eyes) what shall I do? I don't know what I shall do; it won't do me any good anyway."

No one found it strange Dr. Catton was *specifically* questioning Ruth about Jack Halloran—the man who supposedly had nothing to do with the crime.

But two months later, Dr. Catton found an astonishing change in her attitude. In an interview of January 7—twelve days before her trial began—he reported Ruth Judd had renewed faith that Halloran would save her.

"Ruth: Jack Halloran still loves me and always has.

"Dr. Catton: But you told me before that he had forsaken you, that he was just like the rest of men and that he would not raise a finger to help you, now which is so?

"Ruth: No, he still loves me. He has sent word to me in the jail here that he still loves me and that makes things different. He would come up to see me if he could, but you know as well as I do that he couldn't do that because there is a warrant out for his arrest and he would be picked up if he dared to come in here."

Dr. Catton knew there was no warrant out for Halloran's arrest, but he was not particularly surprised that Ruth had fallen for the lie.

Later in the interview, Dr. Catton continued a line of questioning he had pressed many times in the hours he'd spent with her: What story was she going to tell on the stand?

"Dr. Catton: Won't you tell or aren't you going to tell the complete facts of this case?

"Ruth: If things do not go the way they tell me; if things do not go the way they are planned, believe me, I will get up there and tell them everything."

But she never got the chance.

The way the jury would hear it, Winnie Ruth Judd penned her own death sentence.

Something was clogging up the drain in the Broadway store in Los Angeles. In cleaning out the trap, the plumber found a wad of telegraph sheets. In pencil, someone had scrawled a long, rambling letter addressed to "Darling." The pages were falling apart, but the last sentence sent the plumber straight to the police: "I killed in defense. Love me yet, Doctor."

Winnie Ruth Judd wrote the letter in the midst of the manhunt as she hid out in the store. She was apparently contemplating suicide and wanted to set the record straight with her husband. Changing her mind on both accounts, she tore up the letter and thought she flushed it away in the toilet. A few days later, she gave herself up. She had been in custody for forty-eight hours when the plumber made his amazing discovery.

Police painstakingly pieced the "drainpipe letter" back together.

Prosecutors would later joyously present it to the jury.

Here is Winnie Ruth Judd, a jubilant prosecution said, in her own words, in her own hand, to her own husband, submitting her own confession that she is a cold-blooded murderer.

The *Phoenix Gazette* rushed an *Extra* edition on the streets to announce the "bombshell" discovery of the letter.

Telling readers it was quoting directly from the letter, the *Gazette* claimed that Ruth Judd wrote: "I knew that Mrs. LeRoi would give me up to the authorities so I had to kill her, too. Sammy shot me through the hand. I grappled with her and finally gained possession of the gun. Then I shot her twice. I had to kill Mrs. LeRoi to keep her from giving me up."

That's not what the letter says. It's what the prosecutors would pretend the letter said, but that so-called direct quote grossly distorts the actual words of the drainpipe letter.

The press would also surmise that in the letter, Ruth Judd admits to dismembering Sammy's body. They reached that conclusion by these words: "It was horrible to pack things as I did. I kept saying, 'I've got to, I've got to, or I'll be hung.'" Phoenix police officers knew the press misunderstood those words. They knew Ruth was recounting exactly what they had already figured out: Faced with a trunk too heavy to go as baggage, she had repacked the body parts into the second trunk and the hand luggage in her apartment that Saturday night. But no one ever corrected the misperception.

The drainpipe letter is still preserved under plastic sheets in the evidence box at the Maricopa County records annex—the same condition it was in when presented in the murder trial of Winnie Ruth Judd.

In it, Ruth claims the killings happened on Saturday morning. Years later, she would try to explain that ruse by saying she somehow thought that by changing the time, she could conceal from her husband her illicit affair with Halloran. Retired police Captain Hugh Ennis thinks it just as likely she was so confused and psychotic she could no longer correctly place the time of the killings.

Significantly, the letter exonerates Halloran—a point his many supporters would always stress. Burton McKinnell would later argue that his sister tried to protect Halloran because she was convinced he would protect her.

History shows one other crucial point about the letter Ruth Judd intended as her final message to her husband. What she tells him about the fight and the killings is exactly what she has always said happened that night. She would eventually tell this story many times—all of them *after* she'd been convicted of murder. But she would always tell the same story.

Thursday Mr. H. brought the girls a new radio. Mr. Bisch had let them have his, but they didn't like him so hated to use his radio. Mr. H. wants me to get some other girl and go with him out to the house. I know a pretty little nurse who was taking Salvarsan, but she has nothing contagious now. I certainly am not expecting them to do wrong anyhow, so saw no harm. She's pretty and can be interesting, so we went out to the girls house. Dr. Brinker-hoff and a couple of Mr. H. friends were there. The girls didn't like it so Mr. H. asked us to have dinner with them. I refused, so he got dinner and came over to the house— the first time he has ever done this, but it was a nice, clean evening. I truly didn't even take a drink. You can ask. The remains of their drinks are in the ice box.

Next day Anne came over and we had lunch together— the remains of the dinner the night before. She wanted me to go home with her that night. Evelyn Nace was going. I had to do some histories and couldn't. I said, "If I get thru in time I'll come over and play bridge." Evelyn left early and we didn't play bridge, but I stayed all night.

The next morning all three of us were yet in our pajamas when the quarrel began. I was going hunting. They said if I did they would tell Mr. H. I had introduced him to a nurse who had syphilis. I said, "Anne, you've no right to tell things from the office. You know that only because you saw me get distilled water and syringe ready, and she hasn't it contagious. The doctor lets her work nursing."

"Well," Anne said, "I asked Evelyn and she thinks I should tell Mr. H. too, and he certainly won't think much of you doing such a thing. You've been trying to make him like you and Mr. D. too, getting him to move you, and when I tell them you associate with and introduce them to girls who have syphilis, they won't have a thing to do with you and when we tell Mr. P. about it, he won't take you hunting either."

I said, "Sammy, I'll shoot you if you tell that." We were in the kitchen just starting breakfast. She came in with my gun and said she would shoot me if I went hunting with this friend. I threw my hand over the mouth of the gun and grabbed the bread knife. She shot. I jumped on her with all my weight and knocked her down in the dining room. Anne yelled at us. I fired twice, I think.

And since Anne was going to blackmail me too if I went hunting, by telling them this patient of Dr. Baldwin's was syphilitic, and, would hand me over to the police, I fired at her....

Anne said before Sammy got the gun, "Ruth, I could kill you for introducing that girl to [?] and if you go hunting I will tell them and they won't think your so darn nice any more."

I don't want to bring Mr. H. into this. He has been kind to me when I was lonesome at the first place I worked and has trusted me with many secrets of all he did for the girls, such as caring for Anne, giving her extra money and the radio and he's been a decent fellow. It would separate he and his wife and he has been too decent. ...

Doctor, dear, I am so sorry Sammy shot me; whether it was the pain or what, I got the gun and killed her. It was horrible to pack things as I did. I kept saying, "I've got to, I've got to or I'll be hung. I've got to, or I'll be hung."

I'm wild cold, hunger, pain, and fear now, Doctor darling, if I hadn't got the gun from Sammy she would have shot me again. Forgive me....forget me. Live to take care of me, [illegible] as I am sick, Doctor, but I'm true to you. I love you. The thots of being away from you set me crazy. Shall I give up? No, I don't think so. The police will hang me.

It was as much a battle as Germany and the U.S. I killed in defense. Love me yet, Doctor.

It's impossible to read the drain letter today and see how anyone could have construed it as an admission of cold-blooded murder.

"I believe she was trying to explain things to her husband before she killed herself, and to convince him not to think less of himself—it was her problem, not his fault," says Ennis.

The letter is so disjointed and so rambling that Ennis says it clearly shows one thing: "The best it says to me is she was totally psychotic at the time. She was suffering from a total disorientation."

Agreement comes from criminal defense attorney Larry Debus, who would take up her cause in the late 1960s. "If anything, the letter makes it look like she's insane," he says. "The prosecution could argue this letter was self-serving and she was trying to establish a story. But when you read it carefully, she's not being self-serving at all. She says barely anything to help herself, but the letter is full of inculpatory statements against herself."

What most strikes Ennis is how the letter was used. "It seems ludicrous to me that they used this letter to say she was a cold-blooded killer," he says, noting his police training usually aligns him with prosecutors, not defenders. "The letter raises more questions than it answers. As a prosecutor, you'd only use it if you already were confident you had your case made, if everybody was already convinced what happened and the trial was just a formality."

Debus points out that if Ruth Judd's defense attorneys had been on the ball, they could have used the letter to show the basic flaw in the case against her. "What's notably absent from that letter is any hate for these girls," he says. "There's no hint of animosity. The letter tends to make me believe her story of shooting in self-defense."

As Debus studied her case, that point kept haunting him. "Where's the motive for this murder?" he asks. "She killed because she was jealous—that's bullshit. For the jury to believe a certain thing happened, they have to know why. There's no why here. The only why is there was a fight."

But Dogie Andrews wouldn't see it that way. In his best bluster, he repeatedly told the press, "She is guilty of the most cold-blooded murder I ever encountered. If ever anyone deserved to be hanged, it is she."

Chapter 8
The Case Against
Winnie Ruth Judd

"I'm embarrassed to say I was a member of a police department that conducted the Winnie Ruth Judd investigation."

As uncomfortable as those words make him, Hugh Ennis says he can't duck that conclusion. In his thirty years of law enforcement—twenty-two as one of Phoenix's finest—he says he was trained to investigate crimes honestly, not intentionally skew them. By the time he retired from the force in 1981 as captain, Ennis had experience with everything from homicides to narcotics to police intelligence to vice. In all those years, he never saw anything to rival the "lousy" job done by his predecessors in this case.

For Ennis, the Winnie Ruth Judd case is like a hobby. A self-proclaimed "history nut," he feeds his interest through an Arizona organization called the Dons Club—a group of men from all walks of life who study and promote Arizona history. Ennis's specialty is Arizona's spectacular criminal cases. For years, he has gathered bits and pieces of the Judd story wherever he could find them. He also read the Phoenix police report on the case before it was destroyed in a housekeeping move years ago.

In the course of this writer's investigation, Ennis was given the trial manuscripts to review. The 1,700 pages of testimony were among the memorabilia kept by defense attorney Herman Lewkowitz and now owned by his son, Jerry; they are apparently the only transcripts of the trial that still exist. This writer also gave Ennis all the witness statements taken by police during their investigation—many of which were uncovered in the probe.

Hugh Ennis decries the investigation at every single point: how officers collected physical evidence; how they quickly latched onto a theory of the killings and ignored everything that didn't fit; how they blatantly hid all the evidence that undercut their version of what happened that deadly night.

He says the Phoenix Police Department in 1931 botched the case from the moment they stepped into it. And he does not believe it was an accident.

"So much of what happened in this investigation smacks of exactly what it probably was—political interference," Ennis says. "Remember, this was a small town and part of the policeman's job was to know who was doing what to whom—they knew out of self-defense, because that's how you kept your job in those days. They'd know Jack Halloran was prominent. They'd know who his girlfriends were. Some of those cops even knew the victims."

Ennis found proof that Anne LeRoi was no stranger to the Phoenix P.D. one day when he was going through old police records: "I found a mimeographed memo that was a case summation. It was faded and hard to read, but I got interested when I saw the name Agnes LeRoi. I got the sense she'd been at least accused of prostitution. She'd been in the Jefferson Hotel in downtown in the company of a guy and there'd been a scene and the police were called. She wasn't arrested. The memo mentioned that a guy who was then the chief of detectives—he later became the chief of police—took care of the situation. This occurred a few months before she was killed."

So he's not surprised—chagrined, but not surprised—that police "took care" of the murder investigation, too.

Court records show the first officers to arrive at the death house were M. S. Frazier, who had been on the force for twelve years, and George F. Larison, with three years' experience. It was about eight p.m. Monday night, October 19, minutes after the L.A.P.D. had telegraphed Phoenix police of its discovery at the depot. Both officers would testify that reporters showed up instantly and were allowed inside the house.

"I told the reporters not to touch anything, and any time I saw anyone molesting anything at all, I told them to leave it alone," Officer Larison testified at the trial. "I told them to leave that stuff alone until the fingerprint man got there." It was one to two hours later when the fingerprint man finally showed up.

Officer Frazier told the court that during the evening, "there must have been a half dozen people" in the house, both reporters and neighbors. He said the crowd walked through the three rooms of the death house—the kitchen, the living room, the bedroom. "As far as picking up anything, I don't think so because I told them not to," he testified.

Ennis is blunt about the shameful admissions the officers made on the stand. "They sent officers out there who let reporters traipse all through the place. Right then, they no longer had a crime scene. Any crime scene integrity was gone."

Ennis stresses he isn't trying to impose sophisticated crime techniques on the officers of sixty years ago. But even then, he notes, it was standard operating procedure to be sure whatever evidence you had—especially in a capital case like murder—was not destroyed, trampled, or stolen.

"The first thing you do in a homicide investigation is secure the crime scene to be sure all the physical evidence is preserved," he explains. "Every officer knows that. Every officer knew that then. Who knows what evidence was destroyed as those people were milling around? Who knows what was moved or taken away? Who knows what finger-prints were wiped out? Sure, this was a small town then, but this wasn't the first murder Phoenix had ever seen. This wasn't the first time officers had to conduct a homicide investiga-tion. But the police clearly acted like this was a small hick town the way they handled this case. It was just terrible."

And things only went from bad to worse. Ennis says what happened next is "dumbfounding."

The landlord of the bungalow went down to police head-quarters the day after the trunks were discovered and pleaded with police to protect his property because "curiosity seekers were destroying valuable furniture and furnishings," the local press reported. The department did assign an officer to stay at the house, but it appears that was only for show; the officer certainly did not keep the curiosity seekers away.

The landlord quickly ran ads in the *Republic* and the *Gazette*, alerting the public that tours of the bungalow were available for ten cents a head. Newspapers reported "thousands" paid to gawk at Phoenix's hottest attraction during the next three weeks.

And then—after all the first-night intruders, after all the ten-cents-a-headers—only then did police get around to taking blood samples from the site of the crime.

It wasn't until November 13—twenty-eight days after the killings—that the county's chief investigator had collected blood samples. "By the time they got around to taking blood samples, it was a worthless gesture," Ennis complains. "Every-thing in that house was contaminated by then."

That point seemed obvious even then. Defense attorneys clearly did not expect an argument when they objected to all the blood evidence by reminding the judge: "By the advertisements in the newspapers, the entire population of Maricopa County visited that place."

They were in for a rude awakening. Judge Howard Speak-man overruled the objection. In fact, the judge was very for-giving of the mistakes made by police officers and investigators.

Every single objection raised by the defense attorneys about the "tainted physical evidence"—and they objected to virtually everything—was overruled. Eventually, even Winnie Ruth Judd's defenders gave up trying to discredit the case because of the shoddy police work.

Ennis says it got even shoddier, that the unbelievable treatment of the crime scene was only the first clue that the police weren't looking for the truth.

"In a homicide case, you look at the evidence and develop a theory about what happened. Especially when all you've got is a case of circumstantial evidence, and that's what they had here—there weren't any witnesses that came forward and said they saw the shooting. So in a case like that, everything has to fit your theory. If there's one piece of physical evidence that doesn't fit, you have to explain it. But here, they had pieces all over the place that didn't fit their theory. But they didn't try to explain a single one of them."

In fact, Ennis says, he's hard pressed to find any evidence that *did* fit the state's theory of the killing. Not even their contaminated blood samples held up under scrutiny.

The scene the state painted for the jury was that the girls were lying in their beds asleep when Ruth Judd put a gun up to their heads and, one at a time, shot them dead. The state surmised Anne was shot first, dying from a single .25-caliber bullet wound to the head. It further surmised that Sammy was awakened during the slaughter, partially raised up in bed, and threw out her hand in a "defensive gesture" to ward off her attacker, taking the first bullet in her hand. The fatal bullet was in her head. Prosecutors told the jury they'd see how absurd it was to believe Ruth Judd's statements to the press that the girls were killed in a fight in the kitchen.

Ennis points out that the bedroom was really a tiny sleeping porch with just enough space for two single beds and a dresser. Anne's bed was on the north wall, Sammy's on the south wall. There was a walkway between them.

Testimony at the trial indicated the only blood in the bedroom was found under Anne's bed. A corner of the scatter rug under the bed was covered with blood—it had been cut out and thrown into the death trunk. Besides that, there were a few splatters on the floor around Anne's bed that went up the wall no higher than the baseboards. There was no blood on the springs of her bed. There was no blood on the wall by the bed.

And then there was Sammy's bed. There was no blood there at all. None on the walls. None on the springs. None on the floor by or under the bed. No splatters anywhere near the bed. "What, one victim bled and the other didn't?" Ennis asks sarcastically.

Ennis states flatly that the blood evidence does not support the allegation that the girls were killed in the bedroom.

"There just wasn't enough blood in that bedroom," he insists. "If she'd shot the women as the prosecutors said, there would have been blood on the walls beside the beds— especially Sammy's bed, because she supposedly rose up to fight off the bullets. But there wasn't. There should have been a lot of blood in that bedroom, around both beds. You don't kill somebody—especially shooting them in the head— without a lot of blood."

He concludes one of the bodies eventually was on Anne's bed, but the evidence shows she was not killed there.

"The blood in the bedroom alone shows the state's theory was wrong," Ennis sums up. "So if their theory about the bedroom killing is wrong, then where and how were those girls killed? And why would Ruth Judd make up a story where she admits shooting them but puts the shooting in the wrong place? What did she have to gain? If she was there, she's got to know what the physical evidence shows. Why didn't she say the fight happened in the bedroom if that's the only place she knows the blood will show up? It doesn't make any sense that she'd insist the girls died in the kitchen unless that's what she remembered. Those are the questions police should have been asking, but they weren't."

Winnie Ruth Judd's defense attorneys don't earn kudos for the way they handled the blood evidence. Not once do they make the obvious point about the lack of blood on the bedroom walls—a point that could have been easily understood by a jury of men who undoubtedly were versed in firearms and shooting.

Defense attorney Herman Lewkowitz did try to arouse the jury's suspicion that the state was not being straightforward about the blood it found, but he never drove that point home. He raised all the right questions, but let the answers go over the jury's head.

The state's blood expert was Dr. H. L. Goss, who testified that he was taken to the death house by the county's chief investigator John Brinkerhoff (no relation to Dr. H. J. Brinkerhoff). Goss stated the only human blood he found was inside the bedroom. He said he did not make an independent inspection of the house, but took samples *only* where the investigator indicated.

Lewkowitz's cross-examination was filled with leading questions that suggested there actually was blood throughout the house:

> Q: Did he show you on the bottom of the door leading from the hallway to the kitchen a spot as big around as a penny that had what appeared to be hair in it?
>
> A: No.
>
> Q: Did he show you a place under the linoleum in the kitchen?
>
> A: No.
>
> Q: Did anyone pry away the quarter round [molding] in the dining room to show you blood under a baseboard?
>
> A: No.

> Q: Did he show you handprints on the south wall of the hallway?
> A: No.
> Q: Did he show you anything of the same nature in the bathroom? On the bathroom door?
> A: No.

Ennis says those questions should have raised a lot of suspicion in everyone's mind. For one thing, the questions were very specific—was Lewkowitz just fishing, or did his precise questions say he knew there was blood in all those places? For another, the witness was saying there was no blood where everyone should have realized there had to be blood.

"Why didn't they find any blood in the bathroom?" Ennis asks. "The state's own witnesses say the body was dismembered shortly after the killing, so it's pretty clear the dismemberment happened in that house. You mean to tell me an adult woman was dismembered and there wasn't speck of blood left behind? Even if the body was cut up in the bathtub, at the very least there'd be blood around the ring at the drain. Any good forensic examination would have discovered blood in that bathroom. If they found blood, why did they hide it?"

If the defense attorneys knew about all the blood, the obvious question is why didn't they hire their own experts to take blood samples? Modern defense attorneys queried on that point suggest it was a major mistake. But Ennis thinks the defense was simply blind-sided.

"Remember, Lewkowitz didn't know what we know," Ennis says. "He'd never seen the police reports because they weren't given to defense attorneys in those days. He didn't know what the state's evidence on blood samples showed until the state put that evidence on during the trial.

"Besides, the government is supposed to bring forth all the physical evidence. In theory, they're not supposed to be on anybody's side—they're not trying to get a conviction or an acquittal, they're just looking for justice. But it looks like in this case, that wasn't so. It sure looks to me like the prosecution had a predetermined outcome and only put forth the evidence that fit their theory."

The most blatant example of that, this writer's probe discovered, was the blood sample officials lied about on the stand—the most visible piece of evidence the police found the night they first entered the death house.

In the bedroom, a large bloody thumbprint was left on the window shade, as though someone had pulled the shade all the way down. Defense attorneys could not have seen the evidence—it was long gone by the time they toured the house in late November—but Lewkowitz questioned witnesses about it anyway.

He asked the questions because Winnie Ruth Judd had told him who left the fingerprint on the shade. But nobody on the stand admitted to ever seeing that thumbprint, including the fingerprint man who was at the house the night the trunks were discovered.

This probe has found a document in which Sheriff John McFadden admits that he personally cut out the section of the shade with the fingerprint. But that evidence was never produced at the murder trial. Whatever the print showed was lost in the secrecy of the state's investigation.

Ennis says the holes in the state's case just get bigger and bigger, once their evidence is inspected. What they couldn't explain they either ignored or distorted. Consider the missing mattresses.

Neither bed had a mattress by the time police entered the house. Ennis says they should have immediately questioned why the mattresses were gone, where they were, and who took them away. Instead, they ignored the whole issue. The press eventually reported that officers found a mattress miles from the death house. But officers said they did not think it could be related to the Judd case because this mattress *contained no blood.*

"Those mattresses are a clue," Ennis says. "There was either something on the mattresses the perpetrator didn't want seen, or the mattresses didn't fit the state's case—if there was no blood on them, how do you explain a scenario where the girls were shot in their beds?"

Besides that, he adds, the very fact that they were removed from the death house was revealing. "It doesn't take a genius to realize that you had to have some kind of transportation to take the mattresses away," he says. "Ruth Judd didn't have a car. So who removed the mattresses?"

Nor was he impressed with the state's case to prove pre-meditated murder. "To show premeditation, you have to show where the gun was that night. If she came over to kill them, they had to show she brought it with her. They didn't do that. My guess is they didn't because they couldn't explain where the gun was. There were never any tests done to see if she'd ever fired a gun—I've done those tests up to two weeks after the fact. You do a dermal nitrate test. It can even tell what kind of gun was fired."

What the state did with the bullets was just as lax, Ennis says. Police not only had bullets from the bodies but had found both exploded and unexploded .25-caliber shells thrown into the trunks. "One way you show premeditation is, you say to the court, 'Here's a box of shells. The defendant bought them on this day. Six are missing from the box. The six bullets were used in this crime.' But none of that was in the testimony. We don't know where the bullets came from."

Besides physical evidence, the actions of the accused are also important in showing premeditation, Ennis says. You have to show the person had a plan and carried it out. He is flabbergasted that the police investigation of Ruth Judd's activities in the days before the killings revealed no evidence of premeditation.

She met with a realtor on Thursday night—twenty-four hours before the killings—to secure a house big enough to accommodate herself, her parents, and her friends, Sammy and Anne. She told the realtor she and her friends would go by to look it over together on Saturday. On Friday, she and Anne went to lunch together and were seen by Dr. Brinkerhoff returning to the clinic "arm in arm." That same day—hours before her life would be altered forever—she spent all but two dollars of her paycheck making payments on her rent and her grocery bill. Saturday night, without any cash of her own, she was prepared to leave town on the late train, obviously secure that someone was waiting to pay her way. On Sunday, she spent the day trying to borrow the money to get herself out of town.

"None of those things are indicative of a person who is carrying out a murder plan," Ennis says. "She wasn't conserving her resources to make a getaway. The evidence you see presents a picture of a person caught in a predicament who has to improvise. I couldn't take the evidence the police gathered and get the case through a preliminary hearing or a grand jury, to say nothing of a murder trial. You'd pull the stunts today that they pulled and the judge would tell you, 'Get outta town.' He'd throw the case out."

Ennis sees such a pattern of evidence manipulation, such a prepared script for conviction, that he's left wondering just what Winnie Ruth Judd was actually guilty of doing.

"I think it's up for debate if she killed those girls or not," Ennis says. "The whole trail of the investigation and the way the case was prosecuted just raises too many questions.

"If she killed them by herself, there wouldn't have been the need for a cover-up. But we know there was a cover-up. The bodies were stuffed into trunks. One was cut up. She took them to L.A. All that is evidence somebody was trying to cover up the crime. And we know she was incapable of carrying off the cover-up by herself. So why would somebody help her? It makes no sense unless somebody was trying to hide their own complicity in the murders."

Chapter 9
Inside the Courtroom

Stewart Thompson can still see Winnie Ruth Judd sitting there in the courtroom. She looked terribly thin. She was such a tiny thing. Kind of pretty, he thought. That was probably a new dress.

But her eyes seemed so cold. He often wondered if she was paying any attention. Most of the time, she didn't seem to.

She just sat there, day after day, wrapping one linen handkerchief after another around her left hand. Wrapping incessantly until the cloth was reduced to shreds. You could get mesmerized watching that repetitive wrapping. Sometimes she pulled the fabric so tight her knuckles turned white.

Stewart Thompson could see it all so clearly because he had one of the best seats in the house. He and the other eleven jurors were just feet away from the Tiger Woman who had the country in such an uproar. He was only twenty-five years old then, a young clerk who was sitting in judgment in his first trial—the last time he would ever sit on a jury, in fact. He was a little nervous. Being the youngest, he had been honored by the rest of the panel with the job of jury foreman.

Stewart Thompson is now a member of a very exclusive club. He's one of four key players—and the only man—left from those tumultuous days in 1932 when the nation was riveted to "the trial of the decade." Two of the others were witnesses at the trial: Evelyn Nace, who shared the victims' last meal, and pretty Lucille Moore, whose introduction to Jack Halloran caused the fight between Ruth Judd and her best friends. And of course, Winnie Ruth herself has survived all these years.

Everyone else who played a role in the trial is gone—the judge, the prosecutors, the defense attorneys, the rest of the witnesses, the other jurors.

The club has three honorary members, women who weren't participants but had particular reason to pay close attention to the happenings in that courtroom.

County attorney Lloyd Andrews's widow, Francie, is one of them. She sat through the trial every day, and even at the age of ninety has a remarkable memory.

Another frequent trial visitor was Kate Kunze, whose husband, Tom, was a member of the jury. She too can vividly remember the courtroom scene, and also loaned this writer a tape her husband made for his family about the trial shortly before his death in 1989.

The final honorary member is Helen McFadden, the daughter of county sheriff John McFadden. Helen was sixteen years old at the time and was not permitted to visit the courtroom, but her father did let her sneak into the jail to visit with Ruth Judd and gave her regular reports of the trial. The astonishing things her father confided to his family— and the threats they received because of his bulldog determination to get to the truth—have never faded from Helen McFadden's memory.

These few voices are the only ones left to recount memories first hand. Stewart Thompson was interviewed once for a historical article, but none of the others have ever spoken out publicly on the trial until now.

Thompson remembers he was gingerly holding on to his job with the Standard Oil Company in those dark days of the depression when his name came up on the jury pool list. He was still single, still living at home, and his mother met him at the door one night with the anxious news that he was probably going to get on the Judd jury.

The next morning, he reported to the Gothic courthouse, the newest gem in downtown Phoenix. It had been dedicated three years earlier with such hoopla that Colonel John Philip Sousa had come to town to conduct his U.S. Marine Band. Thompson found himself herded into a tiny courtroom along with the other eighty-five men on the jury list. Like most states, Arizona in those days saw jury duty as "a burden the women leave to their menfolk."

The date was January 19, 1932—three months to the day since the bloody trunks had first been discovered in the Los Angeles depot.

Thompson sat in judgment on the longest and best-attended trial Arizona had seen up to then. For three weeks, he listened to the testimony in a hundred-seat courtroom that was so mobbed—mostly with women—that the sheriff had to bring in extra deputies to keep order.

It took two days for the final twelve jurors to be selected. "Some of them missed because they didn't believe in capital punishment or they'd already made up their mind she was guilty," Thompson remembers. "They came to me and I just told them I had read about it in the newspapers—of course, who hadn't? But I said I'd make my decision on the evidence."

From the first day they were impaneled, the men were sequestered in a makeshift dormitory set up on the top floor of the court-house. They were told not to discuss the case among themselves. Newspapers were kept away from them; visitors were denied. When the jurors left their quarters for dinner at a downtown restaurant each night, they would march in double file, with one bailiff in front and another in back. "When they'd take us out to picture shows, they'd buy two rows of extra seats, one in front of us and one in back, so no one could sit near us," Thompson recalls. The jurors were paid four and a half dollars a day.

Thompson says he wasn't surprised that he knew all the other men who sat on the jury with him. Phoenix was such a small place in those days. And he came from a family that was well connected in the community. His uncle was the state land commissioner at the time.

Young Thompson took his responsibilities very seriously. A woman's life was at stake. There was so much confusing evidence he had to listen carefully. And in this courtroom were assembled some pretty impressive members of the bar.

The presiding judge was Howard Speakman, who, like all Arizona judges, was an elected official. He had won his seat on the Democratic ticket in the fall of 1930. Speakman, originally from Oklahoma, had made Arizona his home since 1920. He was a veteran of World War I, and had seen every side of trial work. Six times during the six years he served as a prosecutor, he convicted murderers who paid for their crimes by the death penalty. As a defense attorney, he told the press he had never lost a capital case. In the year he'd already spent on the bench, Speakman had heard nine murder cases. None of those convicted had been sentenced to die.

Speakman eventually became a federal district judge in Arizona. He died in 1952.

The chief prosecutor was county attorney Lloyd Andrews, a popular, handsome figure who'd lived in Arizona most of his life. Most people referred to him as "Dogie," a nickname he'd picked up when he played varsity baseball at the University of Arizona in Tucson. At thirty-six, Andrews was the youngest man ever elected to the office of Maricopa County attorney. He won his seat in the same election and on the same Democratic ticket as Judge Speakman.

Andrews' success in the Winnie Ruth Judd case should have been another notch on his belt. "We thought he had it made," his widow recalls. Instead, he saw his political career evaporate. Just nine months after the Judd trial, he was ousted in his own party's primary, beaten by a young Democratic lawyer named Renz Jennings. In 1934, Andrews tried for a political comeback, running in a four-man contest for the Democratic nomination for Arizona attorney general. The victor got over 34,000 votes. Andrews was in the cellar with only 3,122. "All he went through in the Judd case was hard on him," his widow remembers. He died in 1964.

Winnie Ruth Judd had three defense attorneys—three warring attorneys who would turn on one another after the trial and who she would unceremoniously fire for "mishandling" the case.

The "star" was one of California's old-guard criminal lawyers, Paul Schenck, who was lauded by the press as "distinguished throughout the West." He was a large man with a shock of snow-white hair. Thompson remembers him as "very theatrical—he'd wave his arms around." At the time of the trial, the fifty-eight year old Schenck had thirty years' experience and was famous for introducing the insanity plea in the California courts system. Time and again, he had saved defendants from the death penalty by convincing juries his clients were insane at the time of the crime. He would find that in Arizona, that defense was still considered a novel idea. By the time he took on the Judd case, Schenck had drastically cut back on his legal work to usher in his retirement. He was coaxed into taking the case and secretly paid for his legal services by the famed publisher William Randolf Hearst.

The Winnie Ruth Judd case would be the ignoble end to Schenck's illustrious career. He was banished from the case soon after the trial and publicly blamed for botching her defense. He died ten months later.

Ruth's Arizona attorneys were law partners Herman Lewkowitz and Joseph Zaversack, who headed the very short list of criminal defense attorneys in Phoenix in those days. Both men had busy schedules, and it was common for them to juggle several cases at once. Nothing they'd handled thus far had approached the magnitude of this case.

Zaversack was the behind-the-scenes lawyer who assisted in gathering evidence and organizing strategy. One witness would crucify his name in a humorous parody that cracked up even the judge, referring to him as "Saveherneck." Zaversack died shortly after the trial.

Lewkowitz would go on to handle 114 homicide cases in his career. Ironically, he represented both defendants accused of murder on that bloody night in October 1931. The same day he would lose the Winnie Ruth Judd case in one courtroom, he'd be doing double duty saving Jack West in another. With the blessings of county attorney Andrews, Lewkowitz negotiated a plea bargain for West, the young pharmacist who lay in wait to murder his girlfriend the same night Anne and Sammy died. West's charges were reduced from premeditated murder to manslaughter—killing in the heat of passion. Lewkowitz argued for a suspended sentence, but the judge considered some jail time was necessary because, "I don't believe in cheapening human life to that extent." West was given three to five years in prison, but served only twenty-three months before going free.

Lewkowitz was a thin, bespectacled man whose easy manner outside the courtroom gave way to fierce questioning of witnesses inside. He was considered a formidable legal opponent. He and his partner were also being paid by Hearst. Lewkowitz died in 1951.

Stewart Thompson was surprised that Ruth Judd's "hot shot" lawyers never tried to show she had killed the girls in a fight. Like everyone else, he'd already read that story in the newspapers. How Ruth claimed Sammy had come at her with a gun in the kitchen. How she said she'd reached for the only available weapon nearby and stabbed Sammy with a flimsy bread knife she snatched off the table. How she'd shot Sammy first during their struggle on the floor. How Anne had been "braining" her with an ironing board, trying to break up the fight. How she'd shot once at Anne.

Thompson expected to hear all about that.

But he didn't.

"Self-defense did not come up during that trial at all," he recalls. "The whole defense was that she was innocent because of insanity."

The trial was already seven days old before her attorneys ever made their defense tactics clear. They had made no opening argument to the jury, leaving everyone guessing how they would try to defend this infamous woman. Instead, they waited until the prosecution's case was finished. When Paul Schenck finally addressed the jury, his booming voice slowly announced, "We avow to show that on or about October 16, the defendant was so insane that she at that time—if she did this act—was so devoid of reason as not to know right from wrong and the consequences of such an act."

Carrying the burden of proof, Dogie Andrews himself had delivered the opening statement for the prosecution. He told the jury that Winnie Ruth Judd was on trial only for the death of Anne LeRoi, and that a separate trial would be held later for the death of Hedvig Samuelson. Thompson says that was never really clear in the jurors' minds. So much evidence was presented about Sammy's death—and her dismemberment—that it was hard to distinguish between the two killings. That was a reaction the prosecution was clearly banking on.

Andrews also promised his evidence would prove Winnie Ruth Judd had planned for a long time to kill her friends. He claimed that the relationship between the women had been "deteriorating for five weeks"—getting so bad Ruth Judd had moved out of the duplex in early October. He told the jury he would prove that Winnie Ruth Judd's plan had developed in the weeks following, and she had killed in cold blood—an offense worthy of the death penalty.

Francie Andrews still speaks pridefully about the skillful job her "movie-star-handsome" husband did in front of the jury. "It was a beautifully tried case," she says. "Dogie was really a good lawyer and Judge Speakman was a fair man—he wouldn't put up with any foolishness."

Helen McFadden remembers her father—who is considered the county's first "modern sheriff"—always thought there was plenty of foolishness going on at the trial. "Dad thought there was a lot of cover-up," she recalls. "At first Ruth didn't trust Dad. She thought he was the same as everyone else. But she learned to trust him because he was the one who never stopped trying to prove the truth." But what Sheriff McFadden knew—or suspected—was not part of the prosecution's case.

Jury foreman Stewart Thompson would eventually have many doubts about the evidence he heard during the trial. But that would come later—long after his official duties were over.

At the time, he was convinced that Winnie Ruth Judd killed the girls in the bedroom where they slept. "In those days, every house had an incinerator out in the back where you burned all your trash. And they found these two mattresses all bloodstained, and some of the bedclothes that she'd tried to burn out there," he says. "Whether she did it by herself, I don't know. No one knows. But anyhow, in those days, everyone had a screen porch for sleeping arrangements. And these two girls had two single beds on the screen porch, little space apart, and those mattresses had been found out in the incinerator, bloodstains and all on them, only partially burned."

In reality police never found two bloodstained mattresses. They had found only one bloodless mattress, dismissing it as unrelated to this case. But apparently, Andrews had successfully lodged in the jurors' minds the idea that the missing mattresses must have been bloodstained and must have been destroyed.

Thompson was further convinced when he heard the autopsy report presented by the coroner from Los Angeles.

"According to the medical evidence, the muzzle of the gun was pressed right to [Anne's] temple," he recalls. "And that shot woke the other girl up, and she raised up in bed and the bullet went through her hand and into her arm. And there was a powder burn on her temple, too."

Stewart Thompson says it didn't seem to him that if the girls were fighting, the fatal bullets would have ended up like that. And he knew who had pulled the trigger: "She said she killed them in that letter she tried to hide in the drain."

Francie Andrews clearly remembers the killing scene the same way, just as her husband presented it to the jury. So does Kate Kunze, as did her juror husband.

Of all the evidence the state presented in this case, the autopsy expert was the most damning to Winnie Ruth Judd.

By the time Dr. A. F. Wagoner got on the stand to talk about the wounds, the jury had already heard two witnesses testify they heard three shots ring out in the death house at about ten-thirty that Friday night. Both witnesses—Mrs. Jennie McGrath, who lived next door to the bungalow, and Gene Cunningham, who lived across the street—said they were awakened by one shot, then after a pause, heard two more shots in quick succession.

If the prosecution now showed that there were three bullet wounds in the victims, the whole scene would fit.

It is easy to read Dr. Wagoner's testimony and conclude he confirmed that scene. The testimony is technical and confusing, but one is left with the impression that there *were* three wounds—two in Sammy, one in Anne. That is, in fact, what the jury heard.

But when an expert reviewed the testimony in the course of this writer's investigation, he found the coroner actually said there were *four* bullets in the victims.

Dr. Heinz Karnitschnig was the medical examiner of Maricopa County from 1971 until his retirement in early 1992. He is a forensic pathologist with over thirty years' experience—one of the longest tenures of any in the country. After studying the autopsy reports and the trial testimony, Dr. Karnitschnig said the autopsy clearly discovered three bullet wounds in Sammy, one in Anne.

Anne was killed by a single "contact wound" to the head, with the muzzle of the gun held so close to her left temple that it left powder burns around the entrance wound.

Sammy was struck by one bullet that entered her left chest and traveled through her body, lodging in her left arm. Another bullet penetrated the ring finger of her right hand. Neither of those wounds were life-threatening. She died from a bullet wound to her head, again shot at very close range.

The autopsy found one other wound in Sammy's body— a superficial puncture wound in her left neck. Dr. Wagoner testified he was not certain what had caused this stab wound, but surmised it was an instrument so flimsy it could not inflict much damage.

Winnie Ruth Judd's defense attorneys did nothing to enumerate those bullet wounds for the jury.

They never asked the jury to consider, if the neighbors heard only three shots, when was the fourth shot fired?

They never raised doubt in the jury's mind about the suspicious puncture wound in Sammy's neck. Was this the stab wound Ruth said she inflicted during the fight? What was such a wound doing in a body that the prosecution said was shot in bed, execution style? No one asked these questions.

In the jury's mind, the bullet wounds were the clincher.

"She killed them because she was jealous of them," Thompson says.

That's the way Francie Andrews remembers it too. "The whole case had to do with Jack Halloran," she says now. "He had nothing to do with the crimes, but they were all jealous over him."

Kate Kunze recalls that both she and her juror husband, Tom, also saw it that way. "It was jealousy and rage," Mrs.

Kunze says. Ironically, Tom Kunze did not remember Winnie Ruth Judd as a murderer who had carefully planned out her crime, even though he voted along with the rest of the jury to convict her of premeditated murder. As he told his family in the tape he left behind, the killings were "committed by a frail blond woman in a fit of jealousy—nothing premeditated."

How had Lloyd Andrews instilled the "proof" that Ruth Judd killed because she was jealous? With such vivid memories of the motive, one would expect that he presented a parade of witnesses to show the growing pattern of her rage.

In reality, he presented just two witnesses.

The prosecution's "surprise" witness was Mrs. Arthur Lepker. Her husband, a professional boxer, had recently been prosecuted for murder by Andrews and sentenced to prison by Judge Speakman. No police report exists on Mrs. Lepker's initial questioning by detectives. Her name first shows up in this case the day she testified.

Mrs. Lepker told the court she had seen Ruth Judd only twice in her life—meeting her sometime during the summer and then seeing her at the Grunow Clinic in August when Mrs. Lepker came in for a checkup. At their second meeting, she testified, Ruth confided in her that she was afraid Sammy was trying to take Jack away from her, although, the witness said, she herself had no idea who either of those people were. "She said she got so angry with Sammy and Jack she thought she'd go crazy or die," Mrs. Lepker testified.

During his cross-examination, Lewkowitz basically called Mrs. Lepker a liar. He questioned her harshly, suggesting it was odd that Ruth would share such intimacies with a clinic patient she scarcely knew. "Why would she tell you such a thing?" Lewkowitz asked again and again. Mrs. Lepker angrily answered, "I don't know." Lewkowitz's efforts to discredit the witness did not convince the jury.

The prosecution's "star" witness was nurse Lucille Moore, the subject of the fatal fight. Thompson still remembers how "embarrassed" the jurors were when they were told that Miss Moore was being treated for syphilis. "You didn't talk about those things in those days, and our girlfriends or wives were sitting out there in the courtroom listening to all this," he recalls.

Miss Moore was the centerpiece of the prosecution's case. She was the only witness Lloyd Andrews had to fulfill his "promise" that he would show a long deterioration in the relationship of the three women. And he pegged *that* to a single sentence Ruth Judd had supposedly uttered to Lucille Moore the night before the killings.

From the witness stand, Lucille Moore quoted Ruth as telling her: "I used to live here with Anne and Sammy, but we had a little difference and I moved away—in fact, that is what I moved over, our difference was about Jack."

Ruth's defense attorneys did not ask Miss Moore even one question. Nor did they try to counter the impression that Jack Halloran was the sole reason Ruth moved to her own apartment just seventeen days before the killings.

They could have used Anne LeRoi's own words in the letter to her fiancé to show there was another motivation: "Ruth is leaving us in a few days. Dr. Judd is coming home so she will take an apartment. It really hasn't worked out so well having three of us. We are very fond of her and she is a sweet girl, but there just seems to be a wrong number when one is used to living by oneself and just one other very congenial one."

Or they could have countered with Ruth Judd's own version of why she moved, "I found an apartment $5 a month cheaper and closer to the clinic, so I can walk to work and save the [trolley] fare," she wrote her husband in urging him to return to Phoenix.

The jury never heard any of that.

Nor did they ever hear how Lucille Moore had fled Phoenix because of ominous threats.

Two days after the press first labeled her the "key witness," Miss Moore disappeared. She was found a week later in her hometown of Williams, Arizona, by *Los Angeles Examiner* reporter Russell J. Birdwell.

"Girl Nurse Reticent about Threats That Forced Her to Flee Trunk Killings Inquiry," read the headline on his November 2, 1932 story.

According to the story, Lucille Moore got two death threats before she left town. First a man called on the phone and said, "You've talked too much. You'd better quit." Then an unsigned message was delivered to her home, which read in substance: "You'd better leave Phoenix."

Today Lucille Moore lives in a nursing home in Arizona. Although the media at times portrayed her as a close confidante of Ruth's, she says that wasn't so; the dinner they shared the night before the killings was it. "It was just a brief encounter," she says now. "Our orbits met just that one time, but it was the wrong time."

She looks very frail, lying in the pleasant room at the nursing home. She is kind and calm in answering questions, but leaves the distinct impression she would rather not be forced to remember any of it. "It was a little frightening," she says. "The press were hounding me. They thought I knew more than I did." She well remembers how the press probed everywhere. "They didn't even leave out a dimple," she jokes.

Although her association with Ruth Judd was brief, to this day Lucille Moore remembers her as being "terribly jealous of Jack and terribly possessive of him." She also remembers her "as a very charming lady. She had lots of good friends. They were mad when she was involved with the killings." Miss Moore met Halloran only that one time, but she was well aware of who he was. "Halloran had a domineering personality. When he walked into the room, you knew it. Everyone else knew it too. He was very active behind the scenes in politics, very active. He was a prominent man in Phoenix."

Then Lucille Moore begs off remembering any more. She says she doesn't remember the threats. She doesn't remember fleeing Phoenix. "Lots of people didn't want their names involved," she says, making it clear she wishes she was one of them.

The other one in that club is Evelyn Nace, whose involvement was nothing more than sharing dinner with the girls in the hours before they died. She lives in the West, but doesn't want anyone to know where. After all these years, she still shudders at the taint she experienced when her name was dragged into the case. "Investigators kept asking me who else was there that night, who called," she remembers. "I told them no one was there while I was, that nobody called. But they thought I was hiding something."

Evelyn Nace still thinks there was more to the story than ever came to light. She's always wondered who it was that helped Ruth Judd, because she never believed Ruth was capable of doing everything herself. "It would take a strong person to load those trunks," Miss Nace says, recalling how small Ruth Judd was and what a "good sized girl" Anne was.

Chapter 10
Injustice

Young Stewart Thompson was anxious to hear Winnie Ruth Judd explain herself. She was fighting for her life, and surely she would get on the stand.

He has always felt cheated that she never did.

"All of us on the jury thought it was kind of queer the defendant wasn't asked to tell her story," he recalls. Her silence helped cement the idea she had something to hide. The jury surmised the defense didn't call her because, "being they were using the insanity plea, they didn't want her to get up and act sane."

Kate Kunze remembers the same frustration. "She just sat there, twisting that handkerchief, and I thought, 'She knows what happened—why doesn't she get up and tell us instead of putting us all through this?'"

Young Helen McFadden, who got regular reports on the trial each night from her father, remembers being "disgusted" with Ruth's continued silence as the trial dragged on. "I was disgusted with her for her own sake," Helen McFadden says now. "I thought, 'For God's sake, get up there and tell the truth.' I thought she stayed silent to protect someone, and I remember thinking, 'Could any man mean that much to you, Ruth?'"

But Francie Andrews wasn't surprised that Mrs. Judd remained silent. "When you've got a guilty client, you don't call them to the stand," she says. "Lewkowitz didn't dare put her on the stand."

None of these people had any idea they were not the only ones who felt cheated.

So did defense attorney Herman Lewkowitz.

And to this day, so does Winnie Ruth Judd.

"My father was always frustrated over the Judd case because he never felt he was allowed to do all he could do," Jerry Lewkowitz says. "He always wanted Ruth Judd to take the stand, but Schenck didn't agree. Dad felt he could have won the case if she'd…have testified."

The defense lawyers apparently fought among themselves about that point throughout the trial. Lewkowitz not only constantly advocated her testimony, he repeatedly reassured Ruth that she would get her chance to give it.

And everyone waited. Most of all, Winnie Ruth Judd. As the *Gazette* reported, a newsman overheard her excitedly telling Lewkowitz early in the trial, "I wish I could get up and tell my story." Lewkowitz calmed her down with the promise, "That's all right, you'll be given the chance."

Of all the things that anger Winnie Ruth Judd about the outcome of her case, being kept off the stand tops the list. She still believes that if she could only have explained what happened that night, the jury would never have convicted her. She still believes she could have ended her nightmare there, in that small courtroom where she celebrated her twenty-seventh birthday. And she still believes she was "tricked" by Schenck and Lewkowitz into a silence that punished her until she was sixty-six years old.

"Lewkowitz kept telling me I was going to testify so I could tell my story," she told this writer in a recent interview. "I still thought I was going to testify the day the judge pronounced my sentence. I didn't know it was over. I didn't realize what was happening. I didn't know anything about the law. The judge said it was too late."

Lewkowitz's frustration spilled out in a most unusual legal tactic after the trial. He petitioned Judge Speakman for a new trial on the grounds that Winnie Ruth Judd had not received "adequate defense counsel." He claimed Schenck had "called the shots" during the trial and ignored his advice and efforts in mounting a vigorous defense. The judge rejected the petition.

Francie Andrews still thinks the complaints from Ruth Judd are bunk. "My husband kept begging her to tell her story," she says. "He gave her lots of opportunities—one time he took reporters up there [to her jail cell] and told her she could say whatever she wanted to them, but she never said anything."

Instead of hearing from Winnie Ruth Judd, jurors heard all about her. "They kept pointing out the fact that she kept wrapping her hand in that handkerchief—back and forth, all the time, like a crazy person," Thompson recalls. "And they kept saying she had delusions about having babies. Of course, she never had one. Her parents testified, but they didn't know anything much. She hadn't lived with them for a long time."

The Rev. and Mrs. McKinnell each got on the stand to tell the court about their family's long history of mental illness, recount all the "weird" things Ruth had done as a child, tell again and again how she was constantly pretending she was either pregnant or already a mother.

Thompson remembers the strange phrase, *dementia praecox* was spoken often during the trial and that it was some kind of mental illness. That was what the defense psychiatrists said. They claimed Ruth was insane because she suffered from a mental illness that was tied to the tuberculosis that had plagued her throughout her adult life. Among the symptoms of this particular brand of mental illness were delusional fantasies, erratic behavior, and an inability to carry out a complicated plan.

"But she never opened her mouth once, so how are you going to tell?" Thompson complains. "Her actions seemed like she knew what she was doing."

The defense called three psychiatrists to say Ruth Judd was insane; the prosecution called two to say she was not. Much of the testimony was technical.

"They had all these high-priced psychiatrists on both sides talking about schizophrenia," Thompson recalls. "We didn't know what schizophrenia was. And one of them said she was suffering from that and the other side said she wasn't. So we kind of threw all that out. Who are we going to believe when they're both well-educated psychiatrists and one refuted the other's testimony?"

Tom Kunze's family tape makes the same point: "They had two psychiatrists get up and state she was insane and they had two psychiatrists get up and state she was sane, and here's a bunch of naive jurymen up there trying to decide who's lying and who you should believe."

The jury's confusion over the insanity testimony cleared up once Judge Speakman gave them their final instructions. "We knew it was a very serious matter we were in and we wanted to do the right thing and we wanted to follow the judge's instructions," Thompson says. "The judge told us all we had to determine was if she knew right from wrong. If she didn't, she was crazy; if she did, she wasn't.

"The evidence showed she tried to hide it. Someone who knows the difference between right and wrong—that's what they'd do, try to hide everything." (Actually, the judge gave the jury six possible verdicts—but only the right-from-wrong one stuck in their minds.)

The bodies in the trunks, the plan to dump them at sea, getting her brother to help, even the nonexistent burned mattresses—all those things said to Stewart Thompson that Ruth Judd knew right from wrong.

Francie Andrews has never had any doubts. "She wasn't legally insane—for that, you don't know the difference between right and wrong—but she was nuttier than a fruitcake," Mrs. Andrews says. "She was a mean, bad woman. She killed those girls all by herself. She shot herself in the hand. And she cut up that body by herself too."

But Kate Kunze came away from the trial with two major impressions about what had happened: one, that Ruth Judd was guilty of shooting the girls, and two, that "there was no question" she'd had help somewhere along the way. Like so many others, Mrs. Kunze has always regretted that Ruth Judd's helpers were not exposed during the trial. "We never understood why Halloran was never called," she remembers. "His name was brought up so often in the case. He was sworn in, but he was never called to the stand."

It had created a stir in the courtroom the day Jack Halloran filed in with the rest of the prosecution's potential witnesses. He looked at Ruth Judd, but she turned away. Halloran's name was conspicuously absent when Lloyd Andrews read off his witness list. Even Halloran seemed surprised at what apparently was a last-minute change of plans. The press reported Halloran whispered something to Andrews as he left the courtroom, never to return. They quoted Andrews as saying he only intended to use Halloran as a rebuttal witness—if he needed him.

"People have maligned my husband because he didn't put Jack on the stand," Francie Andrews acknowledges. "I told Dogie, 'Why don't you just call Jack, because everyone wants you to,' but he told me, 'I'm trying this as a lawsuit, not for the scandalmongering public. He has nothing to do with the crime, and people just want to hear dirt.' But it hurt Dogie that he didn't call Jack." She's still convinced her husband was voted out of office in retaliation.

Helen McFadden remembers retaliation for her father, too, but the sheriff got it from the opposite side of the fence.

History shows that Sheriff John R. McFadden—"Mac" to most everyone—was the only law enforcement official in Arizona who made it clear he wasn't buying the pat case against Ruth Judd.

His daughter says simply: "Dad didn't think she was the killer.

"My father tried so hard to solve this case," Helen goes on, noting he wouldn't stop even after the jury had made its final decision. "Dad always thought there was a lot of cover-up about what really happened and he wouldn't let go. Everybody else said, 'Let sleeping dogs lie,' but Dad kept trying to get the truth out.

"He was getting telephone threats that something would happen to his family if he didn't back off."

Helen McFadden still remembers the chilling night after the trial when her father handed her a loaded six-shooter and instructed her to keep it next to her bed. "He told me that when my sister and I went to bed at night, we were to close the bedroom door. He said he'd never enter during the night, and so if the door opened, I was supposed to start shooting." She remembers her father sent some of his deputies over to the house to stand guard.

"Dad was turning up a hornet's nest. He knew who all were involved, but he never once told us, because he didn't want us to have that knowledge. He thought it would endanger our lives."

She also remembers her father—an elected official—was advised his political career could be ruined if he didn't stop. She says it eventually was. And she remembers fighting with other kids over the rumors being spread about him.

"They tried everything to discredit Dad. He was publicly accused of being Ruth Judd's boyfriend. Even Ruth and I would laugh about that when I'd visit her on Sundays."

To this day, when Helen McFadden thinks of Ruth Judd, she thinks about the "very ladylike, well-mannered, very polite" woman she visited so often in the jail. "I just thought the world of Ruth," she says. "I couldn't have felt that way about her if I thought she was a murderer. I didn't think she was, because my dad didn't think she was. Ruth would say to me, 'Do you think they'll hang me?' and I'd tell her, 'Not as long as my dad's got a breath in his body.'"

The case finally went to the jury at 5:12 p.m. on February 8, 1932. Thompson remembers everyone agreed she was guilty on the very first ballot. Then they took a supper break. It took five more ballots to set the penalty. Ruth Judd should hang. Court was reconvened at 9:15 p.m. to hear the verdict.

"I remember before the verdict was read, the judge warned everyone he didn't want any outbursts," Thompson recalls. "But boy, all the reporters made the biggest racket running out to their telephones. I looked at Ruth Judd and she didn't change her expression at all. The ones that were really shocked were her attorneys."

Jury foreman Stewart Thompson would later shock the nation. So would juror Tom Kunze. So would jurors Ed Gray and Ed Landrigan. All four of these men who had voted that Ruth Judd should die on the gallows came forward a year after the trial to plead for mercy.

They announced they had never really intended she should hang at all.

They said they gave her the death penalty "to make her talk."

They asked the state's Board of Pardons and Paroles to commute her death sentence.

Thompson told the board that on second thought, maybe she had killed in self-defense after all.

The jury foreman had been hounded after the trial by Ruth Judd's brother, Burton. "I'd come home from work and he'd be camped on my doorstep, trying to get me to go down to the prison to see her," Thompson recounts. Burton insisted that his sister had always wanted to tell her story but her attorneys wouldn't let her take the stand. He rambled on about all the points that weren't made clear in the trial to support his sister's story. If Thompson would just go down and talk to Ruth, Burton pleaded. Finally, as much to get Burton off his back as anything else, Thompson made the fifty-one-mile trip to the state prison in Florence.

He remembers noticing that Ruth Judd had abandoned the handkerchief twisting around her hand.

"She said she wished that she'd had a chance to plead self-defense," he recalls. "That was her main argument. She was perfectly normal. But she said she wanted to plead self-defense, but her attorneys advised her not to—to plead insanity."

Ruth seemed "a little put out about that," and when Thompson thought everything over, he saw why. "She might have caused just enough doubt if she'd pleaded self-defense," he acknowledges today. He remembered how easily the jury had decided her guilt based on the simple question, did she know right from wrong?

"In a capital punishment case, you have to have a hundred percent of the jurors going along to make it guilty," he says. "If she'd pleaded self-defense, it's a good possibility there could have been doubts created in the minds of the jurors, that they'd have brought in a different verdict. It sort of shows that maybe the insanity plea was the wrong one to have taken."

Thompson felt so strongly about it that on March 15, 1933, he signed a notarized affidavit to the parole board:

"I, Stewart Vaughn Thompson, having served as foreman of the trial jury in the case of the State of Arizona vs. Winnie Ruth Judd, hereby recommend that the present sentence of death be commuted to life imprisonment for the following reasons:

"That if the evidence and facts now brought to light had been produced from the witnesses and during the trial, there would have been sufficient doubt raised in my mind as to whether or not Agnes LeRoi had been killed in self-defense that I would have recommended a penalty of life imprisonment.

"Also, there is now sufficient evidence to show that there were other parties connected with this case that I strongly recommend the present sentence of death be commuted."

Thompson wasn't the only juror to have an astonishing change of mind.

By then three other jurors had come forward to tell a shocking story about what happened inside that jury room during the four hours and three minutes it took to decide Winnie Ruth Judd's fate. All of them pointed an accusing finger at fellow juror Dan Kleinman, a fifty-six-year-old rancher who had once been mayor of Mesa, Arizona, a small community east of Phoenix known mostly as a Mormon settlement. Stewart Thompson remembers Kleinman as an affable man who seemed to know everyone the jurors met on the street during their evening walks to meals. He was a take-charge type known for a strong streak of morality; during his four years as mayor of Mesa, he passed blue laws closing businesses on Sundays, and instituted a nine p.m. curfew for children under eighteen.

It isn't difficult to understand why the other jurors trusted him.

On March 9, 1933, juror Ed Landrigan signed this notarized affidavit:

"I was the last Judd juror who changed my verdict from life imprisonment to the death penalty. I was so worried over having changed, I didn't sleep all that night.

"Never would I have changed as I did had it not been for Dan Kleinman, who insisted that we should vote the extreme penalty. Then, he argued, such a verdict would make Mrs.

Judd talk, involving the accomplice or accomplices. Dan said that he had a good political friend on the Board of Pardons and Paroles and that he would get the sentence commuted if Mrs. Judd would talk.

"Furthermore, all of us jurors made an agreement, as a body, that if new evidence came to light subsequently, and Mrs. Judd would talk, we would immediately urge the Board of Pardons and Paroles to have the sentence commuted.

"If it had not been for the above promise I would not have come over to the death penalty."

Juror Ed Gray signed an affidavit, telling the same story: "I would have held out, but Mr. Dan Kleinman explained to us that he had political influence and a good friend on the Board of Pardons; that he could get Ruth Judd out with life imprisonment; that we should give her a death verdict and that would bring in the other party or parties, and he could have her sentence commuted later."

Juror Tom Kunze agreed. In his affidavit of March 10, he swore: "Dan Kleinman made a suggestion which we thought was all right. That was: If we would vote death, it would make Mrs. Judd 'talk.' I do not now feel that the extreme penalty is justifiable, but we honestly did want the facts brought to light. So we all agreed to give the death verdict.

"Mr. Kleinman's idea didn't strike all the jurors right at first, for a few held out for life. But after Mr. Kleinman talked further, he got them to see his point and they came over. The idea seemed to be a good one, and we voted death."

Dan Kleinman, it turns out, was wearing several hats when he joined the Judd jury. And none of them was white.

Twice his actions inside and outside the jury room would be labeled "juror misconduct" by Ruth Judd's attorneys. Twice they would ask for a new trial because of him. Twice their appeals would be denied.

Long before the Judd jurors made their stunning revelations of his "make her talk" scheme, Kleinman had already been challenged as an unfair juror and had faced the possibility of going to jail.

His actions were first spotlighted shortly after the trial ended, when Herman Lewkowitz was alerted that Kleinman had been anything but impartial. Three people came forward to say that even before he was sworn in as a juror, he had been urging the death penalty for Winnie Ruth Judd.

Armed with their sworn statements, Lewkowitz charged that Kleinman lied to the court when he testified during jury selection that he had an open mind and would decide the case based on the evidence. Lewkowitz charged Kleinman with being "wholly unqualified and unfit to sit as a juror."

To prove his point, the defense attorney brought forth a Phoenix man named A. E. Parmer, who said he'd had a conversation with Kleinman in the Walgreen drugstore in downtown Phoenix in mid-January of 1932, just days before jury selection began. Parmer quoted Kleinman as saying, "This Judd woman is guilty as hell and if I ever get on that jury, I will hang the bitch."

Kleinman was overheard a second time making a similar comment, according to B. H. Ward, one of the potential jurors who was not chosen for the trial. Ward testified he was in the courtroom hallway when he heard Kleinman tell a group of men, "This Judd woman is not crazy and should be hung."

Even a longtime friend of Kleinman's came forward—reluctantly, it was noted to the court—to say that in two separate private conversations, Kleinman "admitted that he probably had said, previously to his being selected as a Judd juror, that Mrs. Judd was guilty and should hang." J. L. Rodgers disclosed in a notarized affidavit that he had kept quiet about his knowledge because, "I thought Dan would do something for Mrs. Judd when the right time arrived, as he said he would. Since he hasn't, I honestly feel it is my duty to tell it now."

Dan Kleinman was not called to the stand to answer these allegations, even though he faced the possibility of jail time if he was found guilty. Instead, the court was presented with his sworn affidavit contending all the charges were "wholly false and untrue." Another statement came from Kleinman's daughter-in-law, who said she had never heard him utter a conclusion about the case.

Kleinman's main defender was a Tempe man named A. N. Smith—a man introduced to the court simply as an old friend who claimed he was present when Kleinman and Parmer talked at the drugstore. Smith declared he had never heard any statement about "hanging the bitch." But he originally swore the encounter he witnessed occurred in mid-December—a month before Parmer's conversation. Instead of rejecting Smith's testimony, the court allowed him to "correct" his memory of when the meeting occurred.

As Ruth Judd's supporters would eventually discover, Smith was far more than a bystander who happened to help Kleinman out of a legal stewpot.

Smith was the link between Jack Halloran and the manipulative juror.

In early 1933, Ruth's supporters were approached by Smith, who claimed he was acting as "an agent for Jack Halloran's powerful and influential friends." According to a sworn affidavit presented to the court, Smith offered Judd's family a deal: "If she issued a written statement wherein she would exonerate Jack Halloran of the part he had in the tragedy, and publish the said statement in the press, Jack's powerful and influential friends, business and otherwise, would see to it that the Pardons Board would commute her death sentence."

But none of these things moved the trial judge—or the Arizona Supreme Court—to declare a mistrial.

◇◇◇

All of that mystifies a man well versed in the thinking of Arizona's highest court: former chief justice Jack D. H. Hays. Retired since 1989, Judge Hays agreed to review the Judd trial and appeals with the eyes of a man who spent nineteen years on the state supreme court. He was elevated to the high court after a decade on the trial bench and seven years as the U.S. attorney for Arizona.

His review was sought because he is a noted conservative. As his lawyer daughter, Rory, puts it, "He'd never be accused of being an ACLUer." His judicial record shows he never coddled criminals, and was a stickler for the propriety of the courtroom. "I have a strong regard for the judicial system, which is constantly under attack," he says in describing the philosophy that guided him through an illustrious career.

Given his conservative bent, Justice Hays might not be expected to find much wrong with the Winnie Ruth Judd case. After all, this wasn't an obscure case that slipped unnoticed through the judicial cracks of Arizona, but one that consumed the state's courts for years under the spotlight of national scrutiny. And three times the Arizona Supreme Court upheld both the guilty verdict and the death penalty.

One would not expect to hear a member of that exclusive club declare that his predecessors were wrong. But that is what Justice Hays says. His reading of the case left him shocked—especially the obvious jury tampering led by Dan Kleinman. Either charge leveled against him—that he was not impartial and that he led the other jurors to their verdict—warranted a new trial for Winnie Ruth Judd, Justice Hays says.

"Dan Kleinman plays a crucial role," he notes. "That screwball made the difference. He just took hold of that jury with his theory—'Look, we can handle this thing and we can get her to spill her you know what, and here's the way we do it and I know the parole board'—he just took that jury, and the jury was going to go his way."

Kleinman's way was to hang her. Without his influence, Justice Hays believes the jury would have issued a far less severe sentence. In fact, without Kleinman's influence, Hays isn't even sure they would have found Ruth Judd guilty of first-degree murder.

"If that guy with the big mouth hadn't gotten into this, I'm sure it at least would have been second-degree," the judge says—a verdict that would have imprisoned her for a maximum of fifteen years. He reached that startling conclusion because his reading of the trial testimony left him unconvinced that the prosecution proved it was a case of premeditated murder. "I don't see the planning" that is necessary for premeditation, Justice Hays explains.

But jury tampering was not the only thing that stacked the case against Ruth Judd, he concludes. As a former criminal trial judge himself, Hays thinks the jury was led to its decision by the instructions from the trial judge. "The judge should have given the jury the option of finding she killed in self-defense," he declares. Instead, Judge Speakman charged the jury with deciding if she was sane.

"There was evidence presented at the trial to support self-defense," Justice Hays notes, pointing to the drainpipe letter Ruth wrote her husband. He stresses it makes no difference whether the defense is arguing self-defense or not. "When you have evidence to support self-defense, there's an obligation on the judge's part to instruct the jury on a self-defense verdict," he says.

But Judge Speakman refused to do that. And when his decision was appealed to the Arizona Supreme Court—on the grounds it was an error that warranted a new trial—the justices agreed with the trial judge.

"The [supreme court] opinion says there's no evidence to support self-defense," Hays reports. "Well, that piece of paper they fished out of the drain has a statement that's pretty obvious and speaks to self-defense. Which, in effect, means

I'm saying the Arizona Supreme Court and a future federal judge [Speakman] were all wrong."

Justice Hays is clearly uncomfortable with this second-guessing of his predecessors. He would prefer to dismiss the mistakes with "Those were the olden days and I guess that's how things were done." But he can't.

He is asked if he thinks Winnie Ruth Judd got a fair trial.

He hesitates for a long time, making it clear he's not sure he really wants to answer the question.

But he finally does: "It appears that she didn't."

Chapter 11
Winnie Ruth Judd Finally Tells All

"Now, Ruth, what we want to know is just what happened out there at the house."

Sheriff John R. McFadden is asking the question. He's a big cowboy of a guy who favors ten-gallon hats and western shirts. At forty-one, he's a little paunchy. Some think he has too easy a smile to be the highest elected law enforcement official in Arizona's most populated county. But they aren't the ones who will vote him into office so often that no one who comes after him can ever match his tenure.

McFadden first won election to a two-year term on the Democratic ticket of 1930, and would go on to be reelected twice to the $400-a-month job. Though it would eventually end badly, that was still years off. For now, McFadden was a popular law-and-order sheriff. He broke up illegal whiskey stills, he conducted regular raids on the whorehouses of Phoenix, and he was admired for assembling an unusual amount of talent: six members of his staff would become sheriff themselves.

McFadden was considered a straight-arrow, no-nonsense kind of guy who worshipped honesty. As his daughter remembers, his personal code was simple: "If a man's word wasn't worth anything, *he* wasn't worth anything."

"Our Mac will not play politics," a booster group bragged during one of his reelection campaigns.

Of all the Arizona officials who touched the Ruth Judd case, McFadden had the best vantage point. Not only had he and his deputies helped the Phoenix Police Department investigate the crime, he had personally spent more time with Ruth Judd than anyone else. He'd been dispatched to bring her back from California in November 1931—accompanied by a female matron. (Those honors went to Jewel Jordan, who would become, in the 1940s, the first and only woman to hold the title of sheriff of Maricopa County. Mrs. Jordan would eventually plead for clemency for Winnie Ruth Judd.)

Sheriff McFadden first heard Ruth Judd tell her self-defense story two days after she arrived at his jail. As he would admit much later, he begged her to sign a statement setting out her story, but she refused. She would only tell it to the court, she told him.

Ruth had sat in McFadden's jail for three months, and almost every day, the two talked. Her attitude toward him covered the gamut: one day, she'd lean on him like an old friend; the next, she'd scream that he was trying to hang her like everyone else; the next, they'd make pleasant small talk. She appreciated McFadden's strict rules that kept the reporters away, but was annoyed that they also meant her husband and parents were not allowed to visit as often as she wanted.

Behind those locked doors, the tough sheriff showed Ruth Judd little kindnesses. Before her trial began, he allowed a local dressmaker to bring four garments to the jail for Ruth's selection, and he saw to it that her hair was marcelled in the style popular in the day. He secretly allowed his sixteen-year-old daughter. Helen, to visit on Sundays. He even broke his own rules to allow Ruth's mother to spend unsupervised time with her.

During the trial, McFadden personally escorted her daily to and from the courtroom. He knew she was waiting for her chance to testify—he could scarcely wait himself. When it didn't happen, he begged her again—was it the twentieth time or the fiftieth?—to speak up. But she would not. The most he or anyone else had heard publicly was her hysterical outburst the day she was sentenced: "Those girls weren't murdered!" she screamed at the judge, who almost broke his gavel restoring order in the courtroom. "You're trying to hang me, and I won't have it," she bellowed, before her husband struck her across the face to quiet her and then held her in his arms.

McFadden had watched over his silent charge during the horrible nights after the death sentence was pronounced, afraid that Ruth Judd would attempt to take her own life. Then he personally drove her to prison in Florence, Arizona.

It was Sheriff McFadden who soothed her out of her hysterics that first night in prison, when officials put her up in the deathhouse with the unconvincing explanation that it was the only place safe from the twelve other women then incarcerated by the state of Arizona. It was McFadden who convinced prison officials that such "protection"—and ugliness—was not necessary.

That had been ten months ago. Ten long months during which the legal maneuvering over Ruth Judd had kept her ever hopeful. A whole new batch of lawyers—working for free—were taking up her cause, filing appeals and trying to overturn a sentence that had sent the country into shock: thousands would write to Arizona officials begging for mercy, including such luminaries of the day as First Lady Eleanor Roosevelt and auto king Henry Ford.

In those 10 months, Ruth Judd had maintained her silence. As much as she had complained that her trial attorneys gagged her, she found her new attorneys also now begged for her silence while the appeals were pending. Let the record speak, they urged her. The supreme court will surely overturn your conviction.

But they had been wrong. And now, seven days after the high court agreed she should hang, Ruth Judd had only one hope left. His name was John R. McFadden. For all her fear and distrust, she had finally realized he was the closest thing to a friend she had—the only official in Arizona who seemed to care what she had to say, who wanted to know what had really happened. Everyone else—even her own defense team, she feared—was content to close the case as she walked to the gallows.

She had less than two months to live. She was scheduled to die between the hours of five and six a.m. on February 17, 1933. Already professional hangmen from around the country were offering their services—some free—to do the deed.

If she was ever to speak, it had to be now.

It is December 19, 1932, 2:15 p.m. Ruth Judd has been brought from her cell to a small room in the Arizona State Prison. She is dressed in standard prison issue, a drab, straight-cut blue dress. She sits on one side of a small table in the windowless room. Across from her is Sheriff McFadden. He has brought along one of his deputies, Jeff Adams, and a court reporter. Prison warden William Delbridge has insisted on sitting in too, as has Ruth's latest attorney, O. V. Willson.

McFadden opens with his simple, direct question—the same question he has asked her so often: "Now, Ruth, what we want to know is just what happened out there at the house." But this time, instead of her silence, he hears: "You want to know about Thursday night. Sure you do, because it was Thursday night when I introduced Jack Halloran to this girl."

The shorthand reporter took down every word spoken during the next four hours. Eventually the words were typed up and enclosed in a cardboard cover. And then they were filed away. No one would see this transcript for fifty-eight years, until it was discovered during the course of this investigation by librarians at the State Archives Office. The document remains the most complete account of the killings Ruth Judd would ever tell.

Even though they are only words on yellowing paper, the reader can sense the tension in that room. Journalists across the nation would have given up a by-line to hear them spoken. All those women who jammed the courtroom each day would have given anything to hear Winnie Ruth Judd defend herself at last.

And there was a cast of characters sitting comfortably in their homes and businesses in Phoenix who would have shuddered at the thought this day had finally come. The day Winnie Ruth Judd would break her silence.

In 103 pages of verbatim transcription, Winnie Ruth Judd speaks. Often she rambles, often she has to be pressed to get to the point, but finally she tells her story.

"There was a girl that came to the clinic, taking treatments for syphilis, she was taking neovalvarsan, and she happened to mention to me that she was going to the White Mountains hunting, and I told her I knew some people that were going and I told her about this Jack Halloran....So arrangements were made for him to meet her on Thursday night."

Ruth Judd tells the sheriff that Halloran was already drunk Thursday afternoon when he called her at the clinic to set a time for the meeting. He picked her up and they drove out together about seven p.m. to fetch Lucille Moore. They headed back to Ruth's apartment. But first Halloran wanted to stop by to see Anne and Sammy.

"I didn't want to go with him, but I finally said, 'All right, if you won't let Anne know that I was in the car,' and he promised to do that. I didn't want Anne to know that I had introduced him to this girl—so we drove up in front of the house and he stopped in the driveway, and I said, 'Don't tell them, don't let them know I am here,' and he said, 'Oh, all right.' I didn't want them, you know, to know that I had introduced him to another woman, because he was practically supporting Anne and Sammy—between Jack Halloran and this L. E. Dixon, they were just about supporting them. The books will show it cost them $150, $175, or $200 a month [to live], and the men were helping them, gave them money, and I didn't want to make any trouble."

To Ruth's dismay, both Anne and Sammy came out of the house. Sammy, she says, gave her a hello hug and kiss. Anne insisted everyone come inside and join the nice new doctor from next door for dinner. "Anne ran up to the car and she said, 'Why don't you come on in, Ruth,' and I said, 'Why, we are going right away, Anne,' and then she saw Lucille Moore and she turned and said, 'Oh, I got to go back' and that was all there was to it. I didn't make any introduction and Anne didn't either."

Two men who had been visiting the girls came out and climbed into Halloran's touring car. They drove over to Ruth's Brill Street apartment, where they ate and had a couple of drinks—these men could always get their hands on bootleg liquor, forget Prohibition—and about midnight, Halloran drove Lucille home.

"The next day Anne came over to my house for lunch," Ruth continues. "I cashed my pay check … I had $30. Anne was with me and I went in and paid my landlady $13 on my rent and then we had lunch and Anne was tired and she went in and laid down to sleep while I got lunch…and we weren't mad at each other at all—and then I paid my rent and we went back to the office together and we had our arms linked, arms around each other when we got to the clinic."

Along the way, Anne asked Ruth to come over for dinner that night and play four-handed bridge. "I said, 'Well, Anne, I don't see how I can. I have been going out looking for houses lately and I am way behind with my histories and I don't believe I better go.'" About five p.m., as Anne was leaving the clinic, she stopped at Ruth's office and tried again. "She said, 'You better change your mind and come on over tonight,' and I said, 'Just look at the stack of histories I have got on my desk to finish.'"

One of the doctors gave Anne a ride home, and Ruth stayed at the office. She worked until about six, then stopped on her way home to pay $15 on her bill at Wade's grocery store. By now she had $2 left in her purse. Ruth apologized to Mrs. Wade for not paying the entire bill, and the grocer said she knew Ruth was good for it because she'd always kept her bill up pretty well. The women talked about a realtor they both knew who was helping Ruth find a house big enough for her parents and her best friends.

"Anne and Sammy said that if I got a house that had two rooms off to themselves, or had an entrance to themselves, that they would try to move in with me and they would help me pay a little on it, and Anne and I were going to look at some houses on Saturday evening, October 17." The realtor had promised to leave the back door open on a house that seemed perfect on East McDowell, close to the clinic and big enough to accommodate everyone. Anne tried to borrow a car from one of the doctors but couldn't get it, so Ruth asked a friend if his car could be loaned on Saturday. "And that is where the dirty low-down policeman was trying to make out a good big lie," she complains to the sheriff, who did not need reminding that the prosecution had used her request for a car as "evidence" she was plotting the murders.

Ruth continues her story, recalling she left the grocery store and continued her walk home, arriving about six-thirty. "I went home and I waited, fixed my cat something to eat, and I waited until almost nine and I thought, 'If Jack Halloran thinks he is going to come out here after this time, I am sure going to be gone,' and I went over to Anne and Sammy's. I walked over and caught the Indian School [trolley] car. I went in the back door because that is the door I always went in...Anne helped me fix the davenport down in the living room because that is where I always slept when I was there... And it was a little cool and we closed the windows in the bedroom.

"Anne was sitting over on her bed and Sammy was lying over on top of her bed and we were talking…and Anne said, 'Ruth, how did Jack Halloran ever meet Lucille Moore?' And I said, 'Why, I introduced them,' and she pitched onto me for introducing Jack Halloran to a girl who had syphilis… and she asked me what in the world I meant by introducing Jack to a girl that had syphilis, didn't I know any better than that? And we started quarreling over that, and I says—I can't remember every word we quarreled over and you can't when you have a quarrel…but I do know what I said. She told me that she was going to tell Jack that I had introduced him to a girl that had syphilis and I told her she certainly had no right to tell things outside of the clinic. And oh, she threw up to me a lot of things, and I asked what difference it made to her anyway, and she told me, 'It will make a lot of differ- ence to you,' in a most insinuating way, and she said, 'I know that he has been over to your house nearly every night since you have been over there,' and I says, 'What difference does that make to you, I know all about you.'… They called me some names and I called them some names. She said, 'I could simply kill you for introducing Jack to some girl that has syphilis, really you know better than to do anything like that,' and she said, 'I am going to tell him.'…So I threatened to tell a lot of things that I know.

"I told the girls that 'every doctor in that clinic thinks you and Sammy are in love with each other and Doctor Sweek and Dr. Baldwin have both told me that you were perverts'— that is what I told them—that is the truth. Dr. Sweek did one day, when Anne was sick. I told him that Anne didn't have enough money to get home on, and I asked him if the clinic would let her have a month or two salary, because she was sick and broke and he said to me, 'What in the world does she want to sleep with her for, that is love's labor lost.' And I said, 'Doctor Sweek, there is not a single word of truth that is being said about Anne and Sammy. They don't sleep together,' and he said, 'Oh, you can't tell anything to me about that, I know all about it. I can't understand why she would want to take care of a tubercular woman, why these two would tie up together.' And then he said, 'Well, the clinic here will let her have $100, and if Dr. Grunow don't like it, I will pay it out of my own pocket, but that is all we are going to do.' And then Dr. Baldwin at one time told me that he wished I wouldn't live with Anne and Sammy because those two girls would get me in trouble, they were in love with each other, and I said, 'They are not,' and he just went off shaking his head. And when I was living with Anne and Sammy, I told them what the doctors had said, because I thought more of Anne and Sammy than I did about any of them up at the clinic. And when we were quarreling, I said I was going to tell the doctors at the clinic that they were perverts…and when I tell them, they will sure believe it.

"I am going to tell you what Anne did up at the clinic. I threw that at her. The doctors at the clinic didn't want Anne back, they had a meeting, and they weren't going to take her back…[Anne's boss, Dr. Charles W. Brown, was on leave and was replaced about this time by a visiting doctor from Oregon, Dr. Lansfield.]

"Dr. Landsfield taught Anne's assistant, Mrs. Rowe, how to make x-ray pictures. Her previous work was just to develop, to keep the developing fluids and to work in the dark room, but he taught her how to make x-ray pictures, and when Anne was ready to go back to work, he told her he didn't want her until Dr. Brown came back, that he had already taught Mrs. Rowe to take x-ray pictures, and it made Anne angry because she said she had spent a lot of money learning how. [Mrs. Rowe] was getting $40 a month and in a few weeks she had been taught to do the work that Anne had taken years to learn and was getting a bigger salary for. Anne had to wait at home a month [before Dr. Brown returned] and she said she would sure fix [Dr. Lansfield] so he would be sorry…So she came up to the clinic one night just at closing time to meet me, and she slipped into the x-ray

department and she turned something on the x-ray machine…
so that the voltage would be real high, so that the rays would
penetrate; her idea was that Dr. Lansfield or his amateur technician would burn somebody with the x-ray and she told me
about doing it…and you know if that x-ray, if someone
would have taken a picture, it would have burned a terrible
hole through somebody.…And I threatened to tell this on her,
to tell that she had done it."

This was no longer just a quarrel between girlfriends that
would eventually end with tears and promises to forgive and
forget. This was now a bitter fight with each side threatening
to destroy the other—socially and financially.

The threat of syphilis has no modern equivalent; not even
AIDS carries all the weight syphilis did in those days. "Syphilis
was the touch of death—it was worse than the plague, it
was worse than AIDS is now" is how it is remembered by
Tom Chauncey, then a young man, who went on to own
the CBS affiliate in Phoenix and become one of the city's
most prominent businessmen. "There was no cure for it
then." Penicillin would not be available for a decade. "You'd
mention syphilis and everyone ran to the hills," Chauncey
recalls. "You were disgraced with that disease. You were
ostracized in all of society." He remembers that newspapers
wouldn't even use its name, referring to it politely as "the social
disease." Besides, he jokes, there weren't any dodges: "You could
only get syphilis one way."

If Jack Halloran knew Ruth had exposed him to a woman
with syphilis, he would surely have broken off their affair.
And what about Ruth's husband? Implicit in Anne's threats
was the revelation to Dr. Judd that his nice young wife was
sleeping with another man. If there was any social taboo
that headed the list in 1931, it was an illicit affair. "Playing
around was murder," Chauncey recalls. "You'd have the
rudest awakening of your life if you were caught." Careers
would be ruined, businessmen would find customers hard
to come by, social standing in the community would be

wiped out. Chauncey does not pretend men didn't play around, but he says they would have gone to extreme lengths to be sure they didn't get caught.

Ruth was being threatened with ruin for an innocent introduction arranged so Halloran could have a successful hunting trip. And she was responding tit for tat.

Lesbianism wasn't medically deadly, but socially fatal. Newspapers didn't even give it a polite name. They used the word "pervert." How would "proof" of this love nest sit with the doctors at the clinic, who all counted Jack Halloran as a friend? How would it sit with Halloran, who was helping support the girls? It wouldn't, and both Anne and Sammy knew that.

Even more significant, they knew Ruth's threat to reveal the X-ray sabotage would cost Anne not only her job but her entire career. What a blow to the one wage earner in a household during the nation's most depressed economic time.

To escape the fight, Ruth tells McFadden, she walked into the kitchen, setting her glass of milk on the counter. As she turned, she saw Sammy come through the breakfast room with a gun in her hand.

"She had the gun pointed right at my heart. And Sammy used to take spells…and she would look—oh, she didn't look like herself at all…and she had the gun pointed right at my heart, and I grabbed the hand with the gun….The table was right there by the door, the kitchen table is right there, and on the table was the bread knife, and I grabbed for the gun and knife right about the same time she shot me through my hand—just before I stabbed…I stabbed her once in the shoulder and once in the head, and the blade of the knife bent clear around. It was a long knife and had a green handle, and it was blunt, and I stabbed her with that and it bent double….And then we dropped to the floor and I grabbed her and pushed her with this arm, and I yelled, 'Give me that gun,' like that, and I grabbed the gun and her hand was yet on the trigger when that shot went through her chest, and she never relaxed on the gun one bit until after she was shot through the chest....

"And then we both grappled on the floor for the gun, we fell on the floor and fought back and forth and I yelled, 'Give me the gun,' and then Anne yelled, 'Shoot, Sammy, Shoot, Sammy, Shoot her,' and she got the ironing board that was right behind [the kitchen door]. When Anne came with the ironing board she hit me a blow immediately... and she said, 'I will brain you,' and she hit me with the ironing board over the head, and I hollered and I yelled, 'Give me that gun,' and she yelled, 'Sammy, shoot.' And she hit me, I don't know how many times it was, but she would knock me flat on the floor with the ironing board, and we rolled around in that way, I don't know how long, until I got the gun, and she had never released hold on the gun at all, not a bit, until we fell, and her hand was on the trigger when she was shot through the chest....

"I kept trying to get up, and when I started to get up, when I was rising [Anne] knocked me down with the ironing board when I was in a half upright position."

Sheriff McFadden asks how many times she shot Sammy.

"There was at least five or six shots, I know there was that many shots fired because there was but one cartridge that wasn't emptied.... All but one, but I didn't see any bullet and I have never loaded a gun in my life, and I have never shot a gun before in my life, in my life before absolutely not, have never shot a gun and I shot to save my life, and now they think they are going to hang me and put my picture in a frame. They are like cannibals; do you know what I mean—cannibals do that with their victims, eat them and hang their pictures in frames, and that is what this country is doing, hanging innocent people and putting their picture in a frame with a rope that is around their neck, and if you can hang innocent me for the betterment of political parasites like Lloyd Andrews and his rotten political friends, this country is no better than cannibals. I fought for my life and I am going to continue to fight for my life."

Her attorney, O. V. Willson speaks up. "We are here looking after you, we just want you to tell what happened." Sheriff McFadden gets the conversation back on track, asking, "Now, where did Anne's body fall?"

Ruth answers, "It fell back towards the stove. Sammy's head…was in towards the breakfast room, the feet towards the kitchen door, because she came that way and fell; when we fell, we were both with heads into the breakfast room. I don't know how long I was sitting on the floor—I must have fell too, afterwards, because I was sitting on the floor and Sammy was lying in one place and Anne was in another place.…"

Her attorney tries to clarify how Anne was shot: "Now in shooting Anne, were you sitting on the floor?"

"I started to get up like this [illustrating]; I was down on the floor and we were rolling back and forth fighting for this gun, and when I started to get up she banged me on the head with the iron board just as I shot, she hit me on the head. And when I come to, I was sitting between two bodies on the floor.…I ran out of that place, I put my dress on and nothing else, just my shoes and my dress.

"I went right back to Brill Street to get my pocketbook. I went home and got my black pocketbook and money, and started out of the door when Jack Halloran came into the driveway."

Ruth explains she was on her way to the Ford Hotel in downtown Phoenix to use their pay phone to call her husband in Los Angeles. But there was Jack on her doorstep.

"We went into the house and I told him what had happened, and he was dead drunk. He wouldn't believe it, and he wanted me to go back over to the house, and he told me, 'I don't believe it.' And I couldn't convince him and I told him, 'I will show you,' and we started over in the car, and in going over in the car I told him how it happened, how we had our fight." She puts the time about eleven-thirty p.m. "We parked the car on Pinchot, on the north side of the road. And let me tell you, that Cunningham—they had a party over at their house and had everything brilliantly lighted up, and he said he was in bed." (Gene Cunningham had testified he was awakened by three shots that Friday night.)

"And Cunningham has been over to see Anne himself with Jack Halloran and we used to go home on the same street car and they always spoke, she and Cunningham, and she told me that he was a friend of Jack's and had been over to the house."

Halloran unbelievingly surveyed the bloody scene in the kitchen, Ruth continues. And then he did something that would forever alter the case.

"He picked up Sammy and he carried her in and laid her on Anne's bed. I don't think he knew that she was shot in the head then. I guess she was dead....If they ever find the mattress, a chemical analysis can be made and they can prove that it is Sammy's blood that is on the mattress, and it is my opinion that it would be on the mattress because of the fact that the woman was bleeding terribly, but the head was not bleeding at all....When he carried her over and laid her on the bed, there was no blood on the clothes any place; he threw the pillows off and he laid her on Anne's bed, and the covers had been turned down, pulled down, and there was no blood on the covers. If you know what they say about that mattress—I know he took the mattress. Jack Halloran took the mattress out away from there."

One can almost hear the questioners thinking to themselves, "So that's how the blood got into the bedroom—in one small corner of the bedroom." And that was why, they finally realized, attorney Lewkowitz had grilled the blood expert about what would cause the scant splattering of blood found in that corner. Even the expert had admitted on the stand that the splattering could have been caused by a body dropped onto the bed—but although Lewkowitz pulled that revelation from the witness, he never did anything to drive the point home to the jury. He certainly never suggested to the jury that Jack Halloran might have dropped Sammy's body onto that bed.

Sheriff McFadden asks Ruth to speculate on the blood splatters. She thinks they might have been drops of blood from Sammy's hair, or maybe Halloran splashed blood when he was mopping up—a job he first ordered Ruth to do but then undertook himself when she cried she couldn't maneuver the mop with a wounded hand.

"Was there any blood on the bathroom floor?" she asks the sheriff. McFadden answers: "Yes, right against the tub." It is unlikely Ruth remembered that the blood expert had said there was no blood in the bathroom, but Sheriff McFadden certainly knew there was.

It was also becoming clear to the sheriff that the search for two bloody mattresses had been in vain—only one had contained any blood. He must have remembered that officers had found a single, unsoiled mattress in a vacant lot miles from the death house but had discounted it as unrelated to the crime. That mattress might indeed have come from the crime scene, McFadden realized. If it had, it supported the story Ruth Judd was telling him.

Her questioners want her to continue the chronology of events that night. But she pauses for a long time when they prod her about Halloran's next moves.

"He said, 'You better let Dr. Brown treat your hand,' and I told him I didn't want him to do it. You know, a long time before, he told me that he had plenty on Dr. Brown...he told me he had enough on Brown to hang him....

"He dialed the phone a couple of times and that is when I told you about this fingerprint on the blind..." She reminds the sheriff that as Halloran used the phone, he pulled down the blind in the bedroom, leaving a bloody fingerprint behind. "But Mr. McFadden, I have heard there are fingerprints on the underneath of the blind, but Lewkowitz told me not to tell it at the time."

McFadden answers, "I cut those out myself."

Ruth doesn't even react to this memorable disclosure. She just continues. "Well, Lewkowitz told me, 'There are fingerprints, but let's not mention it now.'" During the entire trial, those prints were never mentioned.

She's brought back to her narration by a question about what happened next.

"He wanted me to straighten things around the kitchen and I couldn't do anything with one hand, couldn't do anything, and I wanted to call [Dr. Judd] and I was going to tell him about this affair, and he advised me not to do that—he would tend to all this himself, 'If you will let Dr. Brown dress your hand I will attend to the whole thing myself.' Then he pulled the trunk in from the garage. He told me that he was going to take Anne out in a trunk; he didn't say anything about Sammy."

In response to the sheriff's questions, Ruth says Halloran knew Sammy's packing trunk was in the garage because he had put it there himself after he helped Sammy move into the duplex. Now he dragged it into the kitchen and she watched him put Anne's body inside. He told her he would dispose of the body in the desert. He took a mop and cleaned up a bit in the kitchen. Then he took Ruth home.

"He advised me to let Dr. Brown treat my hand for me and never say anything to my husband about this, because he would take care of this thing himself…and that there would be nothing to it. Jack dialed the phone several times in the dark, because he had the lights off in the bedroom and he pulled the blinds down and dialed the phone, and then he took me home because I was getting hysterical, I was raising the dickens and he took me home and told me that he would take care of everything and for me not to say a thing to anybody and he would see me later."

Her attorney interrupts then, as both he and McFadden keep pressing her to quote the words Halloran had used. "You told me," Willson says to Ruth, "that you had come to some kind of a decision that you wanted to give yourself up to the police and he said, 'No, that would never do.'"

"He scared me of the police," Ruth answers. "He scared me of the state attorney—I didn't know who the state's attorney was. Why, he scared the life out of me, what it would mean. He told me not to call my husband or call the police, I must not mention this to anyone, that he would take care of this himself, and that he would see me at once and to keep still and that everything would be all right, and to say absolutely nothing...."

As she and Halloran left the house, she goes on, she picked up the gun from the kitchen floor and put it in her purse. She did not sleep all night.

About noon the next day, Halloran called her at the clinic, telling her he couldn't "take care of those parties" as he'd planned. "He asked me, 'Have you done anything about your hand yet,' and I told him, 'No—I want to go out to Los Angeles, I want to get this bullet out of my hand, I think that is best'—and he said he thought it was a good idea for me to go to Los Angeles, and he wanted me to take [the trunk] to Los Angeles, and I said, 'I will not take those to Los Angeles,' and he says, 'I can't do anything about that trunk,' and he wanted me to meet him that night. He wanted me to talk things over with him, and so I waited outside [the girls' bungalow on Saturday night] and he kept driving around and around the house, and I went inside because it was cool and I was afraid, I didn't know what he was going to do, whether he was going to kill me or not, and then when he stopped the car, why, we went into the house and the trunk was then in the living room, back of the door...

"He told me he had operated on Sammy—Sammy had been operated on. He said Sammy had been operated on but she was dead. He thinks he is Dr. Buckley, every time he gets drunk he thinks he is Dr. Buckley from Buckeye." Ruth tells the sheriff how Halloran had gotten into Good Samaritan Hospital after visiting hours one night by claiming he was this Dr. Buckley, and he used the title when he met nurses sometimes—"He was always wanting me to introduce him to nurses."

McFadden tries again: "Now, Ruth, on that Saturday night out at the house, relate as near as you can the conversation that you had with Halloran and his plans."

Again, she vented her anger rather than illuminated: "That dirty, low-down scoundrel, he won't admit what I want him to admit, where he saw the bodies. I don't care what he does, if he will only admit that. He is a coward, and I am telling you that I am going to get justice from the Supreme Judge of the Universe. I fought for my life there, and I got shot in my hand, and that is where the bodies were lying, and this Jack Halloran was there and absolutely bullied me into going to Los Angeles, and he is too big a coward to admit that.

"I didn't want to hurt anybody. Anne and Sammy were my friends, but I had a fight with them, and I wouldn't hurt them now. Lots of times I think of things I would like to tell them...."

"This is an important part," McFadden insists as he tries to get her to be more specific. "What conversation did you have with Halloran and what were the suggestions he made?"

She ticks them off: "These were the suggestions, and that is what he told me: never to tell about it; that I knew what it meant to me and my family and him and his family; that Sammy had been operated on...."

Deputy Jeff Adams jumps in, trying to get Ruth to talk about the "operation" that had cut Sammy into four pieces. "Did Halloran tell you who done it?" he asks.

"No he did not tell who done it, but you know good and well who did it, if he didn't get Dr. Brown to come over and help him, and pronounce her dead, he tried to do something else."

Attorney Willson asks, "Ruth, did you ask him who cut up the body of Sammy?"

"I didn't and he didn't say, 'cut up,' he said 'operated on,'" she answers. "He cuts up deer all the time. He has been in a butcher shop himself."

The "talk things over" meeting that Saturday night in the house amounted to Halloran giving her instructions. He told Ruth to take the trunk with her on the late train that night to Los Angeles. "He opened his pocket book and he said, 'I'll tell you, I will have to go back past the office and get more money to get a ticket for you to go on to Los Angeles.'" He told her to call the delivery company just before train time and to meet him near the depot for the money.

"He wanted me to take the trunk and he said that there would be someone there to meet me and take the trunk at Los Angeles, that he had a man, by the name of Williams, or Wilson, would meet me in Los Angeles…And Mr. McFadden, you can ask anybody in the depot, and they will tell you that I was there for two hours looking to see if I could find that man that was to meet me, when I got into Los Angeles. I didn't call my brother, I didn't phone for my brother, and there are lots of people that can tell you that I walked up and down that place looking for someone."

It is clear that in Ruth Judd's mind on that Saturday night, the plan would work. All she had to do was get the trunk to the depot and take the ride to Los Angeles. Then Halloran's friend would take over. She could go see her husband and he would take the bullet out of her hand. And nobody would ever know. When someone asks her what she was supposed to do if she was caught, her answer is simple: "I didn't expect to be caught."

But the plan went awry because the trunk was too heavy. Instead of taking the Saturday night train to Los Angeles, Ruth was stuck with that trunk in her own apartment. "I paced the floor all day and night. I said to myself, 'My God, my God, what will I do?' All Saturday night. The Lightning

Delivery came, and when they told me they couldn't take the trunk, I didn't know what to do, because Jack wanted to get them out of that house right away, and I was afraid to stay there any longer. I wanted to get out of there and he told me to take the trunk, and they told me I couldn't take it and I didn't know what to do, so I said, 'Take it over to Brill Street then.'"

Back at her apartment, Ruth realized she could be found out before she had a chance to get out of town, because as the delivery men carried the trunk out of the death house, she had noticed spots on the porch. Spots of blood, dripping from the trunk. So she took the trolley out to the girls' bungalow and used the outside hose to wash off the porch. Then she caught the trolley back. If Sheriff McFadden had not realized it before, he now knew the trolley driver who had testified at the trial had seen Ruth not the night of the killings, but the night after.

"I paced that floor all night long Saturday night, I paced that floor all that Sunday, and I said, 'My God, My God, what will I do? What will I do?'...I went over to Grimm's house and called up, I called up Jack's office, I called his office and there was no answer, and then I called up a party and asked them if I could borrow some money that I wanted to go to Los Angeles, because when that coward didn't meet me and give me money for a ticket, I couldn't go—I only had four or five dollars, and I walked the floor and he didn't come and I waited until Sunday and, of course, he told me to go and I didn't know what to do."

Ruth kept thinking Halloran would realize something had gone wrong and would come by her apartment to see what was going on. But he didn't. By Sunday, she felt trapped. She knew Halloran wouldn't be at his office, and she knew she couldn't call him at home because "I was afraid his wife was there." When it became clear he wasn't coming to help, she went from friend to friend trying to borrow the money to get out of town. "I was stuck with those bodies in my house, and all I could think of was to go to Los Angeles."

The four men in this tiny room know Ruth Judd is trying to hide something. Over a dozen times, they prod her to explain the one thing she does not want to admit. Again and again, she tries to evade the question, getting nearly hysterical at some points. But no one is going to leave the room until the question is answered: Ruth Judd must explain how the bodies that arrived at her apartment in one trunk ended up in several pieces of luggage.

"What would you do if you had two bodies in your house?" she shoots at them. "I didn't know what to do, and I just paced the floor and I said, 'My God, what will I do?' I walked the floor and I walked the floor and my hand throbbed and my brain was gone, and I waited for him to come and nobody came and I didn't know what to do."

As they press, Ruth regresses, pleading that she had loved her friends: "I didn't want to hurt those girls, they were friends of mine, but I had to fight for my life, and I am going to keep on fighting for my life, and if anybody tries to hurt me, because I don't love anyone that just is trying to kill me and I thought more of them than I ever thought of anybody that I ever knew, but they tried to kill me and I am going to fight."

Her attorney tries to lead her into answering the question everyone wants satisfied: "You told me that you used a Turkish towel in transferring the [body] pieces to your little steamer trunk." But she evades again. Deputy Adams tries: "Did anybody help you change these pieces, must have been somebody helped you, must have been somebody help you change part of the big trunk into the other one."

"I told you that I paced the floor and that nobody came there, didn't I?" she answers. Someone agrees she has already said that. "Well, I did. I paced the floor and nobody came."

Sheriff McFadden tries pleading with her: "Have confidence in us, we are not trying to damage you. Was anybody involved there?"

"No," Ruth says. "I will just go to the Supreme Judge and he can judge whether I didn't have to fight for my life."

McFadden answers, "I am confident of that, or I wouldn't have come over here this afternoon. If you want us to help you, you have to tell us a lot of little things that you don't think help you."

"Yes," Ruth says, "but I read in the papers in Los Angeles that you were going to try to hang me and hang Jack Halloran. All I want him to do is tell where he found those bodies."

Since they are getting nowhere, everyone takes a thirteen-minute break.

When the men return, their patience is wearing thin.

Deputy Adams is blunt: "The thing I can't understand is how this stuff got in one of the smaller packages."

Attorney Willson answers him: "She lifted them out. Now, Ruth, go ahead and tell Mr. Adams how you used the Turkish towel and how you handled you—you had the little steamer trunk in the house there, didn't you?"

Little by little, Ruth reveals that she stacked the suitcase on top of her empty steamer trunk, hugging them against the packer trunk that held the bodies. It is obvious just from reading the transcript that the questions were painful and the shreds of information she admitted were excruciating.

"Warden William Delbridge: Tell us what you did, if you opened the big trunk and took parts of them out and put them in the other trunk?

"Ruth Judd: I had to, there wasn't anyone else there to do it, and I walked the floor all Sunday and all night Saturday and nobody came.

"Attorney Willson: You mean that you tumbled the pieces out of the big trunk into the steamer trunk?

"Ruth Judd: I don't know how, I don't know what I did, I don't want to remember, I don't want to know anything about it, because I don't want to remember, because I can't.

"Attorney Willson: She was in a frenzied state of mind, I think.

"Warden Delbridge: She has told everything, and this part of it would be very helpful to her to just tell us all of it.

"Ruth Judd: I think that I walked the floor and I didn't know what to do, and I said, that I didn't lift it, I pulled it out, and there was something messy that dropped out.

"Sheriff McFadden: What did you do with that part that dropped out? [He is well aware that some of Sammy's internal organs were never found.]

"Ruth Judd: It was a dirty, messy towel…it was an awful messy towel stuck inside.

"Deputy Adams: How many packages did you have when you got ready to go to Los Angeles?

"Ruth Judd: I had the trunk and the suitcase and a bag, and I had a little case. I had a little kit and it had tiny, little probes—it was the doctor's that he used to pick out splinters— and that was to cut the bullet out of this hand, and I had a couple of bandages and material, and they tried to say that I had a big knife and I didn't. I didn't have a big knife they operated on Sammy with, because that was a little surgical kit that my husband used—no bigger than a lead pencil, a little tiny, tiny knife.

"Attorney Willson: You didn't see what was in the bottom of this trunk?

"Ruth Judd: I didn't ever find out what was in the bottom of the trunk except what they said in the courtroom; I listened and I couldn't hear what they said was in the trunk and I don't want to remember, don't want to know about it, because I don't want to, I don't know what was in it.

"Attorney Willson: Well, did you pull the pieces out and let them dump into [the other luggage]?

"Ruth Judd: I don't know if I did, because I said I walked the floor all the time and said, 'My God, what will I do,' and I told you there was no one there.…

"Warden Delbridge: I can't understand why she doesn't tell you how she opened the trunk.

"Sheriff McFadden: This is very important that you tell us as near as you can recall how you transferred Sammy's body from the trunk into the steamer trunk and suitcase. Wasn't there a black bag?

"Ruth Judd: That had dirty towels in it. Listen … Anne and I had on pajamas that were alike and I asked her to put one of those pairs on that night when we had our fight…and they were torn…and I opened the train window and I threw them out of the window.

"Sheriff McFadden: Now, in these towels, could there have been anything wrapped in them?

"Ruth Judd: No, they came out of the trunk, they fell on the floor…I threw them out with the other pajamas—the two towels and the pajamas, and I threw them out the window."

As the transcript continues, the discussion wanders all over the place. The men realize Ruth is upset and will not answer their questions, but eventually they come back to this issue.

"Deputy Adams: What was the idea, Mrs. Judd, in changing the bodies into another package?

"Ruth Judd: Because I had to, because that trunk was too heavy to go by express and I didn't know what to do."

Again she tries to evade a direct answer.

"Attorney Willson: Tell us how you lifted those pieces.

"Ruth Judd: I said I didn't lift them, I lowered them. Over the edge and they fell into the lower [trunk]. The piece I lowered, it was on top. I pulled it over the edge into the trunk at the side of it…I had the big trunk and the little trunk at the side and I pulled them over to the edge and lowered it into the other—you can't lift that big trunk.

"Warden Delbridge: How did you get the pieces in the suitcase?

"Ruth Judd: By putting the suitcase on top of the steamer trunk, it made it almost as high as the big trunk.

"Deputy Adams: You just reached down and pulled it over.

"Ruth Judd: Just pulled it over.…

"Attorney Willson: Was there any blood spilled as you transferred the pieces?

"Ruth Judd: There was no blood at all, not a drop of blood ever dropped in my apartment, that I know of; I don't know of any because that body had been cut up over there, and there was no blood on the body."

Again the discussion wanders, until finally, Warden Delbridge comes back to the subject for the last time. "About what time was it when you unlocked the big trunk?" he asks her.

"Ruth Judd: It must have been at least three o'clock, it was late.

"Delbridge: You just made up your mind you had to do something to unlock the trunk.

"Ruth Judd: I had to, I didn't know what to do.

"Delbridge: Well, coming back to that again, what did you take out of there?

"Ruth Judd: I didn't have any idea what I was going to take out and that was on top.

"Attorney Willson: What was on top?"

"Ruth Judd: Portions of a body."

It has been a long afternoon, and Ruth Judd has told a story everyone knows she should have told months ago. Why did she keep quiet for so long, she is asked. Why didn't she tell the truth to her first attorneys in Los Angeles.

"Because I wanted to talk to Jack Halloran before I made statements," she explains. "The first thing I done was to tell them to get in touch with Jack Halloran and they told me, no, that would not be advisable for him to come over here."

It wasn't until she had been in the Phoenix jail for two weeks Ruth admits, that she told her attorneys the same story she is telling now. She says attorney Zaversack took down a full account of the story and later told her he had given it to Judge Speakman. He also told her that was all she needed to say, that she should now "keep still."

"Were you instructed by them not to talk?" someone asks her.

"Absolutely…all they told me, they said, 'Listen, the state is subpoenaing Jack Halloran, and when we get him on the witness stand, we will tear him to pieces on cross-examination, and you will be cleared.' Jack Halloran came in with about thirty people, and he held up his hand when they were all there, but his name was never read off, his name never was. Then they told me, 'All right, we will call him if the state does not, and use him. We will call him. It will be all right, you just keep still, we will put Jack Halloran on the stand ourselves if the state doesn't.' All right, they didn't put him on, and I waited day after day expecting them to put him on but they said, 'If we put him on, then he will claim his constitutional rights to say nothing which would incriminate him and then that is all we can question him about.'…And finally Zaversack said, 'If they don't put him on, I will go on the witness stand myself, Mrs. Judd, and tell the whole story, I will do that.' And until the last day I thought I was going to go on the witness stand myself, and when I didn't—I wrote Judge Speakman the whole story, or Zaversack has it in his possession, and that is the truth, and he told me that he went out to Judge Speakman's house and read it to him."

No one in the room believed Judge Speakman was ever given a private account of Ruth Judd's version of events.

But everyone in the room has a new insight into what actually happened that night. So much of what Ruth has said matches with the evidence.

Armed with her story, the men who have sat in this meeting will fight for her life.

She wouldn't let them leave without once more impressing on them the sliver of justice she still thought was possible.

"All I want that man to do is to tell that there was a fight, and that is all I want him to do. I don't care if he admits another thing…He bullied me and scared me and now he is a coward. He is a bully and a coward."

Chapter 12
A Stab at Justice

Van Beck was four years out of high school, washing windows in the eight-story Security Building in downtown Phoenix for sixty-five dollars a month and hoping to marry his "hon" when he was called for the 1932 Maricopa County grand jury.

He found himself, at twenty-three, the youngest on the twenty-two-man panel, which was kept busy all fall with the usual things—hearing charges on bank frauds and robberies and bootlegging. Van Beck didn't mind that they heard so many cases and issued so many indictments that brought people to trial, considering the "bonanza" he was making: four and a half dollars a day for service, three dollars a day for mileage. It was nice extra pay for these dark days of the depression.

But there was nothing usual about the case Van Beck and the other grand jurors heard—to their great astonishment—for four hours on December 30, 1932, eleven days after Sheriff John McFadden made his trip to the state prison in Florence.

This time, the witness was Winnie Ruth Judd, convicted murderess, who had an execution date hanging over her head. She was quietly brought to Phoenix from the prison, and it was not until she was behind the closed doors of the grand jury chambers that word spread through the courthouse that something strange was up.

Now retired and living in Scottsdale, Arizona, Van Beck has never spoken before about what he heard in that grand jury room sixty years ago. At the time, he remained silent because all the grand jurors were admonished to remember everything that went on inside the room was secret. He wasn't about to risk the wrath of the county attorney and jeopardize his job by being publicly disgraced for disclosing secrets. As the years went by, Beck didn't see how it would help to tell what he knew. But now he does. Because now he thinks the whole story is finally being told and the part he played helps explain many things.

He sits in his comfortable living room sharing behind-the-scenes memories that have always made him uneasy, refreshing his recollections now and then from a worn-out diary he kept when he was a young man and hoped the actions of his youth would be worth remembering in his old age.

To this day, Van Beck can recall the tension and excitement in the grand jury room as they settled in to listen to the woman the whole country had been wanting to hear.

Like everyone else, Beck had followed the infamous trial in the early part of 1932. He had still been working on a Mesa farm then, mowing alfalfa hay for a dollar and a half a day, and couldn't afford to buy a newspaper. But his neighbors had shared theirs, and he figures he read most of the stories about the Judd case. As far as he could see, her trial jury had probably made the right decision. That's what everybody was saying—she wasn't crazy, she was a killer; she wasn't some hapless little thing, she was a cold-blooded monster. Even the state's highest court had just upheld her conviction. Van Beck knew she was scheduled to die soon. He knew everybody in town—if not lots of folks around the country— hoped she would talk before she hanged. And he knew her only way out now—now that there were no appeals left— was to be declared insane. He doubted if anyone would do that. Not after her trial jury had specifically rejected that plea.

So he was a little taken aback when the grand jury was briefed by county attorney Lloyd Andrews, who was finishing out the last days of his term after being defeated in the fall primary. This grand jury hearing, in fact, would be the county attorney's last official act.

Winnie Ruth Judd was finally going to tell the story she didn't tell at her trial, Andrews explained to the jurors. He reminded them that during the trial, he had personally tried to get her to talk, but she had refused. At one point, Andrews had herded a group of reporters into her cell and told her to say anything she wanted to the public; she said she wanted to talk only in a court of law. He would always use those attempts as "proof" that he tried untiringly to get her side of the story aired. Well, on this day—he told the grand jury— she was having her day in court, even if reporters by law were banned and everything said here was protected under a cloak of secrecy.

But Van Beck has always believed that Andrews really had another agenda.

"Andrews told us to be careful, to keep our eyes open because she was rather violent," Beck recalls. "I distinctly remember Lloyd Andrews telling us: 'I want to warn you, she might fly off the handle and she might throw something at you—be on your guard.' But I never saw any person any calmer in her life. She was anything but violent. She didn't do any of the things Andrews warned us about. She was calm, cool, and collected. After seeing her, we figured Lloyd was trying to set us up—to mold our thinking. We saw through him. We felt he wanted us to see her as insane."

Beck believes Andrews did that because he "was trying to save her life—he didn't want her to hang." But considering the history of this case, that would have been a dramatic turnaround indeed. A more likely scenario is that the county attorney hoped Ruth Judd's story would be discredited. An insane Ruth Judd was likely to say anything—even implicate one of the city's most prominent citizens—but who would take her seriously? Who would care about the rantings of a lunatic?

Whatever Andrews's true motivation, it is clear he was forced into this hearing by Sheriff McFadden, who had brought him the transcript of his December 19 prison meeting with Ruth Judd and demanded the information be presented to the grand jury. It is not known what technique he used— whether he threatened to go public if Andrews did not act, or threatened to arrest Jack Halloran himself—but however he did it, McFadden maneuvered the situation.

It would cost him dearly. His daughter, Helen, says her father's political aspirations were scuttled because of the disfavor he fell into for championing Ruth Judd's case. She remembers he was eventually linked to a real estate scandal; he was cleared of charges, but the unsavory association turned off voters. When he died in 1940, he was so poor that his friends had to raise the money to pay for his funeral.

McFadden certainly could see it all coming, Helen says. "He was an honest man—he just couldn't let it drop."

Van Beck remembers the grand jury was "kind of spell-bound" as Andrews asked the questions and Ruth calmly answered. Beck remembers hearing about the fight. He heard about Halloran's actions. He heard about the "operation" on Sammy. About Ruth's horrified Saturday night with the two bodies, and her frantic search for money to get out of town.

The grand jury heard it all and made two staggering decisions.

"We felt—the grand jury as a group—that she was involved in some degree, but we didn't believe it was cold-blooded murder for a minute, not for a minute," Beck declares. "I would have never convicted her of premeditated murder— I didn't think there was any premeditation at all." Manslaughter, yes. I wondered how she ever got convicted. If I'd been on the trial jury, I'd have said, 'I won't make a decision until I hear her story.'

"We felt positive she was unable to cut up the body. We were told it took a professional to cut the body. Most people in the valley knew other people were involved in this crime, but there was nothing they could do—the others involved were prominent married men."

As they listened to Ruth's story, the grand jurors were convinced she "wasn't dangerous and wasn't guilty of any more than getting in a jealous fight," Beck says. "And we didn't think she was insane either, not a day in her life."

He remembers how impressed he was with her testimony—how believable she was. He does not remember exactly what the county attorney asked the grand jury to do. It was a pretty independent-thinking group of men, and they called the shots the way they saw them. Nobody ever dreamed they would call this one the way they did.

This grand jury shocked the nation by declaring it believed Ruth Judd's story of killing in self-defense. It asked the parole board to commute her death sentence to life imprisonment. "I didn't want her to hang for something she didn't do," Beck explains now. "I did all I could to save her life, and I think I helped."

That wasn't all.

That was what the grand jury did to save Ruth Judd.

But they also made a stab at justice.

Van Beck's grand jury indicted Jack Halloran as an accessory to murder.

The indictment was hot news throughout the nation. The *New York Times* reported the next day that a secret warrant had been issued for Halloran, but he had been informed of the grand jury's decision by Sheriff McFadden and had shown up in court immediately. "Standing almost exactly where Mrs. Judd had heard her death sentence pronounced ten months ago, Halloran was debonair and smiling, apparently unconcerned," the *Times* reported. "He posted a cashier's check for $3,000 as bond and at the same time, demanded the earliest possible arraignment."

The Hearst papers had a field day with the charges against "Happy Jack." They described him as a playboy, which was a derogatory title in those days. Or they'd call him "the millionaire clubman," or "the rich sportsman." They often called him "Judd's Aide."

The press in Phoenix gave as much prominence to blasts against the grand jury, including a stinging rebuke from Judd's trial judge, Howard Speakman. "According to their statement—which they had no business to make—all they say is that she acted in self-defense," he blustered. "They don't know any more about it than the trial jury did. In fact, virtually all they had was her own story."

By appealing to the parole board, Judge Speakman charged, the grand jurors had "violated the law and their oaths."

Halloran's few words to the press were boastful and confident: "We'll take our medicine and there's no yellow streak up our spine," he said with his ready smile, as the International News Service reported. "I am glad it is all coming out. It will clear the air and people will not have so much to talk about."

Lloyd Andrews was out of office by the time Jack Halloran's preliminary hearing began in mid-January 1933, and new county attorney Renz Jennings was thrown into the startling case his first day on the job.

Again the courtroom was filled to overflowing and the media from around the nation came to record every utterance from Halloran's accuser.

This was Winnie Ruth Judd's big moment. Already her attorneys were petitioning the Board of Pardons and Paroles to commute her death sentence—just twenty-nine days off— based on the grand jury's recommendation. She was heard to wonder if she might not win a "full pardon" when everyone realized she had really killed in self-defense. In her mind, everything would be cleared up once she had a chance to tell her story publicly.

To allow time for the new court proceedings, the parole board rescheduled her execution date for April 14—Good Friday.

Winnie Ruth Judd was a lousy witness this time.

She was hysterical. She screamed. She cried. She collapsed several times. She was often incoherent. Her story wandered here and there. Anyone waiting for a clear recitation of events felt cheated.

Eventually, she fulfilled her promise to "tell all," but her story was interspersed with "wild cries" and "angry outbursts," as the press constantly reported.

Halloran's attorney, Frank O. Smith, used her hysteria to argue that she was insane and "incompetent" to testify. "It is simply plain she is wild," he declared, asking the court from the start to dismiss the case. Judge J. C. Niles disagreed, and the preliminary hearing continued.

Ruth Judd had now twice been declared sane. In her trial, it had worked to convict her, in this courtroom, it allowed her to tell her story. But as the press noted, those rulings could put her in a terrible bind. Unless the parole board canceled her execution, she could escape the hangman only if she was declared insane. And how could any court do that in light of this history?

If Ruth Judd spent a moment considering that possibility, she showed no sign of it when she finally got on the witness stand. She was not going to be gagged this time—regardless of what questions she was asked, regardless of how painful it was to recount that awful night.

"I am going to be hanged for something Jack Halloran is responsible for," she shrieked, half rising in her chair as she began her testimony. "I was convicted of murder, but I shot in self-defense. Jack Halloran removed every bit of evidence. He is responsible for me going through all this. He is guilty of anything I am guilty of."

At one point, as she cried hysterically, Smith asked the court to expel spectators. "It might be easier for Mrs. Judd if we cleared the courtroom," he told the judge. "I am not trying to shield Mr. Halloran when I suggest this, for he is innocent as anyone—"

"He is not," Ruth Judd screamed from the witness stand. "He is responsible for the death of three girls. Anne is dead, Sammy is dead and I'm going to die." She bounded from her chair and ran to where Halloran was seated, facing him directly. "You don't care what happened to Sammy—that she's dead, and that Anne's dead and that I'm going to die. You sit there and laugh. You still play around. I hope you suffer everything Anne's mother has suffered and my mother and Sammy's mother has suffered."

The *New York Journal* reported that the outburst "brought tears to the eyes of spectators and even the judge."

There had been so much proof to back up her story, she told the court, but Halloran had moved it or stolen it or rearranged it. "I wish that mattress would be brought in here and it would show that no one was shot in bed and I would have been cleared at my trial," she pleaded. When pressed how she could charge Halloran had taken the mattress away, she said everybody knew he had done it. Whom did she mean by "everybody," Halloran's attorney asked.

"Everybody with common sense—I am not accusing him of murdering anyone, but only of operating on Sammy or having her operated upon and obliterating the evidence."

From all outward appearances, Halloran was enjoying the show his former girlfriend put on. His wife accompanied him to court every day, and his mother had flown in from Oakland, California, to be with the family. One morning, when he had to battle the crowds waiting to gain entrance to the courtroom, he told them to let him pass because he was "head man in the show."

He often smiled as Ruth testified, sometimes shaking his head at her recitation of events, more than once laughing out loud. His actions were like a spark for her fuse. He would show some outward sign and she would blow up.

It took nearly three days for Ruth Judd to tell the whole story. The court had to admonish her repeatedly to answer the question posed, not give a speech. She paid little attention to those orders. "I'm not here to exonerate Halloran," she yelled at one point. "He had his chance to help me at my trial and he didn't." Asked any question, she launched into another attack on Halloran, whom the local press referred to as "her former friend." Time and again, her outbursts were stricken from the record as being "unresponsive to the question."

There were no rebuttal witnesses. Jack Halloran never took the stand in his own defense. Officially, he said not a word to this court, which had the power to order a full-fledged trial. His attorney did all the talking for him, declaring everything Ruth Judd said was "absolutely false" and nothing more "than the story of an insane person."

Testimony ended on January 24. Halloran's attorney was on his feet immediately, asking Judge Niles to dismiss the charges against his client. Smith said the issue before the court was clear: Halloran could not be an accessory to a crime if there had been no crime committed.

Where was the crime? he asked. The prosecution's entire case rested on Winnie Ruth Judd's declarations that she had killed in self-defense. That was no crime. Ergo, there could be no accessory. All charges against Jack Halloran should be dropped.

As bizarre as Smith's argument sounds—after all, Ruth Judd was facing a death sentence for murder—Judge Niles alerted prosecutor Renz Jennings that it made sense.

"By your own witness, you proved self-defense," he told the county attorney. "If you can show me any law that will give me anything to weigh here—any question of fact or any question upon which reasonable men might differ—I will feel it my duty to overrule this motion for dismissal."

Jennings came up with nothing. As he would recall years later in his autobiography, "I had previously had some experience with the judge who tried the case and I felt that his 'stinger' was out for me. In addition, before the trial was over, I felt that he had some kind of a close relationship with the so-called conspirator [Halloran]." Jennings's widow, Leola, sounds like so many other Phoenix old-timers when she reflects on the case. "Winnie Ruth Judd was such a sweet and refined person, people couldn't believe she was involved in such a thing. I had the impression Halloran was mixed up in it and let her take all the blame."

On January 25, 1933, Judge Niles set Halloran free.

He told the court that Smith's argument held. "Mr. Judd's testimony is most persuasive," Niles said. "The state of Arizona has definitely proved that Mrs. Judd acted in self-defense. Therefore, there was no crime committed."

Jack Halloran jumped up and kissed his wife. Smiling, they walked out of the courtroom together.

And Winnie Ruth Judd went back to death row, still facing the hangman's noose.

The bizarre turns of the Halloran case were "certainly one for the law books," as the *Los Angeles Examiner* put it. "It leaves Mrs. Judd convicted of murder and sentenced to be hanged and yet virtually exonerated of the crime by another court, before which she told the story she was not permitted by her previous counsel to tell at her own trial."

It gave hope to all those who saw Ruth Judd as a victim. Her attorneys quickly seized the situation, telling the press, "Based on the findings of the Maricopa County grand jury that it believed she killed Agnes LeRoi and Hedvig Samuelson in self-defense, and upon the decision of Judge Niles in the Halloran action, we are confidently hopeful that the Arizona Board of Pardons and Paroles will grant Mrs. Judd a full parole at her hearing to be set next week."

Privately, the attorneys told Ruth Judd her ordeal was almost over.

For Jack Halloran, it was over. The law had exonerated him. But Phoenix was not as forgiving. His secret business partners, the powerful O'Malley family, forced the sale of the Halloran-Bennett Lumber Company. The lumberyard he had opened on his own in an unfashionable section of South Phoenix never gained any particular prominence. His family name was tainted. The house he owned in the silk-stocking district of Phoenix would still be his home forty years later, when the neighborhood had fallen into disrepute.

Jack Halloran walked out of court a free man, but his glory days were over.

Today his name has been all but lost to history. A television documentary on the Judd case in 1969—the first televised interview with her—bleeped out his name. A book written in the early 1970s used the fictitious name "Carl Harris" for Halloran. Some newspapers have referred to him only as "Mr. X." Even people who were close to the case in the thirties have forgotten he was ever charged.

Private detective Howard Sauter says all of that was orchestrated. As he found during an investigation in the early 1970s, there was a concerted effort to erase Halloran's name from the case. Sauter, who was working for Ruth Judd's attorneys, recalls doing a routine records check at the courthouse for a copy of the indictment against Jack Halloran.

"There was no record. There was nothing that showed he'd ever been indicted," Sauter recalls. "The register of documents didn't have it. But I found a torn piece in the record book, and in checking the numbers, I saw a page was gone.

I went to the state, and thankfully, that page had already been copied before someone tore it out."

Sauter, a former San Diego cop who moved to Phoenix in the late 1960s and is still a private detective, says his reading of the evidence left him with nothing but disgust for Halloran.

"The more I read, the more I knew Winnie was involved in a case of self-defense," he says now. "All that happened to her was to protect a Phoenix Country Club man—the whole criminal justice system was subverted to protect him. The movers and shakers allowed all this to happen to her to protect the image, reputation, and marriage of Jack Halloran. Winnie was the sacrificial goat. The system was aware of the truth, Halloran got involved because her trial would inevitably bring out his affair with her, because he was the subject of the argument. He's thinking, 'If I can cover up what she's done, I'll never get exposed.' He wasn't doing it for Winnie. He was doing it for his own purposes, but his purposes compounded the case."

"You talk to people in this town, they don't know Jack Halloran's name anymore. They don't know he was her lover. They don't know he was indicted. He succeeded where it counted to him—in this town."

For Winnie Ruth Judd, life looked rosy in the weeks after Halloran was granted his freedom. Her attorneys were almost certain that Judge Niles's ruling would give her freedom too.

And her list of supporters grew spectacularly.

A total of thirty lawmakers—more than a third of the entire state legislature—signed a petition on her behalf to the parole board. Citing both the grand jury and Judge Niles, the legislators told the board, "Since the state of Arizona itself has proved that Mrs. Judd acted in self-defense, we feel that it is highly offensive to our sense of justice, to allow our fair and sovereign state of Arizona to hang Mrs. Winnie Ruth Judd."

A second impressive petition for justice came from an ecumenical group of thirty-four ministers and priests—an unusual union in the days when churches seldom joined voices and there was almost open warfare between Protestants and Catholics. A total of twenty-seven different parishes were represented by their religious leaders on the list, including the associate priest from Jack Halloran's parish, St. Mary's Catholic Church. The chaplain from the state prison in Florence joined the group, as did a variety of Baptists, Methodists, Lutherans, and even the Salvation Army.

Most notably, members of three of the state's religious hierarchy added their names to the plea: Walter Mitchell, bishop of the Episcopal Diocese of Arizona; G. W. Griffith, bishop of the Free Methodist Church; and Hill A. Betts, district superintendent of the M. E. Church in Arizona.

The clergymen gave the parole board two ways out: either follow the lead of the grand jury and Judge Niles, and commute the death sentence, or give Ruth Judd an "indefinite reprieve" until she could be tried for the death of Hedvig Samuelson. They reminded the parole board that three arrest warrants had been issued in the Samuelson case—Mrs. Judd and two unnamed accomplices, or John Does. The clergymen said they wanted all three brought to trial, with Ruth Judd's punishment based on the outcome of that forum.

"If a trial jury on the Samuelson charge find that Mrs. Judd acted in self-defense and their verdict is not guilty, then a full pardon should be issued on the LeRoi charge," the petition suggested. "If the trial jury on the Samuelson case determine Mrs. Judd is guilty to the extent of manslaughter, then a commutation of the death penalty should be made to that of manslaughter on the LeRoi charge, etc."

Waiting in her prison cell for the parole board to act, Ruth Judd was being reminded what happiness felt like. Her joyous parents, who had moved to Florence to be near her, were allowed to spend most days and evenings with her inside the prison walls. Ruth told her parents she wanted to leave this "land of strangers" and return to Indiana, where she'd grown up. Her parents were just as anxious to return to Darlington, to retire in the community they had served for so many years.

For now, they were homeless and penniless and forced to rely on the generosity of the strangers who had entered their lives. During the trial in Phoenix, they had been looked after by various ministers who took them into their homes and provided their meals. That was to be expected. The McKinnells would have done the same.

They were surprised—and grateful—to find the people of Florence just as openhearted. The residents in this small rural town, where the prison was the major employer, enthusiastically befriended the aged couple. Many shops in town put donation cans at the checkout counters to support them. The town's two cafés filled up pails each night with soup or leftover dinners so the couple could eat.

Someone in town gave Ruth a pregnant black cat she promptly named Egypt and kept in her cell. As the hearing before the parole board neared—the last formality, her attorneys called it; her "last stand to cheat the gallows," the *Republic* called it—Ruth wondered if she would be free before the kittens arrived.

The Arizona Board of Pardons and Paroles was unmoved by the grand jury.

It was unmoved by Judge Niles's ruling.

It was unmoved by the lawmakers.

It was unmoved by the impressive list of clergymen.

It was unmoved by more than three thousand letters from across the nation begging for mercy.

It was particularly unmoved by the trial jurors who had come forward with their "make her talk" scheme. When Ruth's attorneys attempted to call those jurors before the parole board, they were rebuffed. Board member Arthur T. LaPrade, the new attorney general for the state of Arizona, spat, "I wouldn't believe them if they said they did it with an ulterior motive. Go before the Superior Court and take those jurors there and let them 'confess their sins' and let the Superior Court prosecute."

During six days of testimony, the board heard Ruth Judd tell her story, watched as she reenacted the deadly fight with the girls. It called Jack Halloran to the stand and heard him categorically deny her every charge. It heard William C. Judd recount how his wife had told him several versions of what happened that night—versions he knew were lies because there were too many pieces that did not fit. He said it wasn't until two weeks after her surrender that she told him the self-defense story. And he admitted he now understood she had lied to him at first to conceal her illicit affair.

And the board heard plenty from Sheriff McFadden. As *The Arizona Republic* reported on March 21, 1933, the sheriff "strongly substantiated portions of Mrs. Judd's self-defense story." Most significant, the paper reported, "McFadden told of finding considerable evidence of blood in the breakfast room and the kitchen…supporting Mrs. Judd's story of her fight for life."

But the board was not moved by the sheriff's revelations either.

On March 30, the Arizona Board of Pardons and Paroles declared that Ruth Judd was a cold-blooded murderer who had shot Mrs. LeRoi in bed as the woman slept.

It said Winnie Ruth Judd should hang by the neck until dead.

It set a new execution date—avoiding the distasteful thought of killing her on Good Friday—of April 21.

Van Beck well remembers reading in the *Republic* about the parole board's decision. He made a few notes in his journal: "March 31, 1933: Parole Board did not commute. I heard her story and did not believe she was completely guilty; do not believe she was guilty of a crime that should be called murder; did not think she should hang."

Chapter 13
Thirteen Steps to the Gallows

No one could really believe Arizona was serious about killing Winnie Ruth Judd.

While the death penalty was imposed often throughout the nation in the 1930s, the debate over its morality was as strong as it is today. And Winnie Ruth Judd's case became a cause *célèbre* for those who argued that legalized murder was barbaric.

"If the death penalty is ever justified, it can be only in a case where there is no doubt," argued Rev. W. C. Reynolds of the Free Methodist Church in Phoenix, who preached and wrote extensively to arouse public support on Ruth's behalf. "But here is a case shrouded in mystery. The more we study its various angles, the more the mystery deepens. To hang any person under such conditions is a monstrous crime against civilization and a blot on the state that does it."

In the California statehouse, the "spectacle" of her pending execution was cited to bolster arguments that the state should get off the capital punishment bandwagon. (It didn't.)

Public opinion throughout the nation seemed to side with Ruth Judd. Thousands wrote on her behalf, including First Lady Eleanor Roosevelt, who received national recognition for bringing the case to the attention of the President. Many enumerated all the strange twists and turns of the case; some argued that Ruth's testimony would be needed later, if Arizona ever brought her accomplices to trial; some maintained that it was inconceivable to execute a woman; some begged that she be spared for the sake of her aged parents.

But a handful wrote to support the state's desire to visit the "ultimate punishment" on this wayward woman, according to the records still kept on file at the Arizona Archives. A woman from San Antonio wrote: "If women are allowed to give way to their passions thinking public sentiment will insure them leniency, we could all cut and slash and shoot on the least provocation." From Hollywood came a letter saying, "I feel that the thirty legislators who signed the petition for this murderess's pardon should be sterilized pro bono publico."

It was painfully clear to Arizona—its business leaders, its politicians, its journalists, and its citizens—that the negative publicity the case was generating was the last thing the state needed. Its intense booster campaigns had told people this was a mecca, a place where good people were raising healthy families in a climate that—except for the summer months—was the envy of the nation. How could it now explain executing a woman who many believed was not even guilty?

But Arizona was up against the wall.

State law puts the final word in the hands of the parole board. The governor of the state is prohibited from acting without a recommendation of leniency from the board. The board then harbored no leniency.

There was only one slim, unlikely chance left. Arizona law at the time allowed the state prison warden—who served at the pleasure of the governor—to call for a sanity hearing for death row inmates. But since two different courts had declared she was sane, it seemed like political suicide for new Warden A. G. Walker to use his power.

But that's what he did. Nobody ever thought he acted without at least a reassuring wink from the governor.

On April 12, 1933—nine days before her scheduled execution—Warden Walker petitioned the Pinal County Superior Court: "There is good reason to believe that... Winnie Ruth Judd has become insane after the delivery of the said Winnie Ruth Judd to the Superintendent of the Arizona State Prison for execution."

Judge E. L. Green of Pinal County—the home county of the prison—set the trial to begin immediately; after all, there was no time to waste. The jury was selected from the citizens of this rural county in one day.

Ruth Judd's latest batch of attorneys was hastily assembled. O. V. Willson—now an old man with health problems who had retired after a brilliant career as a defense lawyer—headed the list. He was assisted by young law partners who would both leave their mark on Arizona: Tom Fulbright, who would eventually become a judge himself, and Ernest McFarland, who would become the state's best-known citizen, with a thirty-five year career in public service that included terms as United States senator, governor, and chief justice of the Arizona Supreme Court.

Years later, *Life* magazine would spotlight McFarland as a rising Democratic star and note that his favorite case had been defending Winnie Ruth Judd. But that was not how McFarland would remember it in his 1979 autobiography, *Mac.* He admits he "did not enjoy" the case and got into it only because of a misunderstanding: Ruth's father thought he and Fulbright had volunteered their services, and showed up at their office to proclaim how "proud" he was to have them on the team. "We didn't have the heart to turn him down," McFarland recounted.

As Fulbright remembered in his memoirs, none of the attorneys were paid, except with the experience of handling one of the most watched trials the country had ever seen. With only days to present their case, they scrambled to find experts who would testify Ruth Judd was insane, knowing the county attorney was going to rely on the San Francisco psychiatrist who was very familiar with the case—Dr. Joseph Catton.

The sanity hearing began at 9:40 a.m. on April 14, 1933. Anyone who had expected officials to zip through the trial soon realized that would not happen. There wasn't enough time before the execution date to cover all the witnesses. Ruth's attorneys argued it was ludicrous for the state to execute her while her insanity hearing was still in progress.

On April 18, the parole board delayed the execution until April 28. That gave the trial some "breathing room," as everyone remembers it.

Winnie Ruth Judd put on a good show for the twelve men who would decide if she lived or died. From the first day of the trial to the last, she acted crazier than a loon.

"Her hands clutching her hair, her body rocking back and forth, and her almost continuous laughter or tears made Mrs. Judd a pitiful sight at today's session," reported Marjorie Driscoll of Universal Press Service on April 15, the first day of testimony. "She stared into space and laughed or sobbed while her husband now and then, took her groping hands in his own and endeavored to calm her. Occasionally she relaxed a little, but her lips moved as she muttered incoherent sentences. Once she turned to her husband and pleaded with him to permit her to throw herself from a nearby second story window of the courtroom. At another point, she threw the court into an uproar when she jumped to her feet and shouted to the jury: 'You're all a bunch of degenerates—gangsters. You're just here to see me suffer. You're all crazier than I am.'"

Two days later, the Associated Press reported: "Shrieking imprecations in a wild voice, Winnie Ruth Judd was removed forcibly today to her state prison cell from the courtroom where a hearing was in progress to determine her sanity. After a drive around country roads in the custody of Warden Walker, the convicted 'trunk slayer' returned to the courtroom meekly, sat down, placed her chin in her hands and stared at the floor. The outburst, her most violent since the hearing began last week, came while her husband was on the stand testifying to a belief she was insane."

It went on like that for ten days.

In his 1968 autobiography, *Cow-Country Counselor*, attorney Fulbright remembered it differently. What he saw in the trial was the blank stare, the monotonous twisting of the handkerchief—now a trademark of Winnie Ruth Judd inside a courtroom—and the inattention. He remembered only one outburst, but it was a lulu: "When the name of the Phoenix playboy was mentioned, she jumped to her feet yelling and screaming and said, 'That damn Jack Halloran, I would like to take his head and break it against the ceiling and spatter his brains like a dish of oatmeal.'"

Ruth Judd turned on the psychiatrists—both pro and con. She turned on her parents. She swore at her brother for not coming to her side at this crucial moment. (Burton McKinnell was there, Fulbright notes in his memoirs, but the strange young man was wearing a disguise of "false red whiskers, a wig and dark glasses.")

Her attorneys now did exactly what her trial attorneys had done. They put her mother on the stand to recount the family's "history of insanity"; they put her father on to detail Ruth's teenage acts of lunacy; they put her husband on to tell how she had pretended to be a mother for years. To that old story, they added the testimony of prison officials who had overseen Ruth Judd for months.

Matron Ella Heath told the jury she thought Ruth Judd was "absolutely insane." She said the other female inmates in the state prison were "all afraid of her." Matron Heath described how Mrs. Judd had beaten herself on the head with her shoe, thrown herself on the floor, and torn her hair, many times without apparent reason except that some word or incident had excited her. "And a minute later, she will be laughing and playing with her kittens and calling them her babies."

There was nothing normal about Ruth Judd, the press quoted Matron Heath as telling the court. "She didn't seem to realize the seriousness of her situation. She believes that she is being persecuted. She says over and over that the doctors want to kill her so that they can examine her brain. She doesn't speak of it as punishment for anything she has done, but she thinks that someone wants to hurt her for their own satisfaction."

Tom Fulbright's widow, Edna, sat through each day of the trial and still remembers how embarrassing and uncomfortable all this testimony was. She also came away thinking that Ruth's entire clan was a little nutty. "Winnie Ruth was the sanest one in the whole family," she said in a recent interview.

"There were very strong feelings against Winnie," Edna Fulbright recalls. "Most of the women in town were very much against her. The disposition of the bodies ticked people off. At that time, I was opposed to her too. As time went on, in thinking it over, I got considerable sympathy for her. It was widely suspected other people were involved. There was talk she did not get an adequate defense [in her criminal trial in Phoenix]."

Dr. Catton got on the stand and repeated much of what he had said in the trial. He told the jury Ruth Judd was faking insanity. In his professional way, he lectured the men sitting in judgment. He said he had found Ruth Judd perfectly capable of understanding what was happening and of putting on an act to save herself. He should know, Dr. Catton told them, because he was a trained psychologist.

Tom Fulbright later wondered if Dr. Catton himself wasn't a little off. He recounts in his memoirs the story he was told after the trial by deputy county attorney Charlie Reed. "Every damn night Dr. Catton insisted on sleeping at a different place. Then he would lock the door behind him and crawl under the bed."

Grand juror Van Beck drove down to Florence to testify at the hearing. He explained how the grand jury had reached its conclusions that Ruth Judd had really killed in self-defense and should not hang. He also told the court that he thought, yes, she was insane. He did it, he says now, because he couldn't bear to see her die with a rope around her neck.

McFarland delivered the closing arguments, remembering in his memoirs: "I told the jury that we had just passed through the Easter season, and reminded them that the thief had asked forgiveness of Christ, while they were on the cross. I said that was what we were asking for Ruth Judd. If she were to be executed, it would be at a time when she was sane and able to ask for forgiveness. A reporter from the *Los Angeles Times* told me my speech to the jury won the case."

It took the jury only minutes to decide Ruth Judd was insane.

"When I saw the jury file into the box with the verdict, my interest was in Winnie Ruth Judd," Fulbright wrote. "If she was faking and the verdict was one of sanity, I expected to see a feeling of hopeless despair upon her face, for it meant her execution at daybreak the next morning. If it was insanity, then I expected to see the blank stare fade from her eyes in a look of relief. But there was no change. There was not even a cessation of the manipulation of the handkerchief. She walked out of the courtroom surrounded by her family and sympathizers."

McFarland visited with Ruth Judd the day after the verdict. "She was all dressed up, and told me what a wonderful speech I had made," his autobiography notes. "I said to her, 'How do you know? You're crazy.' She laughed at that."

For some in the press, the jury's decision meant Ruth Judd had "cheated the hangman."

For others, it meant she had received justice.

But looking back, it seems clear what it really meant was Arizona had finally wiggled its way out of a ridiculous situation.

By now no one really wanted to see her hang—not with such widespread public suspicion about what had happened the night of the killings. Executing her would make her a martyr for the vigorous opponents of capital punishment. It would give Arizona a black eye the state could not afford.

But at the same time, Arizona was tired of the "nastiness" and "taboos" that the Winnie Ruth Judd case represented. It wanted to hear no more about Phoenix playboys and lesbians and syphilis and infidelity. And it certainly had no stomach left for body parts in trunks.

Arizona wanted this case over and it wanted to silence Winnie Ruth Judd, and many think it did both in that Pinal County courthouse.

Some today view the insanity ruling as a graceful way out for everyone. It meant Ruth Judd lived. It meant Arizona closed the door on the case. But others think it was more devious than that. "She was declared insane to shut her up," says Larry Debus. "It was all part of the cover-up."

Agreement comes from former *Republic* reporter Logan McKechnie, who investigated the case in the late 1960s: "A governor might not let a woman hang. But if you put her in an insane asylum and then she talks, nobody's gonna believe her."

Whatever the true motivation, Winnie Ruth Judd was not going to die on the gallows—although the hangman's noose was always a shadow in the background. By the ruling of the court, she would be held at the Arizona State Hospital for the Insane in Phoenix "until her reason is restored." Then the state of Arizona would exact the punishment it demanded for the killing of Agnes LeRoi.

At 12:50 p.m. on April 24, 1933, Ruth was escorted to the "crazy house," as everyone called it. She was allowed to take her cat with her. She'd found homes for the four new-born kittens with the good people of Florence.

She was greeted at the gates of the asylum by a throng of photographers and reporters. As the flashbulbs blinded her, she was escorted through the group. She looked back over her shoulder once before she entered the big wooden doors.

Her parting words to the press were hissed: "I never saw such a bunch of morbids!"

Nobody heard much about Winnie Ruth Judd for the next six years.

Chapter 14
The One with the Scalpel

Who cut up Hedvig Samuelson?

Of all the lingering questions in the Winnie Ruth Judd case, this one tops the list. Former governor Jack Williams says after all these years, it's the one he still wants answered.

It is the question that needed to be answered when Samuelson's dismemberment made the Judd case "the trial of the decade." Instead, at least officially, it wasn't even asked.

As far as the state of Arizona was concerned in 1931, Winnie Ruth Judd did it. Period.

That's what history says happened.

That's what the media and authors who write about notorious crimes have reported all these years.

As the press at the time claimed, she "admitted" it in the drainpipe letter when she said, "It was horrible to pack things as I did." The press surmised she would not have packed the bodies if she hadn't done the cutting. And every "official" voice maintained that conclusion was correct.

Most of the public believed the widespread press descriptions of Samuelson's body as being "hacked to pieces." They believed she had been "butchered." Since the autopsy pictures were seen by so few, those descriptions were all the public had to rely on. But it wasn't just erroneous newspaper reports that had people believing a lie about the condition of Sammy's body. The lie was long perpetuated by one of the few men who had actually seen the autopsy pictures: the man who prosecuted Winnie Ruth Judd.

Lloyd J. Andrews always took pride in the fact that he had convinced a jury to convict Winnie Ruth Judd. And it clearly rankled him that as the years passed, rumors about the Judd case refused to die—rumors that she didn't get a fair trial, rumors that she was railroaded, rumors that she had had accomplices.

In a 1952 interview with the *Arizona Republic*, Andrews said he wanted to be sure the record was clear. "Judd Rumors Called Bunk," the headline read.

The rumor Dogie Andrews most wanted to put to rest was that someone with skill had to have dismembered the body. "It was brought out at the trial that the defendant could have done the job unaided. People say now that she must have had the help of a skilled surgeon. More baloney. In trying to sever a leg, the person doing it attempted to go through a thigh bone. Does that sound like the work of a surgeon or of an amateur butcher?"

In asking the question, Andrews thought he was presenting the clear answer that it took only an amateur like Winnie Ruth Judd to do the awful deed.

No one noticed that Lloyd Andrews rewrote history in trying to put this rumor to rest.

There was no testimony at the trial about who cut up the body. There was no testimony about how much skill it took. The questions were never even raised, because Winnie Ruth Judd was not standing trial for Samuelson's killing. Prosecutors said at the time they would try her first for the LeRoi murder and then hold a separate trial on Samuelson. But they never did, despite repeated claims from Ruth Judd's attorneys and defenders that the whole story of what happened that night could not be told until the questions about what happened to Sammy were finally asked.

Attorney Larry Debus, who reviewed her court records over thirty years later when he hired on as her attorney, decries the "convenient" way Arizona split the trial. "Why try her on the death that had tentacles into Phoenix society?" he asks sarcastically. "If they tried her on the body that was cut up, then they'd have to explain it and ask who cut her up—especially because of the way it was cut up. So they split the trial as part of the cover-up."

It still angers him. "If there hadn't been a dismembered body, this would have been a very different case," he declares. "Without that, you wouldn't have had these personalities involved, you wouldn't have had a cover-up. At the worst, she'd have been convicted of manslaughter and been out jail in three or four years."

It is not just a view reached all these years later. A 1933 letter to state officials begging for mercy for Winnie Ruth Judd makes the same point. O. G. Morrow, editor and publisher of Arizona's *Ash Fork Record*, stressed: "If the body had not been mutilated AFTER the crime, I do not believe a verdict of FIRST DEGREE would have been brought in. And it seems to me that the death sentence was imposed, not because of the crime itself, but because of the means used to dispose of the bodies."

Dogie Andrews was not interested in pursuing those questions—he was the one who decided the trial should be split. But he was very interested in perpetuating the notion that Winnie Ruth Judd deserved what she got because she was "an amateur butcher."

This writer's investigation wasn't two days old before cracks started showing up in that historical conclusion: "Ruth Judd didn't cut up that body," one old-timer after another said with certainty. At first it seemed she was just getting the sympathy vote. Grown women who were girls when the crime was committed—like Rita Grimm and Edna George— said they would never believe she'd done the cutting. Larry

Debus, said the same thing, but that kind of talk is to be expected from a defense attorney.

What one would never expect to hear is her last living juror saying: "We thought she killed them but she didn't cut them up, we were all pretty agreed on that." Stewart Thompson didn't even see anything remarkable in that revelation.

In over a hundred interviews, the only person who still thought Ruth Judd was a butcher was Dogie Andrews's widow, Francie.

The autopsy pictures are shocking. Not only for what they depict but because they so belie the thousands of times they were incorrectly described.

The cuts are clean.

There are no slashes, as though the cutter was hacking away at the flesh.

They are so clean you instantly think you're looking at a body that underwent an operation.

And Ruth Judd's haunting recitation of the story comes back: "Halloran said Sammy had been operated on."

Sammy's body was hemisected—cut in two major pieces—at the waistline. Then her legs were severed at the knees. There is also a ten-inch-long, two-inch-deep gash at the hipbone in her right leg, as though the cutter had intended to sever her torso from her legs but then quickly abandoned the idea.

During this investigation, retired Maricopa County medical examiner Heinz Karnitschnig studied the photographs along with the autopsy reports and all the trial testimony. Dr. Karnitschnig, a bear of a man who still speaks with a heavy German accent, is one of the few people around who is never shocked by such pictures, but then he's performed thousands of autopsies himself.

It takes Dr. K., as everyone calls him, only a few minutes to review the evidence shown by the pictures and described in the reports. These are his first words:

"The person seems to know what he or she was doing. Being able to hemisect the body, going through the spine by cutting through two vertebrae, is not the easiest thing to do. The knee joints were disarticulated. Without some skill either as a doctor or as an operating room technician or as a butcher, it wouldn't be all that easy to do."

He is asked directly if that unsuccessful incision around the hipbone shows the cutter didn't really know what he or she was doing, as prosecutor Andrews claimed. "No, it doesn't," he answers. "Disarticulating at the hip joint can be done, but it's very hard to do. You need a long and very thin knife to do that."

Dr. K. is very clear on what is obvious from the autopsy reports and photos. "I don't see any butchery to it," he says. "This is not a rage case where people get really butchered. This is utilitarian stuff. I think it's a straightforward case of dismemberment for the ease of packing {the body in a trunk}. It takes somebody with skill to do it."

There has never been any evidence that Winnie Ruth Judd was skillful with a scalpel.

That was apparent even to one of the psychiatrists hired by the prosecution. Although his job was to help send her to prison, Dr. Joseph Catton grilled Ruth so relentlessly on this point that it was clear he never believed her capable of the dismemberment. Time and again, he posed the question in various ways, getting an evasive answer if he got any at all. Finally he asked her bluntly: "Mrs. Judd, as a matter of fact, you have never cut a human being in your life."

Her answer sounds almost weary: "Dr. Catton, I have never even cut a chicken."

Sheriff J. R. McFadden was among the handful who had actually seen the autopsy pictures of Samuelson's body. He had seen that the cuts were so precise the coroner had been able to stitch her back together. His daughter says he believed Ruth Judd's protestations.

"What made my father try so hard to solve the case were the pictures of the girl's body," Helen McFadden says in a recent interview. "He said it had to be done by a professional—a surgeon or a doctor. He said Ruth was incapable of doing it."

Former governor Williams long ago reached the same conclusion. He says it was common knowledge in Phoenix that even as the media were portraying the dismemberment as a "butchery," it was no such thing. He says he's known for as long as he can remember that the cuts were so skillful the cutter "had to be a doctor."

But if Ruth Judd didn't do it, then the question is, who did?

At first Ruth thought Halloran had done it, posing as his "Dr. Buckley." But she also knew he had tried repeatedly that first night to reach his old friend Dr. Charles W. Brown. She never saw Dr. Brown at the bungalow, however. And she never asked Halloran to explain who—he or his doctor friend or somebody else—had performed the "operation."

The first clue in answering the question came from a highly unlikely source: jury foreman Stewart Thompson.

Thompson has always believed a doctor was responsible and that he knows which one. He says he reached that conclusion a few months after Ruth Judd's trial when he went down to the prison to see her at her brother's insistence.

While he was waiting for Ruth to be brought from her cell, Thompson recounts, the prison warden told him about a strange incident. "He said a Dr. Brown had been down to the prison three or four days before, drunk as a skunk, waving his hat around and yelling he was the only man alive who knew the truth about the Winnie Ruth Judd case."

As Thompson remembers it, Dr. Brown died only a few days later. He says he always wondered if he committed suicide.

Thompson's conclusion could be dismissed as wild conjecture—except that Dr. Brown's passing resulted in a most extraordinary letter from one of Arizona's most extraordinary citizens.

Editors at the *Los Angeles Times* were alerted to Brown's death by Colonel J. H. McClintock, one of Arizona's pioneer journalists, whose name still adorns a major street in Phoenix's sister city of Tempe. Colonel McClintock—a decorated soldier who had been one of Teddy Roosevelt's Rough Riders—had a career that encompassed everything from justice of the peace to teacher to, at the time of the Judd trial, postmaster for Phoenix. Through it all, he was also a prolific journalist who would always be remembered as one of Arizona's "great historians." As one admirer put it, in his numerous articles that ran coast to coast he "never neglected to boost for Arizona."

It was natural for McClintock to pass on a news tip to the *Times* because for twenty-five years he was the Arizona correspondent for the California paper.

During the course of this investigation, librarians in the Arizona Room of the Phoenix Public Library were cataloging McClintock's private papers—a collection that is the pride of the historical room.

Among the thousands of documents he left, they found a letter he wrote on June 6, 1932. It is addressed: "My dear Trueblood and Hall." Ralph Trueblood was then managing editor of the *Times*, and Chapin Hall assistant managing editor.

McClintock wrote: "Dr. Charles W. Brown, formerly county physician, died at his home here Friday, apparently of heart disease, though in the right hand of the corpse was clutched a sharp butcher knife. Apparently, he was stricken while at least contemplating suicide.

"This especially may be of interest to your men who took in the Ruth Judd trial. I understand that no evidence has been produced publicly, probably never will be produced, but I have heard a report that Brown was the individual who did the deft job of dissection.

"For a year or so he has been almost irresponsible and is believed to have been under the influence of narcotics."

There is no evidence the *Times* ever did anything with the information. And if reporters in Phoenix heard the same report, no mention of it was made in the local press. The Hearst papers, however, could not ignore the rumors. As the *New York Mirror* reported the day Halloran's indictment was announced: "A second man would probably have been indicted, according to widespread rumor, if death had not intervened. Mrs. Judd's story included the declaration that a physician, who has since committed suicide, was summoned to the murder bungalow to aid in the disposal of the bodies."

It was 1936 when a nurse at the state mental hospital first heard the story of Dr. C. W. Brown's involvement, from two different people.

Mrs. Ann Miller was thirty-three then, just three years older than the "awfully nice" Ruth Judd who was held in Ward B as a murderer.

The two women often worked together, Mrs. Miller as a paid staff member, Ruth as a patient who assumed so many chores to help the other patients that she seemed like a member of the staff too. The two women became friends. And as the friendship grew, so did the level of trust.

Ann Miller eventually remarried and became Ann Keim. She still lives in Phoenix, and is anxious to finally tell the story she has kept secret all these years.

"Ruth told me a lot of things," Mrs. Keim said in a recent interview. "She told me about killing the girls in self-defense. I believed her because she wouldn't kill in cold blood. That wasn't Ruth. And I knew she couldn't have cut up that body—she didn't have the skill or the strength."

It took some time, Mrs. Keim remembers, before Ruth Judd trusted her enough to talk about who had dismembered Sammy's body.

"Ruth told me that a Dr. Brown had come to see her while she was in prison and told her he was going to confess everything. But for some reason he never did. Then one day I was talking to an attorney I knew in town named Ed Scarborough and I told him what Ruth had said about Dr. Brown. Ed said, 'I'm sure she told you that. Dr. Brown came up to my office and wanted to tell the whole story. He made an appointment for the next week, but he died the day before the appointment.'"

Ann Keim still wonders what would have happened if Dr. Brown had kept that appointment with the lawyer, who has since died. She still wonders if the confession he promised would have helped free Ruth Judd in the mid-1930s, when she was still a young woman. She has always lamented that none of that happened. "I think it's awful what they did to Ruth," she says today.

Dr. Charles W. Brown earned his medical degree in Atlanta, Georgia, in 1917. He was licensed to practice medicine in the state of Arizona in 1928, according to records at the Maricopa County Medical Society. In 1929, he was the physician at the state prison in Florence; he held the post for a little over a year before moving to Phoenix. In September 5, 1930, he was appointed by the county board of supervisors as the county physician, in those days a political patronage job that paid $3,300 a year. He also held that job for one year, and was in private practice at the time of his death. Although he was married and had four children, he and his wife were apparently separated, because his obituary notes they lived at different addresses. He was forty-four years old when he died.

A news story on his demise said the coroner considered calling an inquest into the cause of death, but abandoned that plan and declared Brown had died of a heart attack.

Ruth Judd herself does not like to talk about these things. In interviews with this writer throughout 1990, she refused to discuss the details of the night her best friends died, saying she could not bear to think of it.

And so the grisly subject of the dismemberment was approached gingerly. It was brought up, most carefully, one night during a telephone interview.

With bated breath and hoping she wouldn't hang up, she was asked the most nonthreatening question possible: "I wonder what Dr. Brown meant when he was down at the prison saying he was the only man alive who knew the truth about your case."

"I know what he meant," she answered immediately.

"I know you know. Can you tell me?"

She was silent for a long time. Afraid of losing her, a chancy offer was made: "Could I tell you what I think he meant?"

There was another long pause before she said yes.

"I think he meant he was the one who dismembered the body."

There was just a moment before she answered, "I've always thought that too."

Chapter 15
The Asylum

Arizona couldn't get rid of Winnie Ruth Judd.

It couldn't hold her, it couldn't silence her, it couldn't make everyone forget.

She became not just a suspicious and embarrassing chapter of the 1930s but a haunting piece of Phoenix history in the 1940s. The 1950s. The 1960s. The 1970s.

It was most disturbing for Arizona—which started growing like a weed after World War II—that Winnie Ruth Judd's name remained one of the state's most prominent for four decades.

Many would look back on her first six, quiet years in the asylum as the only peace Arizona would ever get from the infamous "trunk murder case."

Because Winnie Ruth Judd started escaping. Again and again and again. Bring up her name today, and people across the nation will remember her more as an escape artist than a convicted murderess.

She was still a young woman when she started pulling off her disappearing act, to the startled reaction of Phoenix. She was still at it as a middle-aged lady, and by then Phoenix was mainly mortified that she could steal her freedom at will. She was most successful at it as an old woman, by which time most were simply bemused.

The first escape was October 24, 1939—eight years to the day after she surrendered herself to the Los Angeles police, exactly six years and six months after she was committed to the asylum.

She did it again on December 3, 1939.

Again on May 11, 1947.

Once more on November 29, 1951.

Again on February 2, 1952.

And again on Thanksgiving Day of 1952.

The last time was October 8, 1962—just eight days short of the thirty-first anniversary of Anne's and Sammy's deaths.

By that time, "Winnie's Gone Again" was a very familiar headline throughout the country. Nobody could remember anyone else who had escaped from custody seven times. But then nobody could remember anyone who had been incarcerated—either in a prison or in an asylum—for thirty-one years either.

Along the way, another generation grew to know the name of Winnie Ruth Judd. Even if they were fuzzy about what she'd supposedly done, the children of Phoenix in those years were quite sure she was dangerous.

As the escapes began, newspapers were filled with hysterical stories. Bloodhounds were brought to Phoenix from the state prison to track Ruth down. Manhunts were marshaled throughout the West. Officials particularly kept their eyes on the border between Arizona and Old Mexico, as the nation of Mexico was known until the fifties. With her command of Spanish and familiarity with the country from the years she spent there with her husband, most assumed she would try to hide in Mexico, where the long arm of the law would have trouble reaching her. Phoenix children wondered if she would have time to kill again before she was captured.

"My folks would tell me if I didn't behave, Winnie would come in the night and *get me*," remembers attorney and Phoenix native Michael Pierce, echoing stories told by many.

Some children were told she was a crazy murderess. Somewhere along the line, the idea that she was an "ax murderess" became part of the folklore. Some were told she was driven crazy because Arizona had railroaded her for a crime she did not commit. Some were just told the story was too sordid to explain.

But all of them were told there was something peculiar about the way this woman seemed able to escape the state hospital at will.

Everyone assumed Ruth Judd had "powerful friends" who helped her to escape. There are even Phoenix stories about limousines picking her up at the hospital. Many have long believed she spent as many nights out of the hospital as in, amusing herself by going to parties and dinner and the movies and the theater—hardly the kind of punishment expected for a convicted, insane murderess.

"Every time she'd escape, I'd secretly pray, 'Go, Winnie, go—get away this time,'" remembers Rita Grimm, whose father hauled those infamous trunks to the train depot. Rita knew she wasn't alone. It would be such a relief if Winnie were done with Arizona and Arizona with her.

But for every sympathetic prayer, there was a public demand for retaliation. The Phoenix dailies, in particular, were not amused by the way Winnie Ruth Judd snubbed her punishment. Each escape earned another angry editorial demanding that Arizona get tough about keeping "the trunk murderess" locked away. The papers called for investigations to discover the identity of her helpers, and suggested if hospital officials were the culprits, they should be fired. It was a black eye for Arizona to allow this notorious murderess to make such a mockery of her incarceration, the papers fumed.

Oh, her escape befuddled and angered Arizona for so long.

But it really was not as hard as everyone thought.

Winnie Ruth Judd still has the key to the front door of Arizona State Hospital.

She giggles like a schoolgirl as she presents it for inspection now, her wrinkled, speckled hand holding the precious, long-kept secret.

It's such an ordinary key to have caused so much commotion—not much bigger than a common house key, the numbers 634 stamped on one side. It was her most sacred possession over fifty years ago when she first used it; it is her most treasured keepsake today.

She holds it out so lovingly it's clear this was never an ordinary key to her. "They always wondered who helped me escape—oh, they went on and on about it," she says with conspiratorial glee.

She needs to be prodded to admit the key didn't just happen into her hands by accident. She wishes her explanation that she "just got it" would suffice, but when she finds it won't, she finally concedes that the key was a secret present from a nurse at the state hospital—a benefactress still so dear to her heart that she promises the nurse's identity will go to the grave with her.

Ruth Judd is sitting in her Stockton, California, apartment in January of 1990, a white-haired, stoop-backed eighty-five-year-old woman who was finally paroled and set free in 1971. For three days she talks to this writer about her forlorn life. She dredges up the sad parts, the happy ones, the painful ones. She gives names and faces to every kindness shown her over the years. The same for every insult and broken promise.

She is never more animated and playful than when she talks about the escapes that proved she had some control over her life.

From the time she was twenty-six until she was sixty-six, so many others made the important decisions. Her boyfriend, her husband, her lawyers, police, prosecutors, judges, juries, all had their say. Prison wardens, nurses, doctors, hospital administrators, politicians, had theirs.

She had only an ordinary-looking key.

"This is my survival kit," she says as she reaches for a lacquered box she keeps next to her bed. Inside it are a portable radio and a metal coin purse with such a worn cover you can barely tell it was once a "Souvenir of Florida."

The radio let her monitor the frequent news reports on her latest escape. She mimics the stories it used to broadcast: "'Police report Winnie Ruth Judd was sighted at the corner store buying two packs of cigarettes.' And I thought, 'Now isn't that a lie. I never smoked in my life.' And I was laughing. They'd say, 'She was sighted in Michigan…Well, now they've sighted her down in Mexico.' I would listen to that little radio all the time."

But the real treasure was the coin holder a nurse brought back from a vacation in the Sunshine State. Nurses kept it filled with coins that fit into the various slots and a dollar bill that slipped behind the clip on the lid. The purse still holds a quarter, a dime, and a penny. No one ever realized that if you pried off the lid, inside was the priceless key.

"They never thought to look in here," she whispers as her bony fingers fumble to remove the lid. "Oh, I hung on to that key. Whenever they brought me back, I wouldn't let it go. One time, one of the men from the male unit banged my head on the bed: 'You cost me forty-eight hours of sleep,' and he beat my head. But I wouldn't let loose of the key."

There's something else she continues to hold on to.

To this day she believes the greatest injustices she suffered in Arizona were in the state hospital. That is the story she is most anxious to tell.

It seems strange. She doesn't rail about her conviction, her date with death, her insanity hearing. "My case was in politics" is how she'd like to leave it. She refuses to discuss the night the girls died. She has little now to say about Jack Halloran. She keeps a boxful of papers—mainly newspaper clippings—about her case, but even they are too painful to handle.

"I won't talk about it, no. Won't talk about it," she says adamantly. "It's out of my mind, and my family has told me I must destroy all papers I have saved, like Ollie North. And when I go to shredding, I read things and I get so upset I can't bear it. I have to get away, and I get on the bus and take a ride because it's so far, it is so far from my mind, because I have lived in another world and I cannot be reminded. I go all to pieces, and I would be very, very sick, deathly, I would die. I would absolutely curl up and die."

But she talks for three days about all that Arizona did to her while it pretended she was insane. Some of the stories are so painful they still make her cry. Some are so hateful she screams out loud at the memories.

And some are so funny she laughs about them to this day.

Arizona State Hospital was a horrible place in 1932.

Overcrowded, understaffed, cruel, dirty, corrupt.

There was little pretense of "treatment." Like its sister facilities throughout the nation, it was not a mental health facility, it was just a warehouse. And it was a political pawn— patronage jobs were dished out directly from the governor's office; so were contracts for supplies.

The hapless souls who found themselves locked inside were not just the insane. This was the warehouse for epileptics, too. For orphans. For alcoholics. For old people unable to care for themselves.

In a town that had no nursing homes, no facilities for the handicapped, and hospital beds only for the temporarily sick, the state hospital was the destination of final resort.

Mental health officials look back at those days with shame. But it would be years before anyone seriously considered this place inadequate or inappropriate or even inhumane. Not until the 1940s was there any attempt to clean it up. By then its rotten plumbing pipes had led to outbreaks of typhoid. By then its rotten politics were so entrenched that a reform-minded board demanded the resignation of every single staff member. But reform would come hard to this institution many in the community tried to ignore. In the early 1950s, Arizona State Hospital won its first national recognition—as the most overcrowded public insane asylum in the nation.

Phoenix had been so proud to capture this "plum" in 1885 when the 13th Territorial Legislature handed out public facilities—"The Thieving Thirteenth" that session would always be called because of the blatant corruption of the lawmakers.

Given the choice of a university, a teachers college, or an insane asylum, Phoenix used all its political muscle to get the crazy house. It wouldn't be the first time—or the last— that the city would grab for a brass ring while letting the gold ones go by. In a pattern that some think is still prevalent to this day, Phoenix went for the short-term profits: the legislature appropriated $100,000 to build the asylum, while it gave only $25,000 to establish the University of Arizona (now the state's most prestigious institution of higher learning), and $5,000 for the Tempe Normal School, which today is Arizona State University and holds the distinction of being the nation's fifth-largest public university.

By the time Winnie Ruth Judd arrived, the state hospital was no longer a plum in anyone's eyes. A total of 277 people were confined there, with the state spending only 61.7 cents a day to house, feed, and care for each of them. Even by the standards of 1932, spending $225.20 a year for a person's total care was pretty chintzy. Apparently, Arizona cared more for its criminals than it did for its mentally incompetent: the state prison in Florence was spending 77.5 cents a day on its inmates.

Officials would say they could get by so cheaply because both institutions were supposed to be self-sufficient. The state hospital had is own ice plant, its own laundry and bakery and cannery and shoe repair shop. It had a sewing room to make patient uniforms, its own mattress factory and carpenter shop. It had a farm that grew wheat, barley, corn, and alfalfa, a fifteen-acre orchard of oranges and grapefruit, and a twenty-acre garden. Add to that a dairy herd of about a hundred head, a few mules, and some hogs.

It also had an untrained staff that neither understood nor was able to cope with the peculiarities of people confined in an asylum. Brutality was used more often than counseling; neglect was used most often of all.

It is an ironic twist in its twisted history that Arizona State Hospital became a better place because Winnie Ruth Judd was there.

Unlike most of the other patients, she was not bedridden or helpless or mentally incompetent. She was a young, attractive, bright woman who was used to taking care of herself. She found within the brick walls of the institution a whole community that needed her.

"She was more like a member of the staff than a patient," remembers Ann Keim, who was a paid aide at the hospital. "She worked unusually hard—did more for that hospital than any two or three people. She wasn't crazy either, she was as sane as anyone—except when Halloran came out to harass her." Mrs. Keim recounts how Jack Halloran started showing up at the Saturday night dances at the asylum. "Halloran would sneer and laugh real nasty at her, and she'd just go to pieces and they'd have to take her back to the ward," Mrs. Keim relates. Finally hospital officials banned Halloran from the grounds.

"I was helping with patients, making their beds, helping bathe them," Winnie Ruth Judd recalls now. "And I was doing patients' hair. I was dolling them up to go to the dances. I did a hundred heads of hair one time. I got up around four or five to do that. I was making everybody happy."

She tells the story as though it's the most ordinary thing in the world for a convicted murderess who is supposedly insane to have her own beauty parlor inside a crazy house.

Ruth Judd had always had a knack for fixing hair. She'd seldom had the money to have her own done professionally, so she learned to do it herself, for her pocketbook and her vanity. She always felt better when her hair was done. It seemed logical to her that the patients might feel the same way. They had so little else, she remembers. They were outfitted in plain blue hospital gowns that erased their individuality. They spent their days alone in their beds or wandering the halls, without any organized recreation or entertainment. They ate off tin plates, sometimes with only a spoon. They were fed in an assembly line, a mass-feeding situation that made even the homegrown food taste like institutional slop. Washing and fixing and styling the women's hair might seem like a puny gesture in this setting, but it was the first thing Ruth Judd saw as helpful.

She told someone, who told someone, who told a local beautician that she wanted to set up a hairstyling salon in the state hospital. To her joy and amazement, beauticians arrived at the hospital with boxfuls of shampoos and hairpins and combs. They brought her washbasins and curling irons and rods for permanents. Ruth never knew why these women were acting like such angels of mercy. She might have guessed they were sympathetic because their beauty shops had been hotbeds of gossip about the inside story of her case.

"I didn't charge the patients anything," Ruth stresses. "Then the nurses would come in and they would want me to do their hair, and they would put a quarter in my little saucer there. And I bought the supplies to do the patients' hair— down at the supply house. I bought Conte's Castile Shampoo, the very best. I bought a rinse—what was it called? After fifty years, I forget. It was a blue rinse. You diluted it, it made four gallons. And I bought wave set. But when I first started doing wave set, guess what I used? What they call wood shavings. You put these wood shavings into water and it forms kind of a jelly, it thickens. I used that." Soon the women in town started arriving, along with their daughters, to have their hair fashioned by Winnie Ruth Judd.

Edna George, whose father had secretly cleaned out the drain the night the trunks were discovered, remembers she and her sisters were often customers. "I was a little afraid when she cut my hair, but not enough not to go to her," Edna says. "She treated me and my sisters like a dear aunt. She warned us about men. She didn't talk much, she asked questions. She was so shy and withdrawn, like she'd been whipped like a dog. I've always felt sorry for her. I've never believed she killed them."

Ruth's helpfulness and popularity at the hospital even earned a few words of praise from the Phoenix newspapers. "She lavishes her love on the other patients," the *Gazette* reported, noting the patients adored her for it.

Part of this graciousness was natural enough for Ruth Judd. Her mother had instilled in her the duty to care for those less fortunate. Ruth had demonstrated that unselfishness before. She'd nursed her husband when his drug addiction left him helpless; she'd nursed Sammy in the months before the "tragedy" that had destroyed so many lives.

But part of the graciousness was due to the fact that Winnie Ruth Judd had been assured—by some of the top officials in the state of Arizona—that she was not going to be locked up in the hospital for long.

"I had free rein of the grounds. There weren't any fences. I could have walked off any time. But I wouldn't because I was on my honor," she says with fierce pride.

Ruth Judd promised not to cause any trouble because she was just biding her time. She stayed put and didn't even think of trying to escape because she thought she had a deal.

That was the lie she believed for a long time.

It is impossible to verify the stories she tells about the behind-the-scenes maneuvering. The people she talks about are dead, and secret meetings of this sort aren't written down for posterity. But the stories she tells now mirror those she wrote out in long letters during the 1940s. They are the same stories she told attorney Larry Debus in the late 1960s.

"I believe her," Debus says. "I'll tell you why. If I had been those people in those positions, and allowed to happen what they allowed to happen, I would have had guilt, and at some point, I would have tried to do something for her."

Old-timers remember the widespread rumor that Ruth Judd would only spend a few years in the hospital if she kept quiet. Rita Grimm recalls her mother telling her a story like that after Mrs. Grimm had been to the state hospital to see Ruth in the mid-thirties. About the same time, Ann Keim says, Ruth told her she was going to be given her freedom if she behaved herself.

So whether the visits she describes are a flight of fancy or a recitation of cruel games, this is how Winnie Ruth Judd remembers it.

She had been at the hospital just over a year, she begins, when two members of the parole board came to see her. She remembers being called into a small room at the hospital to meet with attorney general Arthur LaPrade and superintendent of public instruction Herman Hendrix. "We're your friends," she recalls LaPrade telling her, just as she recalls spitting back, "No you're not." But the men insisted she could trust them, and they told her they had a plan. "They told me, 'We have commuted a man by the name of Janavitch—J-A-N-A-V-I-T-C-H. We commuted his sentence; he's been deported to Syria. Just as soon as public sentiment dies down, we're going to do something likewise for you.'"

Department of Correction records verify that George Janavitch, a convicted murderer who was judged insane, was deported to Syria on July 17, 1934.

Ruth recalls the parole board members telling her, "You're getting along here just fine and you just keep on doing what you're doing."

And she remembers her dashed hopes: "That was the end of it. Six years went past."

She continued to behave herself year after year, never misusing her privileges, she boasts. And she had more privileges than any other patient.

"I could leave the hospital grounds if I wanted, but I'd only go to the little store across the street if I wanted this or that. But I never considered running away. Somebody, one of the nurses or doctors, would take me to see my father once a week—he'd had a stroke."

The weekly visits were unsupervised. Ruth would be dropped off at her parents' home—they'd settled in a modest place in Phoenix so they could stay close to Ruth—then picked up late in the evening to return to the hospital. Usually she brought home the makings for dinner; nurses often gave her meat and fruit from the hospital storeroom to share with her aged parents.

The small family would talk about many things—relatives, how Burton's new marriage was going, what was happening in the hospital. The one thing Ruth did not want to discuss was her case. She kept reassuring her parents that her days at the hospital were numbered and they just had to be patient.

The McKinnells were never as trusting as their daughter. If they believed authorities had a secret plan to free her, it did not lessen their constant efforts to see she got justice.

Mrs. McKinnell bravely told the press, "We're getting old. But we are going to live long enough to see our daughter free. We want a pardon for her because we believe that's the only fair thing. From all evidence, the women were killed after a terrible fight in which Ruth received a bad beating."

Until he was incapacitated by the stroke, H. J. McKinnell wrote unceasingly to officials. His passionate letters are filled with the agony of a parent who believes his child has been unfairly judged. He begged the governor to reconsider the death sentence that still hung over Ruth's head. "As it now stands, recovery means execution," he wrote. "This condition is intolerable."

But even her parents had to admit Ruth was making the best of it for the time being and the hospital was being more than kind.

"And do you know what?" Her voice starts to rise and you can feel her anxiety, even all these years later. "I was jumped on for operating a beauty parlor without a license and every privilege I had was taken away from me. Everybody told me I was doing good work. The governor did, the Board of Pardons and Paroles told me I did. And then for them to come in and take it all away from me just broke my heart."

The uproar over her popular beauty shop was apparently orchestrated by a society woman in town who was active on the Board of Cosmetology, Ruth says. The woman complained that Ruth Judd was stealing business from licensed beauticians, not caring that the "payment" was a mere quarter. Governor Robert Taylor Jones was so angry, Ruth says, he came to the hospital to see her, telling her that the complaints were a way of criticizing him. "He said, 'If in order to get at me, they have to stoop to pick on a patient out here, they're getting pretty low.' And he said, 'Now listen—I'll be out here to talk to you in a few days. Pretty soon you're going to get your beauty parlor back, pretty soon you'll get your privileges and you'll get to see your father.'

"So anyhow, he didn't come out and didn't come out. I didn't get my beauty parlor. I didn't get my ground privileges. So I just took the key and went to see my father."

It was the night of October 24, 1939.

To camouflage her absence, she filled her bed with a mound of boxes, bottles, and cakes of soap. The ruse worked so well nurses didn't discover she was gone for twelve hours.

"RUTH JUDD FLEES ASYLUM," read the banner headline in the *Arizona Republic* the next morning. The paper noted that once again she was "the West's most widely hunted woman."

For six days she was free. She says she visited her mother and her ailing father in their Phoenix home and hid out—of all places—in a cornfield on the hospital grounds. While on the lam, she wrote to the governor, complaining the hospital administration was being cruel to her. "You promised me I could go and see my father," she reminded him.

The *Los Angeles Examiner* paid the fare for Dr. Judd to come to Phoenix from L.A. to help search for his wife. He went first to her parents' home, where Mrs. McKinnell recounted Ruth's visit. "In the dead of night, I heard a scratching at the back door and thought someone was trying to break in," Mrs. McKinnell was quoted by the *Examiner* as telling her son-in-law. "I caught the shadow of a form and asked, 'What do you want?' There was no answer and I looked more closely into the blackness outside and saw it was Winnie Ruth. Neither of us said a word. I turned, walked slowly into the bedroom to look at her father, lying weakly in bed. Then I decided that—at all costs—he must see the daughter he loved so much. She walked with me to the bedroom. There was no word spoken. Then, with sobs, she knelt beside her father and they both cried and prayed. After a few moments, she arose, kissed him gently and said, 'I must go now.' Then she gave me a letter which she asked me to take at once to the governor, and walked out of the house. That was the last we saw of our daughter. I believe that Winnie Ruth will show up safe and sound and the Lord will take good care of her and guide her safely to us."

Ruth was "recaptured" when she showed up at the back door of the hospital and blithely told superintendent Louis J. Saxe, "Well, here I am!"

She was shoeless, her stockings were ripped, her legs were bruised. She had used her girdle to fashion a brace for a sprained ankle. The *Republic* said she was caught while "foraging hungrily for food like a slinking wolf."

"They tied me down in a straightjacket and beat my head up and down on the bed," she remembers. "But I still had the key. They didn't get my key."

Ruth was put in solitary confinement for the next month. She was uncomfortable, angry, nervous. Officials finally let her out, believing she'd return to normal if they let her mingle with the other patients.

She was back in the general ward only two weeks when she was convinced it was time to leave again. She remembers the story clearly, acting out the parts as though relating a scene she is seeing right now before her eyes.

"One of the nurses announced, 'All the patients are going to be moved to the new hospital ward tomorrow, except Ruth.' I asked, 'Where am I going?' And she said, 'They're going to hang you and I hope I see them do it.' And I said, 'Ohhhh, *I believe you.*' So that night I took my little key and away I went. And I didn't have a coat. So I went to a minister's house and I got in and I took a coat and something for my head, two bath towels, and a box of crackers. And I wrote them a note saying, 'I'll either return it or Mama will make it good to you.' I drank all the milk I could before I left. I went like a streak of lightning down the railroad track. I ran as fast as I could. I went all the way to Yuma."

It was a 180-mile trip.

Another banner headline. Another bout of hysteria. "RUTH JUDD AGAIN ESCAPES," the *Republic* blared the morning of December 4, 1939. At 6:30 p.m. the night before, she had been sitting on her bed, the paper reported. At 7 p.m., she was gone. Bloodhounds from the state prison were brought to Phoenix to follow her trail, but lost her scent at a well-traveled highway. The paper noted that officials suspected she had used a passkey to gain her freedom, but everyone was mystified at how she could have disappeared after only a half hour's head start. The Associated Press reported "numerous tips" on her whereabouts had been called in to the sheriff's office—all to no avail. A deputy sheriff said officers were busy checking out the tips but felt most of them came from persons having "Judd jitters."

"In the daytime, I went clear out in the fields and slept under the mesquite trees," Ruth recalls. Then she would go back to the railroad tracks, always heading west. She found refuge one day in a shack used by men on the state's road crew. "Here was a little stove, potbellied stove, and a thermos of water and some sugar. So I poured the water on the sugar and drank it because I was starved. All I had was crackers and water. I could see the gas stations all along the track and I'd go over there and I'd drink water from the hoses at the gas stations. But I needed some other stuff, sugar. I got drunk on the sugar. Drunk as a lord, and I went in the wrong direction, I think."

"So finally I got to Yuma and I got into some cockleburs and tore all my stockings. My legs were all scratched and bleeding."

Inside her metal coin purse, she had a dollar bill and a few coins. She found a store and watched as people bought milk, afraid if she tried, she'd be found out. But she was so hungry she finally got up enough nerve to buy a bottle of buttermilk that she thought would soothe her stomach.

She took the buttermilk and sat drinking it on the most public place in town—the courthouse steps. "My husband always laughed at me, saying, 'Ruth, who'd ever think of looking for you there.'" She used one of her dimes to call friends of her husband, hoping they could get a message to him in California about where she was so he could come help her. She had just finished the call when a police officer spotted her. She wouldn't tell them who she was. "They went and called up the mayor's wife, because she was a friend of mine. And she comes into the jail and she said, 'Oh Ruthie!'

They let me go up to her house and I took a nice hot bath and she fixed me a couple poached eggs and then we went back to the hospital.

"And they kept me in solitary confinement for two years. In a little tiny cell, and the bed was soldered down to the floor. I had no shoes. Barefooted and in pajamas, for two years."

Dr. Otto Bendheim, who later would create the state's first private psychiatric hospital—Camelback Hospital—had just arrived in Arizona when Winnie Ruth Judd started escaping. He worked then at the state hospital and got to know her well.

"The [psychological] treatment she got was rather mild," he remembers. "She was considered nondangerous. She gave us no problem except for running away."

He recalls her as being "very nice" and not showing signs of insanity. Such a patient today would be discharged, he says. "But the emphasis on patient rights came after the war. Before that, we did warehousing. The courts would commit to us all kinds of people who couldn't care for themselves, senile people, retarded people, people who had nowhere else to go."

And few ever asked about the validity of housing Ruth Judd there as though she were a crazy person. "In those days, we didn't have these questions," Dr. Bendheim admits, although the question of whether she had ever been insane would plague this case. "I guess we were a little cowardly and let well enough alone."

But this writer's investigation has found that some hospital officials at least made a stab at helping Ruth Judd. On April 23, 1933, hospital superintendent Jeremiah Metzger had written to the parole board asking that her death sentence be commuted to life imprisonment. "Such action would undoubtedly result in making Ruth Judd a better patient, a better worker and improve her morale....Living continually under the death sentence is not conducive to either cure or improvement." There is no record of the parole board seriously considering the doctor's request.

Dr. Bendheim remembers he was so sure Ruth Judd was fine he wouldn't have had any qualms letting her "work in my household with my children."

"My memories of her are very positive," he said in a recent interview. "Watching her, I would never guess she was a murderess."

Even to the layman's eyes in those days, this woman was an unlikely murderess, an even less plausible crazy person.

Harry Whitmer was the business manager at the state hospital from 1942 to 1952. He remembers Ruth Judd as "a smart, good-looking woman who was very intelligent and very well liked by the women on her ward." And he never thought she was crazy.

"Oh no," he says. "She did some foolish things, but as far as being insane, no." It was widely understood she was in the hospital either as a ruse or as the state's only out, he goes on. "There was a major question in a lot of people's minds if she did [the killings] or not, or if she was just taking the rap."

Dr. Loreen Fox-Shipley was a young girl in the 1950s who went to the hospital on Sunday with her parents to bring punch and cookies to the residents. Now a psychologist, Dr. Fox-Shipley recalls the "warm feelings" she had about Ruth Judd. "I had trouble understanding all the fuss about her," she says. "In the community, there was a lot of sympathy for her—unlike what was being said in the media, there wasn't a feeling that she was guilty. There was a feeling she was a scapegoat. I remember people saying it was kind of a shame, and when she'd escape, people would say 'I hope they just don't get her this time.'"

In the first good press Ruth Judd ever got, a 1933 *Gazette* story about her life in the asylum, the paper called her "the Queen of the Hospital."

Three-year-old Diane Gales had a more cherished title for Ruth Judd. She thought of her as a mother.

Diane and her baby sister were sent to the asylum in the mid-forties when their mother was declared insane—a situation unfathomable now but common in that day. For the little girl, the institution was a big and scary place where children were regarded as a nuisance.

Then came this angel of a woman named Ruth who "treated me like a mother would," remembers that girl today. She is now Diane McClinnon, and still believes that, "Because of Winnie Ruth Judd, I'm not crazy."

As she explains it in the first interview she has ever given about her background, "Children have to be cared for and talked to and loved, or they regress. I saw children there who weren't retarded but acted that way because no one cared for them. Because of Ruth Judd, I didn't regress. I've always wanted to thank her." She remembers Ruth talking with her, carrying her around the grounds, making her feel loved. "I've wondered all these years if she remembers the little black girl she used to carry around," Diane says today. "My sister and I were the only black children there, so maybe she does."

Diane was eventually adopted, grew up to graduate from high school and raise six children, and now dotes on her grandchild. But there's still a message she has always wanted to deliver to Ruth Judd: "Here's one person you helped stay normal. I escaped that place too."

Ruth remembers little Diane Gale well. "She was cute as a bug," she recalls. "I'd rub her with good Pond's cold cream. I'd braid her hair. I put her in a bed in the entrance hall and folded a curtain across. Some of my friends brought clothes so I could dress her up."

Ruth Judd was finally a mother, even if it was informal and assumed rather than legal and binding. Helping a child like Diane filled that vacant place inside her. She didn't need to create any more fictitious children—here was a real live child who needed her and loved her back.

Whatever else motherhood signified to Ruth Judd, her own mother had shown her it meant you would always have someone on your side. Carrie McKinnell never wavered in the belief that someday her only daughter would be cleared. She stood by Ruth throughout the trial and even lived at the prison with her for a time.

Now, inside the Arizona State Hospital, Ruth experienced the most bittersweet twist in her strange life—she became a "mother" to her own mother. Mrs. McKinnell, eighty years old and senile, was committed to the hospital in the mid-forties because she had nowhere else to go. By then the reverend was dead and Burton was living in California with a family of his own. Dr. Judd died in a veterans hospital in October 1945. So these two women—convicted, incarcerated daughter and old, senile mother—clung to each other as only sole survivors can.

Ruth gladly took over most of the daily care of the old woman. For a while, she was allowed to sleep in the same room with her mother. But a change in the hospital administration put an end to this cozy and calming situation. It is not clear if the new administrator disliked Ruth Judd in particular or just thought such an arrangement too coddling, but all of a sudden, her access to the most important person in her life was strictly limited. Some days, she was permitted no visit with her mother at all. Other days, she could see her only for a couple of hours.

Ruth worried that her mother was not getting all the care she needed, that she wasn't eating properly. She feared her mother might think Ruth had abandoned her.

On Mother's Day of 1947, Ruth begged to spend the day with the old woman. Word came down that she could visit for only five minutes, and then only with three guards present. But even that scant allowance was never given. Ruth Judd was not permitted to see her mother on this day when the entire country was honoring motherhood.

In her fury, she escaped for the third time. It was May 11, 1947.

"They took my mother away," she cried to reporters when she was found twelve hours later hiding in an orange grove at the Arizona Biltmore resort. "She is all I have now that my father and husband are dead." Without her mother, she was left lonely and anxious, with nothing to do but "sit there and brood."

She is remembering those days now as she shares a family picture, kept like most of her mementos in an old shoe box. "A nurse told me my mother had cancer," she recalls bitterly. "For three months I believed Mother was dying of cancer. And then somebody told me it wasn't so." Although she is wearing an old blue sweater and her two-bedroom apartment is overly warm, she still shudders as if the very thought of that lie lets in the cold.

After her capture, the administration played a seesaw game with her. Sometimes she could see her mother; sometimes she couldn't. She resigned herself to the situation for four years. But then the rumor mill at the hospital led her to believe she would never see the old woman again. Some patients started taunting her that she would be moved into a new "criminal ward" that was kept segregated from the rest of the hospital. Although administrators tried to convince her the rumors were untrue, she would not believe them. For days she busied herself in the hospital laundry, washing uniforms for the nurses, gowns for the patients. No one knew she was also secretly washing her own dress, again and again. At ten-thirty p.m. on November 29, 1951, she put on the dress and slipped out the window of her mother's room on a rope she had fashioned from rags. The bloodhounds were unable to pick up any scent. Every police agency in the state was called out to help in the search.

For her few hours of freedom, Ruth hid in the empty house of hospital nurse Ellen Evans, who was at work. She ate food from the cupboard, wrote letters that she mailed from a box in front of the federal building downtown. She took from the house a fur coat, a sports jacket, a pair of hose, a purse, and a flowered scarf. When Mrs. Evans returned home, she reported the theft. A police officer spotted Ruth on the street wearing the flowered scarf. "Why did you have to pick me up?" she asked police officers, according to press reports. "I've served 20 years out there and I think I should be turned loose. I had a tragedy 20 years ago that I wasn't wholly responsible for. I wish you boys would turn me loose."

Mrs. Evans later told police, "If I had known Ruth had my clothes, I never would have reported her." She refused to press burglary charges. "Winnie Ruth Judd couldn't steal anything," Mrs. Evans declared. "She wouldn't steal anything from me. I would give it to her. Besides, a lot of people do not realize what good she has done at the hospital. She has helped many of the inmates."

Two months later, on February 2, 1952, Ruth escaped once more, evading capture for five days this time. Friends hid her out, she admits, moving her from place to place. To this day she refuses to name those friends. One of them anonymously called hospital director M. W. Conway and promised Ruth would turn herself in if she was permitted to tell her story again before a grand jury. The request was quickly granted and Ruth kept her word, appearing at the front door of Conway's home.

◇◇◇

On February 11, Ruth Judd testified for four hours behind the closed doors of the grand jury room. By now women were permitted to sit on Arizona juries. By now the state had seen six governors since the day Ruth gave herself up. By now Ruth was no longer a movie star beauty but a middle-aged, plump woman of forty-seven.

Once more she told her story. Killing in self-defense. Halloran's orchestration after the fact. Her suspicions about who had cut up the body.

And history repeated itself. This grand jury too said they believed her story. They recommended her death sentence be commuted to life imprisonment, or, as Ruth Judd likes to report it to this day: "We recommend that her sentence be commuted to time served without further punishment or humiliation."

The parole board agreed, recommending the commutation to the governor.

Governor Howard Pyle removed the hangman's noose from around Ruth Judd's neck. He signed the order on May 11, 1952.

The term "life imprisonment" did not mean she had to stay in prison for her natural life. It meant she had to serve about ten years. By now she had been confined for twenty-one years. If her time in the hospital was counted as "time served"—a phrase that normally means time in prison—then her life sentence had already been generously met.

And that was what everyone told her, she repeats now. "They said I was going to get my freedom."

This turn of events greatly disturbed Lloyd Andrews, who was now in private practice. He told the press her story was "tripe" and "twaddle." He said the "ugly facts" were that she was a cold-blooded killer who had confessed in her own handwriting with the drainpipe letter. She wasn't railroaded, he insisted, she wasn't covering up for anyone else, she acted alone. "I've been listening to this eyewash for years, but the current outburst is pretty hard to stomach," he said.

Ruth was convinced it was almost over. She thought she would get herself a little place in Phoenix so she could visit her mother every day in the hospital. Then, after her mother went—and Ruth knew the woman didn't have long—she dreamed of going to South America and working in a leper colony [Ruth's mother died in November 1953]. She shared her dreams with one of her attorneys from the sanity hearing, Tom Fulbright. As he recalled in his memoirs, he spent an afternoon visiting her in the hospital, getting a tour of "her small, spotlessly clean bedroom" and hearing about her work with the other patients. "She wound up our visit by expressing the hope that she could realize her ambition of going to South America and living out her days by helping in the leper colony in Asuncion, Paraguay, operated by her church. I could not help but feel she was sincere in this, and it was and still is my private thought that this would have been a sensible, humane solution for her and for Arizona."

There was only one formality left before Ruth Judd could walk out of the asylum, and Arizona, a free woman.

"Dr. Conway came in and he said, 'Well, Ruth, you're going to get your freedom, but first you have to have a sanity hearing.' He told me what day it was to be....And my guardian brought out a cute dress for me to go to the sanity hearing in, and I didn't even get to go."

Tears well up in her eyes when she remembers the awful day she sat there, convinced she was on her way to freedom. She remembers her guardian, Elizabeth Harvey, had made a point of bringing her a dress in her favorite color, green. Mrs. Harvey also brought along a camera, and someone snapped a happy picture as the women waited to be called. Ruth remembers sitting in that dress all day, carefully so it wouldn't wrinkle. But there would be no sanity hearing that day. Nor any other day.

Ruth got tired of waiting. She had been promised her freedom. She had earned it. And when they didn't give it to her, she stole it for herself.

For weeks she worked patiently on the heavy metal screen that covered the bathroom window in the women's section of the asylum. "I never chew gum, but I chewed it then and put a little wad of chewing gum there to hold the screen," she recounts. "Next day I would take a shower, cut four more little bits. Then I cut a big enough hole my head would go through, I could wiggle through."

On Thanksgiving Day, 1952, Ruth ate a turkey dinner with her mother, whom she was now allowed to visit twice a week. At about seven p.m., she complained of a headache, saying a nice hot bath might give her some relief. Attendants agreed, and watched her go into the bathroom fully clothed, carrying a bathrobe over her arm. A half hour later, when they checked the room, they found the bathrobe on the floor and a fifteen-inch hole in the screen. This was escape number six.

"She makes escaping from institutions look easy," news stories reported. Editorial pages were blunter. The *Phoenix Gazette* was so exasperated it ran an editorial asking, "Is Mrs. Judd bigger than Arizona?" It suggested: "If a dungeon has to be constructed, that should be done. And every effort should be made to find out who is helping the murderess. Ruth Judd and her friends have thumbed their noses at the sovereign State of Arizona long enough."

After forty-six hours of freedom, she was found under a pile of clothes in the closet of her guardian, who was away for the weekend. "I've been locked up long enough," she pleaded to reporters, who had taken to calling her "Wily Winnie."

In December 1952, she wrote a long letter to Governor Pyle: "Being of sound mind and in possession of all my mental faculties, I am hereby requesting a sanity hearing. I am not insane. I do not hear voices, have no delusions of grandeur or persecution, and know the difference between right and wrong. I have a clear and active mind."

No hearing was held.

The next year, her guardian petitioned the court for a sanity hearing, arguing, "Winnie Ruth Judd is not insane within the meaning of the law." By then Dr. Conway had resigned to go into private practice and Dr. Samuel Wick had become the hospital superintendent. He too promised Ruth she would get a hearing, she insists.

No hearing was held.

Even with the commutation of her death sentence, even with all the lingering questions about her conviction, even with the widespread belief her insanity was a ruse, nobody but a small handful of ineffectual friends championed her cause.

And nothing happened.

Attorney Arthur Mackenzie Johnson says anyone in the know in those days should not have been surprised. He remembers he was approached by a couple of Ruth's friends and asked if he could lend her some legal help. But he was warned off the case from the start.

"When I first went out to see her at the state hospital, I talked with a hospital administrator," Johnson recalled in a recent interview. "He gave me the opinion Winnie Ruth had really gotten screwed. He told me, 'The best advice I can give you, son, is forget about it.' He implied there were forces that were going to keep her there, no matter what."

Johnson says he was never able to do much for her, but he clearly remembers that "every human being I came in touch with loved her and believed in her." He remembers getting angry one night as he listened to the Bob Hope show on the radio and the young comedian made a joke about "bad girl" Winnie Ruth Judd. Johnson knew he was not the only one who didn't laugh.

Whoever was pulling the strings behind the scenes is lost to history. Was Dogie Andrews keeping this final door closed to Ruth? Was Jack Halloran calling in his last chit? It isn't hard to imagine the fear in some circles that if this forty-seven-year-old woman were to be declared sane and freed, somebody would listen to her stories and the whole ugly mess would be revived—maybe reopened as a criminal case.

Ruth Judd herself can't put a face to her tormentors. All she can do is recount the torment. How Dr. Metzger tried to console her with the words, "Nothing but dirty tricks are being played on you." How Dr. Conway told her his call for a sanity hearing had been overruled because "someone had more power than he did, but he would not tell me who, except that it was not the governor."

Nor was it the Board of Pardons and Paroles, this probe has discovered. Because, unknown to anyone, the chair of that influential body was trying to help Ruth Judd win her freedom.

Walter Hofmann did what he could, he would later tell Ruth's friends, but even the chairman of the parole board could not get her a sanity hearing. Hofmann tried to intercede with Dr. Wick when Wick became superintendent of the hospital in December 1953.

This investigation has uncovered a handwritten note Hofmann penned in 1972 to one of Ruth's friends in California. The letter reads: "If Dr. Wick had listened to me, Ruth would have been free 15 years ago, but she was the victim of state hospital politics. Dr. Wick passed away several years ago. The last time I saw him…he told me, 'Hofmann, I'm sorry I did not follow your suggestion. She should have been released years ago.'" Hofmann died in 1979.

Almost everyone else forgot about Winnie Ruth Judd as the 1950s became the decade of rebuilding, starting new families. Phoenix was booming with an influx of soldiers who had been stationed in the area during World War II and swore if they made it through, they would move back. A young veteran named John F. Long used his G.I. Bill to build an entire community of affordable homes on the west side of Phoenix that he named Maryvale, after his wife, Mary. He got the spokesman for General Electric to hawk the project, and actor Ronald Reagan did a good job. Veterans lined up around the block to buy Long's "starter" homes. Air conditioners were now being mass-produced, and the living was easier in the summertime.

Democrats had started to lose their grip on the state's politics. In 1952, they suffered one of the great political upsets in Arizona history when Ernest McFarland—a former attorney for Ruth Judd who was now the majority leader of the United States Senate—was defeated by a handsome young Republican named Barry Goldwater.

The promise of Phoenix was being built before everyone's eyes. In a single year—1959—the city saw more construction than in all the years from 1914 to 1946. Population increased 311 percent during the fifties. By decade's end, nearly 440,000 people sprawled over the 187 square miles within the city limits. Local government was controlled by a group of civic-minded businessmen who called themselves the Charter Government Committee. They had taken over during the war to rid the city of corruption and open debauchery—as much for economic survival as for any sense of moral outrage. When officials at Luke Air Force Base west of Phoenix threatened to put the city "off limits" to servicemen, these business leaders finally got serious about cleaning up the town. Their brand of politics—a handpicked mayor and slate for the council every two years—would rule until the mid-1970s.

Winnie Ruth Judd no longer warranted banner headlines when she escaped for the seventh time on October 8, 1962. A small story in the *Republic* simply declared, "Winnie's Gone Again." There was none of the frenzy of her first half dozen escapes. No dogs were called out. Police agencies did not mobilize their forces. "Nobody seems to be looking very hard for the 56-year-old 'Tiger Woman' who is no longer considered dangerous," the *Republic* noted.

This time it wasn't hours that she was free.

Nor days.

Nor months.

This time it was six and a half years.

She took her key and she walked away.

To begin the fairy tale years of her life.

Chapter 16
Glorious Freedom

Winnie Ruth Judd ceased to exist. No one bore that name anymore. No one carried the fame or the shame. One day there was an infamous woman by that name who had been deposited at Arizona State Hospital for twenty-nine years and the next day, she was no more.

In her place was a fifty-seven-year-old, matronly, soft-spoken woman with merry eyes and an easy smile. Her name was Marian Ruth Lane.

There was nothing remarkable about her. She certainly was no beauty, and whatever figure she'd once cherished had gone decades ago. She wore heavy-rimmed, unfashionable glasses to help her failing eyesight. She had a most ordinary background.

She was a widow who had spent the last twenty years caring for her dear mother, now departed. She was a good Christian—her father had been a minister. Her only remaining family was a brother and a couple of nieces and nephews. She was trained in nothing more than loving care for the sick and aged.

That was the sum total of the life that Marian Ruth Lane presented. Nobody asked for more.

She perfected the story of her identity in the five days she hid out in a warehouse that was just a stone's throw from the state hospital in Phoenix. A nephew had been waiting for her with a car outside the hospital that October night when she walked away for the seventh time, had arranged her hideout until it was safe for her to travel. Each night, she admits now, "churchwomen" in Phoenix fixed her a hot meal that her nephew brought to the warehouse. Finally, when it seemed the coast was clear, they headed for Oakland, California. Brother Burton gave her enough money to set up housekeeping; a niece found her an apartment.

The destination was chosen for several reasons. She had a niece and nephew in the Bay Area and it would be nice to be near them. Also, it was a place she thought no one would look for a woman named Winnie Ruth Judd. There was nothing in her background to suggest she would settle there. Los Angeles, yes. Mexico, yes. Indiana, yes. Not Oakland, California.

But she almost got caught immediately.

Her new apartment needed linens and she had noticed a sale at J. C. Penney. Her niece drove her down but had to go to work, so Marian said she'd take the bus home. "And my goodness, when I got off the bus, there was an attendant from the state hospital. And he said, 'Hello, Ruthie.' My goodness, he scared me to death. I just stared at him like I didn't even know him. And he looked at me, and I stood on the corner until he got across the street, and I think he thought he'd made an awful mistake. I had a little brown scarf over my head, tied under my chin, and a little brown sweater on, and a pink cotton dress. And I think he thought it was somebody else, that he'd made a mistake. I watched to see if he looked back and he never did. I was just scared to death. And you know, I wouldn't get on the bus for months after that. I was just so scared from it."

She figured the best—and safest—solution would be to find a live-in working situation. She found a job with an invalid blind woman who was crippled and completely bedridden. The family asked few questions and was willing to pay dearly for someone to care for the woman. But the work frightened Marian Lane. "I was supposed to give her a shot each day and I just wouldn't do it," she remembers now. "Because I was afraid she might die, and I didn't want to feel like I had given her a shot and she never woke up." To hide her fear, she told the family she couldn't physically handle the strain of moving the woman. "The family offered me three thousand dollars' bonus if I'd stay," she recalls. "They said, 'If she lives six weeks or she lives three months, we'll give you three thousand dollars if you'll stay with her.' I said, 'No, I'm going to go,' because I wouldn't give her a shot."

She had to find another job. The day she walked into an employment agency, she was terrified, praying she would fake it through the background check somehow.

What happened next was like something that happens in the movies. Movies that begin, "Once upon a time…" Then again, even Hollywood would have trouble selling a script where an infamous fugitive, supposedly a crazy murderess, ended up in the lap of luxury caring for a delightful woman who showered her with gifts and affection and loved her so much she considered her a "sister."

Some would say Marian Lane got incredibly lucky all of a sudden. She still thinks the Almighty was finally watching out for her, leading her to a new life that would erase the pain and misery she had suffered for so long.

The very day that Marian Lane walked into the employment agency, the wealthy Nichols family had asked the agency to find them a maid and companion for the family matriarch. Pleasant Marian Lane seemed just the ticket. The agency staff did no more checking than calling the family of the blind woman. They were told Mrs. Lane was a caring and capable worker. Marian was sent out to the Nichols home in Piedmont, California—a twenty-three-room mansion overlooking San Francisco Bay. She got the job instantly.

◇◇◇

To this day the woman once known as Winnie Ruth Judd answers only to the name of Marian Lane. No wonder. She has had so much more success in this persona.

Winnie Ruth Judd was reviled. Marian Lane was trusted. Winnie Ruth Judd was feared. Marian Lane was loved.

Winnie Ruth Judd was confined in a stark room with bars on the window. Marian Lane lived in a lovely suite off a formal garden.

Winnie Ruth Judd had only a shrunken coat she wore like a cape. Marian Lane had a fine coat that cost $350.

Winnie Ruth Judd was always too poor for concerts and movies. Marian Lane went all the time. In a chauffeured limousine.

She herself says it best: "Imagine all those years of eating out of aluminum bowls in the hospital and then ending up in that beautiful mansion eating off beautiful china—some plates cost one hundred dollars a piece."

Marian was surrounded by opulence and beauty. "Piedmont has very restricted zoning," she explains. "There's no apartments allowed, only single homes, and they're all millionaires. And we lived in the very nicest part, the corner of Crocker and Lincoln." The house was filled with the fine sterling silver of people who entertain lavishly; the walls were covered with family portraits done in oils. "There were beautiful chandeliers, crystal glass—cut glass that sparkled like so many diamonds," she remembers.

Soon she began meeting the neighbors, finding they were names recognizable throughout the country. "The Gerbers of Gerber baby food lived just a few houses above us," she recalls. The Oppenheimers lived down the street. But then, so did some families that could have meant her ruination.

To her horror, one day she was introduced to the Swenson family from across the street. She smiled pleasantly and left the room as quickly as possible. The Swensons never recognized her. Fortunately, she looked quite different than she had thirty-five years earlier when she had first met them. Mr. Swenson had then managed the silver mine in Mexico where Dr. Judd was employed.

Another day she met the King family, who owned a food company that employed her brother-in-law, Dr. Judd's brother. "Lord, I was just in the thick of everybody," she says, still amazed nobody ever made the connection.

Next to her own mother, Marian Lane still speaks with the greatest reverence for "Mother Nichols"—Ethel Nichols, whose family was old money. She can go on for hours about what a considerate, loving woman Mrs. Nichols was—how generous and joyful, how sweet. "She paid me very well, four hundred dollars a month, and my room and board and all my social security," Marian explains. "Mother Nichols bought my clothes for me. She bought my uniforms—twenty-five dollars a uniform. She bought my aprons, fifteen dollars each. She would buy me a lot of stuff. She bought so many pairs of kid gloves for me."

It became embarrassing at times, Marian remembers. "I didn't dare admire anything or she'd buy it for me," she says, still pleased at the memory. "If I picked up a scarf and told her I thought it was pretty, she bought it for me. If I remarked about a beautiful vase, she bought it for me."

When Mrs. Nichols ordered herself monogrammed handkerchiefs, she would order some for Marian, too. Marian has them, each a fine white linen with the initials "M.L." in one corner.

Of all the gifts, two will always stand out for Marian Lane. One was the expensive coat. "I never told Mother Nichols that my last coat had shrunk at the cleaners and I had to wear it like a cape," she says. "She never knew how much that new coat meant to me."

The other was a sapphire ring her employer gave her for a Christmas present one year. A simple message had been inscribed: "E.N. To M.L., Love."

As a maid and companion, Marian worked long hours, but she never minded. "I was with Mother Nichols constantly," she recalls. "I just had my days off that she insisted on my taking. I always got up early and ate my breakfast and took her tray. And she took her bath while I was making her bed, and then I would go to the market—the chauffeur would take me."

In the morning, she wore a starched white day apron. At night, she served dinner with the formal apron, cuffs, and collar expected in homes of this ilk. She still has several sets, all carefully stored in tissue and plastic.

Once a week, a laundress would come in to do all the washing and ironing. There was also a gardener, and a full-time chauffeur. Marian did the cooking and the light cleaning; a woman came in every other week to do the heavy cleaning. "I hadn't cooked in twenty-nine years, so every night, I took the cookbooks to bed with me and studied them. I was determined to make good," Marian recounts.

Mother Nichols loved to entertain, especially at afternoon tea parties. And Marian soon became the favorite tea cook in the exclusive neighborhood. "I used to have teas for sometimes eighty people," she remembers. "And do you know that all those women, they just loved my cookies. I used to bake about five different kinds. And those millionaires—you'd be surprised—but they all wanted to take some to their husbands. They were my friends."

At the age of sixty, Marian Lane went back to school in her spare time. She enrolled in night school at the Oakland College of Medical Assistants. "I graduated with twenty-year-olds," she brags. "I made good grades too. I got a little patch on my sleeve and I got a little cap on my head. They got me a job in a doctor's office, but I didn't take it." She preferred to stay with Mother Nichols. Not only was this "home," it was better financially. "I made more money cooking, with my room and board, than you do in an office, where you have to pay room and board," she explains.

She woke up every morning thankful for this new life, went to bed each night with prayers that it would never end. She now had the freedom to do what she wanted. That did not include men.

"I never even dated," she stresses when asked why she never married again. "I never met anybody that was half as nice as my husband. I never went out. Well, you see, I was the companion to Mother Nichols. I was with her all the time."

The memories Marian keeps—the ones she brings out to share, as opposed to the ones hidden away that she still intends to shred—are memories of these years. Inside her shoe boxes she keeps the pictures of those dear times: posing with the Nichols grandchildren at Christmas; relaxing in the garden; cuddling the two poodles that, like all cherished pets, ran the place; prancing in her formal maid's costume. She remembers the lovely mornings when she'd sit with Mrs. Nichols in the upstairs master bedroom with its sweeping view of the bay. She would end her days the same way. "When I got through with the dishes at night, she'd want me to watch television with her," she remembers. "I'd turn her bed down and get the little dogs. Oh, Mother Nichols was so sweet with them. She had all these treats for them. She'd get her gown on—she wore beautiful blue, filmy gowns—and she had these gorgeous sheets, all embroidery, and mono-grammed, and she'd brush her hair and braid it down her back—white hair. Then she'd get out these five boxes of treats for Mickey and Cutie. The poodles would sit there begging for the treats. It was the prettiest picture."

They would watch the evening news together, discussing the events of the day, of the world. There was one subject they never mentioned: Mother Nichols never knew the real identity of her trusted companion. Marian Lane was always thankful for that. Among the things they did talk about was the restless youth who were marching and protesting and causing such a ruckus. The 1960s were an era of campus unrest and social upheaval, of The Doors and Janis Joplin and Vietnam. Sex and drugs and rock 'n' roll was the mantra for a generation trying to find itself before it was lost forever.

But this was Marian Lane's Age of Aquarius too, even if it bore no resemblance to the happenings down at Haight-Ashbury. She had been reborn into a life she had never dreamed possible, had found love and respect after so many years of snickers and catcalls. For the first time since she left home as a bride, she had found a safe harbor.

"Of course, they never thought of looking for me in a chauffeured limousine with two little poodles—sassy little poodles," she giggles.

Every now and then during those years, some newspapers somewhere would write a story wondering whatever happened to the infamous Winnie Ruth Judd. Many speculated she had escaped to Mexico and was probably living in a hovel somewhere, helping the sick. Phoenix police would be quoted in the stories as saying they checked every tip on her whereabouts, but the tips were far and few between as the years passed.

Marian joined a church. She produced one lovely crocheted item after another—a skill she had learned as a girl and had practiced all her life. She became friendly with the service help from the other mansions and occupied a special place among them because her employer treated her so lovingly. She didn't even worry about getting old.

"Mother Nichols promised me I'd always have a home," she recalls with pride. "She said that even after she went, she wanted to be sure I was taken care of. In her will, she willed me all the furniture in my rooms, and ten thousand dollars. She had already given her daughter eighty-five thousand because she was going to buy me a prefabricated octagon house. We went down to San Jose and looked at it. It was awful cute. But Mrs. Blemmer says, 'I can do much better than this, Mother.'"

Mrs. Nichols's daughter, Ethel, and her husband, John Blemmer, owned a farm north of San Francisco, in the shadow of Mount Diablo. There was a small guest cottage on the property. If they fixed it up and added on a few rooms, it would make a perfect place for Marian, Ethel suggested to her mother. Marian loved the idea. It would give her all the privacy she wanted, but still keep her in touch with the family she had adopted as her own. Mother Nichols agreed it was a fine idea. The work was already under way when Mother Nichols died in December 1967. Marian stayed on in the big house in Piedmont for the next year and a half, watching over it until it was sold. Then she packed up her many belongings and memories and moved to the country. She was sixty-four years old.

"My house was awful cute. It was cozy. I had two apple trees—one outside the kitchen and one in the yard, and there were a couple of lemon trees. Mrs. Blemmer fixed a runway for my dogs, and had a hole cut in the door so they could go in and out. I had beautiful wisteria. So fragrant, like clusters of grapes, all over the trellis, and I had a white one all over my porch."

She was still unpacking, still settling into the house where she expected to live out her life, when she gave her first party.

It was June 27, 1969.

One of Mrs. Nichols's friends, an elderly woman who was dying, insisted on coming out, saying that if she waited, she might never get to see the lovely place Marian had so often described. "She and her cook and her maid came and I didn't have much. I had a little chicken salad and served some cream of tomato soup and some strawberries. We ate on the porch.

"While we were eating there, here came the police."

She remembers her guests had no idea what was going on. She somehow convinced them to leave, saying only that she had business to attend to. She went to the "big house" on the farm, telling the maid and handyman that she was going to be gone for a few days and to lock things up. She picked up her two dogs—Skeeter and Toto—and rode in a squad car to the Martinez police station. "And of course, at the police station they took the dogs away from me, and I worried about them—I was just sick."

Marian Lane's worst nightmare had come true. Winnie Ruth Judd was back. But she refused to admit it. She still remembers the questioning: "They said, 'Did you ever know of any Ruth Judd?' and I said, 'I've heard of a Senator Judd in Washington.' They looked at each other. 'And then there was a Governor Judd in Hawaii, I've heard of him. But Winnie Ruth Judd—it doesn't ring a bell.'"

She had been discovered by the most bizarre of circumstances. Although she didn't drive, she had bought a car that she loaned to her nephew. It was not just an act of generosity. It was a payoff. Although she is loath to use that word, she finally admits that this nephew wasn't shy about asking for money, asking for the car, asking for help whenever he wanted it. "He reminded me, 'I could have turned you in,'" she says. "And I told him, 'But you won't.'" Her constant handouts were added insurance.

The car was found parked in a San Francisco neighborhood where a woman had been killed, and a routine check found it registered to one Marian Lane. The name rang a bell with an old-timer on the police force, who thought it might be an alias. Somewhere along the line, somebody remembered that when Winnie Ruth Judd escaped to Yuma, Arizona, in 1939, she had tried to pass herself off as Marian Lane. It was worth checking, police thought.

Marian was fingerprinted and the hunch turned into a spectacular bust. Once again, the name Winnie Ruth Judd went out over the newswires. The Tiger Woman had been netted.

John and Ethel Blemmer were vacationing in Belgium at the time. "They were riding up an elevator," Marian remembers, "and they had a newspaper and Mrs. Blemmer said she almost fainted when she looked at the picture and said, 'My God, that's Marian.'"

The Blemmers flew home immediately, retrieving the dogs and the car that police had impounded. And then they showed the trusted maid how much she meant to the family. "Dr. Blemmer wrote beautiful letters in my behalf. They told me they loved me, they'd do anything for me. Mrs. Blemmer never questioned me at all. Never did. She saved all the newspaper clippings, if I ever needed them—had a big box full of them."

She was Winnie Ruth Judd again. She was old and tired and unused to the shame.

The nation's most notorious fugitive hired one of the nation's most famous defense attorneys, Melvin Belli. By 1969, he was so famous he was a household word in America. He was handsome and urbane and impressive. He was flamboyant and bombastic and bodacious. And he was so good he usually won.

Belli remembers the day he got a call from Winnie Ruth Judd and, without even a private visit, took her on as a client. As he explained in a recent interview, he first heard about her case when he was in law school and she was perfecting her disappearing act from the state hospital. "She went over the fence more times than Babe Ruth," he jokes. This was Belli's kind of chutzpah, Belli's kind of case.

From the moment he signed on—paid with Ruth's savings and the help of the Blemmers—he bellowed that it was outrageous for anyone to punish this woman further. His first line of attack was to fight her extradition to Arizona, charging that California had to be insensitive to send her back, Arizona sadistic to want her back. Face-to-face, he argued with the aides of then governor Ronald Reagan: "This woman who stands before you now has been as rehabilitated as any woman can be, or rehabilitation is a mockery."

Reagan signed the extradition papers anyway.

Belli's second move was to take Ruth's plight to the public—a jury he understood better than most. On the eve of her extradition, the famous attorney sat next to his famous client as a Phoenix television crew recorded an "exclusive"— an hour's worth of questions.

The documentary was hosted by reporter Joe Patrick, who was Phoenix's most famous television newsman of the day. He had a voice and presence that recalled the style of Edward R. Murrow. The story was such a coup that KTAR-TV gave "Winnie Ruth Judd: Then and Now" a full hour in prime time.

Belli used the show to argue for compassion. "If she was insane, certainly she's rehabilitated," he told Patrick. "If she was guilty of the crime, she has done her time three times over. In California and Arizona, seven to ten to twelve years would be the most in a first-degree case. She's done thirty-eight years. I don't know anyone else, at least in the West, that has done more time for murder than Mrs. Judd."

Belli looked right into the camera: "I have never, in thirty years of practice, had so many people phone me, write me from all over the West—people who knew her, or knew where she worked, and people who had just heard about her—saying, 'She's done her time; if jails and asylums aren't hypocrisy, then this woman, who has done her time, and is penally and psychiatrically rehabilitated...should be out.' And I don't think she should have to spend much more time before the wheels of justice grind over there [in Arizona] and turn her out."

While Belli was succinct and convincing, Winnie Ruth Judd was rambling and confusing. She mumbles and stumbles through the interview just as she did on the witness stand when she testified against Jack Halloran nearly forty years earlier. Although the 1931 crime was the main thing on Joe Patrick's mind, Winnie Ruth Judd had a lifetime of complaints she wanted to air—those promises to her made and broken in the state hospital, the mistreatment from some asylum directors, her fury at being made to remember all this after she had proved herself a solid citizen for six years.

Her story of self-defense came out in befuddling bits and pieces, jumbled with stories from her current life: how she still put violets on her husband's grave in the Golden Gate National Military Cemetery, how good Mother Nichols was to her; how much she wished everyone would leave her alone. It is pathetic to watch the only copy of this documentary that still exists—the one Patrick keeps in his private collection. To hear Ruth talk of violets and bullets in almost the same breath—giving casual conversation and deadly encounters equal weight—is disturbing. She sounds like a frightened, foggy, whiny old woman.

But anyone listening closely—anyone who could separate the junk from the juicy parts—heard about the fight, about the boyfriend who interceded, about the "Dr. Brown" who cut up the body. Once again, it was the same story she has always told. Jack Halloran's name was never mentioned on the air. Every time she used it, it was disguised and a male voice inserted the name John Doe. Halloran was still alive then, in a nursing home in Phoenix.

Patrick was a skillful interviewer, letting Ruth wander for a bit to show her thinking process, then bringing her back to the point with direct questions. "Now, do you feel in 1931 you received a fair trial in Phoenix?" he asked her at one point. She shot back: "Do you think it's a fair trial when you can't even take the witness stand and state anything in your behalf?"

Interspersed with her story was an interview with a retired Phoenix police officer named Charles Arnold—the same source the Phoenix dailies were using to present "the other side of the story," as they scrambled to report on this latest development.

Arnold claimed that he had directed the investigation of her case in 1931. He told the camera he never had any doubts she had done it in cold blood and had done it alone, out of perverted jealousy. He described interrogating her when she was brought back to Arizona from California; "Now, Ruthie, they weren't fighting you. Ruthie, your story's all wet—you went out to kill them because one rejected your love."

Several times during his interview, however, Charles Arnold misstated undisputed facts about the case. He claimed, for instance, that one of the mattresses from the death house had bullet holes in it. It didn't. He claimed a mattress was found with two big spots of blood. It wasn't. He maintained Sammy's body was slashed "four to five" times as the cutter tried to find a joint. That wasn't true either.

But Charles Arnold sounded as if he knew what he was talking about. He was presented as the cop who had the best inside information on the case and a razor-sharp memory of the facts. Anyone new to the case could easily have found his points convincing and concluded that Arizona had once again nabbed a vicious killer.

The problem is that there was no Charles Arnold directing the investigation of the Winnie Ruth Judd case. Nowhere in the thousands of pages of police records uncovered in this writer's probe is his name even mentioned. And although the Phoenix police were initially called into the case, the real investigation was done by a separate agency—the county attorney's office. If Charles Arnold was involved in the case at all, it was not the exalted position he presented to the media.

Patrick concluded the show with a dramatic wrap-up. Maybe, he said, the whole story of Winnie Ruth Judd would finally be told. "There are still hundreds of unanswered questions that only Mrs. Judd may answer, for some of her answers are accusations that so far have been neither confirmed nor denied," he told his audience. "This film report, while only a crack in a thirty-eight-year-old closed door, could be the opening of a legal Pandora's box."

Now a free-lance writer living in Tombstone, Arizona, Patrick remembers he was impressed by her story. "She was not real bright but she was very sincere," he says. "There's no doubt in my mind that she did the killings, but as far as I could determine, it was not premeditated at all—it just happened. I never believed she cut up the body. It was done with precision and she didn't have the skill. I think the morals of the time were such that it was demanded they punish her in some fashion."

Newspapers, of course, also retold the story that was now a part of Arizona history. But many persisted in misreporting the facts. Most still claimed both bodies had been mutilated. Interestingly, not a single story mentioned the weird litany that had raised so many doubts for so long: the jurors with second thoughts, the astonishing ruling that freed Halloran but left Ruth in the lurch, the widespread belief that she was not responsible for the dismemberment.

Open-and-shut. That was how the case was presented, just as it had been forty years earlier.

But there was some joyous news too. Arizona attorney general Gary Nelson declared that the law was clear: Ruth must get credit as time served for the years she spent in the state hospital. Subtracting the time away from the hospital in her seven escapes, that amounted to 29 years and 154 days. Nelson noted that prisoners sentenced to life terms—as she had been in 1952 by Governor Pyle—served on the average from eight to ten years.

The highest law enforcement official in the state of Arizona had freely agreed with her famous defense attorney that Winnie Ruth Judd had already served the equivalent of three life terms. Nelson hinted broadly that Arizona could hardly ask for more.

When Winnie Ruth Judd got on the plane in San Francisco in the custody of an Arizona sheriff, she had every reason to believe it would be a short visit.

That's what she was told attorney general Gary Nelson had indicated.

That's what Melvin Belli promised her.

Finally, she thought, people with power were speaking publicly on her behalf. No more secret deals. No more broken promises.

All she had to do was endure this pain for a few weeks more and she would finally be a totally free woman.

She could go back to her cottage with its expansive view. She could dote on her dogs. She could be Marian Lane again. Forever.

But Arizona was not through with her yet.

Chapter 17
The Last Pound of Flesh

Larry Debus, today one of Arizona's pre-eminent defense attorneys, was a young man in his early thirties in 1969. He had already done a stint as a Phoenix police officer and a public defender. That year, he had decided to open his own office and scraped up enough money to rent a cubbyhole in the Luhrs Building in downtown Phoenix.

He had yet to have any case of note when Melvin Belli called asking if he would sign on as the Arizona attorney for the Winnie Ruth Judd case. Debus says he never jumped so fast or so hard at any case in his entire career.

Debus met the plane that brought Ruth Judd back to Arizona on August 18, 1969. "And the first thing I did was something defense lawyers never do," he recounts. "I got her *into* prison."

As he explains, "As far as Arizona was concerned, she was still insane and had to be held at the state hospital. But the only way to get her a pardon was to get her out of the state hospital and put her in prison." He handed officials a writ of habeas corpus, claiming she was not insane and was being improperly held at the asylum. It worked. Four days later, she finally got the sanity hearing she had been wanting for seventeen years. The panel declared Winnie Ruth Judd was sane. She was sent immediately to the state prison in Florence.

The minute she arrived, Debus filed a request with the parole board for a commutation of her sentence, arguing that she had already served so much time that Arizona had no right to hold her any longer. He reassured her it would all be over when the parole board next met, on October 27.

Winnie Ruth Judd thought she had sixty-six days to go.

The state prison was a far different place from what she remembered. The only thing that stayed the same was the identification number she had been issued in 1932: number 8811. By now so many had come through those gates that the prison's consecutive numbering system was up to 29,466. There had been a scant dozen women incarcerated in Arizona when she entered a cell here as a young woman. Now there were several hundred.

Today Ruth does not like to talk about the prison. "It was very different" is all she wants to say. But friends she made there tell a frightening story. Some of the female inmates threatened her, demanding "protection" money. Some of them pushed her around. Many taunted her. She finally met a young female inmate, far more streetwise than Ruth Judd would ever be, who became her friend and helped ward off the others.

Belli flew in just hours before the parole board hearing, and he and Debus drove down to Florence together. Belli says he'll never forget that day. "We went down and it was a hot day, but they all sat in a formal room with stiff collars—they looked like a Grant Wood painting. I knew when I saw them they were never anyone *I'd* want on a parole board."

As usual, the meeting began with a prayer. When Belli rose to address the board, he remarked how touched he was that they would seek divine guidance in their deliberations. And then he brought forth a parade of witnesses to plead for Ruth Judd.

One after another, they told the board she was "completely rehabilitated." The minutes of the meeting show her supporters included a professor of psychology, a doctor from the state hospital, John and Ethel Blemmer, and Ruth's second cousin. The Blemmers promised they had a lifetime job for her and would assume her care in old age. She would never be a burden to the state of Arizona, they assured the board.

Four days later, on a vote of two to one, the board said Winnie Ruth Judd did not deserve a parole. Their decision meant she had to spend at least a year behind bars before her case would even be considered again.

"The board finds that Mrs. Judd in the past has been the benefactor of much gracious and charitable treatment, far in excess of that usually granted to one guilty of so grave an offense," their formal denial reads. "From the standpoint of punishment and incarceration, Mrs. Judd has been very fortunate, indeed. She completely escaped the verdict of the jury and the penalty [to hang] prescribed by it, whether by subterfuge or providence…While in the Arizona State Hospital, she enjoyed privileges not extended to like inmates. To observe the application of punishment in this case from beginning to end, one wonders if it could not be singled out as the case more disposed to induce and encourage crime, rather than act as a preventive."

Belli immediately bawled his outrage to the press: "I think the board was born too late. They should have been born at the time of the Inquisition and the Star Chamber." At a San Francisco news conference, he announced that Debus was filing a lawsuit against the board for unconstitutional behavior: it was improper, Belli contended, to begin a public meeting of a governmental body with a prayer.

An astonished Debus told the press he knew nothing of any lawsuit and certainly did not intend to file any. Privately, he cursed that Belli's grandstanding was doing nothing but entrenching the stubborn board, which, like many other Arizonans, saw the flamboyant California attorney as an upstart.

Debus filed for another parole hearing as soon as the mandatory one-year waiting period was up. In the meantime, Ruth helped out in the prison hospital and Debus politicked.

As he recalls it, every reporter in the West was clamoring for an interview with the famous Winnie Ruth Judd. He steadfastly refused all press requests. But one of his friends in those days was the *Arizona Republic*'s investigative reporter Logan McKechnie. "Logan wanted exclusive access to her in prison. I had to create good public opinion, so we made a deal," Debus says. He traded an exclusive interview for a promise the *Republic* would print a positive editorial. McKechnie, now a defense attorney in San Diego, acknowledges such a trade "could have happened."

His interview did. So did the editorial: The *Republic* opined that Arizona had taken its pound of flesh from Winnie Ruth Judd and "enough is enough." The editorial declared: "We believe Arizona will be serving the joint causes of justice and mercy if it turns Winnie Ruth Judd loose to live the rest of her life as a functioning member of society."

"Winnie Tried to Forget" was the headline on McKechnie's exclusive interview with her. "I've had six years of love and happiness. I have been in heaven," she told him. "I was somebody else and I tried to forget the past. In this atmosphere, with all the love I had, I was happy for the first time in my life. These people loved me. I was not insane Winnie from the insane hospital. I was Marian Lane and I was loved."

She told the reporter she had felt so secure that she wasn't even afraid of the police. "I was walking down the street when a small boy—about 2 years old—was almost hit by a bus. I ran out and picked him up and I spent all that morning riding around with a policeman looking for the boy's mother," she related. Her only scare during her stolen freedom was when a ruby ring disappeared from the Nichols household. "Oh, I was so scared," she admitted. "The ring was insured and the insurance investigators would be all over me because I was responsible for everything in the house." The ring was eventually found in a repair shop.

She wanted her freedom, she pleaded to McKechnie. "I will prove to everyone who has been kind to me that I can make them proud of me."

That interview whetted McKechnie's appetite and he started investigating the old files about Winnie Ruth Judd. He found the case so fascinating he even considered writing a book, but never got around to it. He had gathered boxes of information, though, and came to a startling conclusion: "I was left wondering if she pulled the trigger," he says now. "She was such a fragile person at that time, she could have been convinced she killed them. I never was."

There was a decidedly different atmosphere by the time Ruth got her second parole hearing, on February 16, 1971. Public opinion had shifted in her favor. And once again, Arizona was being chastised by the national media. How much should this woman suffer? some editorial pages asked. What is it that makes Arizona so heartless to this old woman? others wondered. In-state papers wondered the same things.

The *Arizona Republic* printed sympathetic letters from her supporters—they were no longer labeled "sob sisters." One touching letter was written by Genevieve Podratz, whose mother had been a patient at the asylum. "We came to love and admire Winnie Ruth Judd very much as we watched the self-sacrificing service and love she gave to the patients at the hospital. No one knows how many thousands of dollars she saved the state by the work she did in relieving the nurses and helping wherever needed." And from the details Mrs. Podratz enumerated, Ruth Judd had been needed every-where. "When she was in the building with the elderly, she planted flowers and put bouquets in their wards, preparing foods they could eat, reading with them and feeding them. She took complete care of six babies and children when the children's wing overflowed. She did all the washing and ironing, cooking, feeding and care. She was placed in the young women's wing. There Mother got her a sewing machine and gathered formals and party dresses. These Ruth carefully washed and ironed and altered so that the girls could dress up for the dances and programs arranged by the therapy department. She helped in the craft work and made beautiful things to brighten the rooms and develop the skill of the patients who had lost their ability and will to go on.

"As anyone who ever knew her would tell you, she was a help and comfort and inspiration to all who came in contact with her. Surely the years of service have earned her the right to peace and an end to the persecution by the newspapers."

Debus handled the parole board hearing alone. He called only two witnesses, Dr. Herbert Collier and Dr. Otto Bendheim. Both had done psychological evaluations of Ruth Judd. Bendheim who had known her since the thirties, concluded: "This person is sound, sane and absolutely harmless. She presents no danger whatever to society or to herself. There are no suicidal, homicidal or violent tendencies. She has a potential for constructive and meaningful contributions to society."

Dr. Collier reached the same conclusion. As he recalled in a recent interview, "My initial impression was this woman couldn't have killed anyone. She was a sweet grandmother type. She looked as normal as anyone I'd ever seen."

The board again split two to one, but this time it was in Winnie Ruth Judd's favor. Board member Keith Edwards had changed his mind. He wrote the final report:

"This case is not one you sweep under the rug and forget about. The people of Arizona are very much interested in this case...She has served more than anyone else, possibly in the history of Arizona. Mrs. Judd has served approximately 32 flat years, with a total of 75½ years with two for one and statutory time credits added.

"Prior to her first hearing, I was contacted by many people who were not in favor of her being commuted. Apparently, there has been a change in public opinion. Prior to the hearing of Feb. 16, of all the people who contacted me, only one was for denying Mrs. Judd a commutation.

"As time passes, more and more people will join the ranks of those who think her sentence should be commuted. What we will see is not a question of modern penology, but the portrayal of out-and-out persecution of an elderly, grand-motherly type, unfortunate woman.

"A family in California is very anxious to have her back as their housekeeper, and they have promised her a cottage of her own and employment. Mrs. Judd has a means of livelihood now. It is incumbent upon the board to give her a commutation of sentence now, while she is physically able to work, or forget ever giving her a commutation of sentence."

Edwards noted that her "excellent adjustment" while an escapee in California showed she had been rehabilitated. "If circumstances had been different and she had been on parole instead of an escapee, Mrs. Judd would have been classified as an 'outstanding' parolee," he said.

But he also stressed that the board believed strongly that "crime doesn't pay" and wanted her parole to include assur-ances that she would never profit from a book or movie about her life. Some remember that Hollywood had already expressed an interest.

Debus has never believed that final caveat was as pure as the board made it out to be. He suspects the stipulation was meant to ensure that her story never again embarrassed Phoenix's old-time power brokers. "I always wondered how much of old Phoenix was still pressuring, forty years later," he says.

Debus called Ruth as soon as the recommendation was announced, and remembers she cried with joy over the phone. "[Then] all we had to do was have Governor Williams sign the commutation. We waited and waited and waited."

Jack Williams had risen through the political ranks over the forty years when Ruth Judd was a fixture in Arizona's penal system. From radio newsman who reenacted her trial each night to mayor of Phoenix to chief executive of the state, Williams was a man who evoked strong emotions. Having lost an eye in a youthful accident, he was referred to as "One-Eyed Jack" by his detractors. He is the first to tell you he's an old-fashioned kind of guy with a strong sense of male supremacy, an advocate of traditional law and order. He was just the kind of establishment official who was out of favor in the late 1960s and early 1970s.

During his eight years as governor, he made enemies of supporters from every single "liberal" cause that touched Arizona. University students hated him as a right-winger who scoffed at "student rights." The farm labor movement saw him as a racist. He seemed to delight in the most outrageous snubs. Farm labor organizer Cesar Chavez was in the governor's outer office, waiting to plead against a bill outlawing unions on Arizona farms, as Governor Williams was inside his office signing the bill. That action launched a recall effort against Williams in the mid-seventies—a drive that apparently collected the required signatures but was subverted when the Republican attorney general found a nitpicking technicality that disqualified most of the petitions.

This was the man who held the fate of Winnie Ruth Judd in his hands.

He well remembers those days now, as he sits in his comfortable living room in Phoenix. He remembers the pressure to free her. He remembers the pressure to leave her in prison. He remembers his own uneasiness with the notion that Arizona should forgive and forget. "I didn't want her to be rewarded for escaping," he explains. "I wanted her to spend a month in prison for every year she'd been on the loose. I don't think we should foster the image that crime pays."

Some attempts at pressure still make him laugh. He was scheduled to speak at the University of Arizona in Tucson—an engagement he was less than anxious to fulfill, since he'd already been through a riot at the sister university, Arizona State in Tempe. "But I had to go through with it," he recalls. "I got to the podium and you could just feel the hate coming from those students. And just as I started my speech, along the balcony they unfurled a big banner that read, 'Free Winnie Ruth Judd.'"

Months went by, and he refused to sign her commutation.

Ruth Judd bided her time.

Debus got anxious, then furious, then anxious.

Governor Williams was obviously agonizing over the recommendation. He called Tom Kunze, who had sat on her 1932 jury. As Kunze recalled in the tape he made for his family, "I told him, 'Jack, why don't you pardon the gal? She's paid her price, in my book.'" Williams also called Stewart Thompson, the jury foreman. Thompson remembers the governor asking if he had any objections to her release. "I told him I had no objections at all," Thompson says.

More months went by.

Ruth Judd bided her time.

Debus got frustrated, then angry, then frustrated. As he recounts it, "Unknown to me, Belli calls Governor Williams and they meet at Williams's home. Belli talks him into signing the pardon, but Williams makes him agree they'll never disclose they had that meeting. Belli goes back to San Francisco and immediately calls a press conference and reveals the meeting."

Belli says he doesn't remember that, insisting, "I'd never do that." Governor Williams says he can't recall it either, but it could well have happened. But while Belli remembers Williams well—"I was very comfortable with him"—Williams had a totally opposite reaction: "I didn't like him at all."

Enter Debus, who can vouch for the dislike the governor harbored for Ruth Judd's primary attorney. "I got a call to report to the governor's office," Debus recalls. "The meeting was very short and quick and to the point. I was told, 'As long as Belli is her lawyer, I'll never sign.' I got back to the office and typed up a letter for Ruth. I go down to Florence and tell her what happened and ask, 'What's your pleasure?' She told me, 'Fire him.' She signed the letter firing Belli. I delivered a copy of Ruth's letter to the governor, and…the next day, he signed the commutation. In the middle of the night—literally. They sneak her out of the state. Nobody knew she was gone."

The precise time is two a.m., December 22, 1971.

Governor Jack Williams's signature has finally been affixed to official papers with the magic word parole. It's taken him 245 days.

Ruth Judd has gathered together her few belongings, said her few goodbyes.

A nephew carries her suitcase to the car. It's already gassed up, ready for the two-day drive to the Blemmers' home in California.

Her leaving is nothing like her coming.

The warden is there to say goodbye. That's all.

There are no reporters. No photographers with flashbulbs popping, although she is not sure photographers even use flashbulbs anymore.

It's not a Packard now but a Plymouth.

There are no gawking crowds, just empty streets.

And she's not a pretty lass anymore, just a 66-year-old woman with a stooped back.

It seems such an ordinary ending to such an extraordinary story.

But everyone is so tired of it, so glad it is finally over.

Arizona has owned Winnie Ruth Judd's hide for thirty-eight years, eleven months, and twenty-two days.

She gets in the passenger seat and holds her black pocket-book on her lap.

She never once looks back.

Chapter 18
Free at Last

It was raining on Christmas Eve of 1971 when Ruth Judd arrived at the Blemmer home in Danville, California. But she didn't care that the weather had turned bad. This was going to be the most joyous Christmas she had ever known.

She no longer was a fugitive or a convict. She no longer had to answer to prison guards or consult with attorneys.

She was a parolee who just had to be a decent and good citizen in order to keep her freedom.

And once again, she was Marian Lane.

That Christmas, she became Marian Lane for good.

The Blemmers welcomed her with open arms. Ethel Blemmer told the *Phoenix Gazette*, "She's a wonderful woman. We saw her at dinner at least twice every week for six years and she always came at Christmas loaded with toys she had made for our grandchildren—mostly stuffed animals—and crocheted doilies and placemats for the adults. She does beautiful work. It looks like it's going to be a great Christmas after all."

Marian Lane still remembers it took her hours to open all the gifts the family bought for her that year. In pictures taken during the celebration, she is smiling brightly. It's hard to look at her face and imagine the tribulations of this woman's life.

The *Phoenix Gazette* of December 12, 1972, ran this, by reporter Lois Boyles: "The major worry facing Marian Lane of Danville, California, today is whether her lemon tree will survive the unusual frost and the nibbles of wayward horses driven by hunger to try the sour fruit. A year ago Marian Lane was better known as Winnie Ruth Judd, Arizona's trunk murderess of the 1930s. And her main concern was whether she was going to get out of Arizona State Prison in time for the holidays."

Boyles noted Marian Lane had spent her first year of freedom living quietly in a snug little house on the Blemmers' estate. "And Mrs. Blemmer is certain most of the people of Danville have forgotten the kind, matronly woman has a past which is still a matter of frequent conversation and speculation in the Valley of the Sun." Marian Lane had "a dear little garden" and "an assortment of animals" that included a couple of cats and dogs, the story went on. "Everything is fine. It couldn't be better," Mrs. Blemmer was quoted as telling the paper.

Marian too remembers those first years as idyllic. "When I got back, Mrs. Blemmer gave a tea. She had twelve people and they all kissed me and hugged me and were so glad I was back."

There was only one sore spot. To celebrate her first birthday in decades as a free woman, she went out with the Blemmers to a fancy restaurant. They were having a gay time, she remembers, when Dr. Blemmer said to the waiters, "Do you know who that is? She's Winnie Ruth Judd!" She still cringes in relating the incident. "And then everyone came over and looked at me," she says, reliving the humiliation.

◇◇◇

Winnie Ruth Judd: The Trunk Murders by two Phoenix advertising executives, J. Dwight Dobkins and Robert Hendricks, was published in 1973. It was a history of the case, drawn primarily from newspaper clippings. It provoked a small flurry of renewed interest in Winnie Ruth Judd, who was not interviewed for the book and to this day says she has never read it. Both men gave interviews to the Phoenix press, which allowed that maybe the case was not as open-and-shut as it had always been portrayed. The name Jack Halloran is not found in the book. Instead, the authors refer to him as "Carl Harris."

On July 7, 1975, the *Arizona Daily Star* wrote: "Winnie Ruth Judd, now 71 and collecting Social Security, has led a quiet existence since the Arizona Board of Pardons and Paroles ordered the convicted murderess freed nearly five years ago. 'She's doing just fine—splendidly,' said a parole official in Phoenix. 'She's been leading a very, very quiet life—there have been no problems at all.'"

No, no problems in 1975. Or 1976. No, the problems started when Ethel Blemmer died in January 1981.

By then Marian Lane had spent a decade in her lovely cottage on the farm. She attended church, did her fine needlework, helped out her family whenever she could. She also helped the woman who had been her "protector" in the state prison—a woman now paroled herself, who found work for a short time with the Blemmers and then moved to a town nearby. To this day the women remain friends and visit often.

The Blemmer children were now adults themselves, with children of their own, and Marian was like a loving aunt to this next generation.

"I loved Mrs. Blemmer," Marian repeats now, often. But she had never really gotten along with Dr. John Blemmer. She worried about that as she attended Mrs. Blemmer's funeral, but then reassured herself that her lifetime care had been promised by two women: Mrs. Nichols and Mrs. Blemmer. There was sufficient public record in the files of the Arizona

Board of Pardons and Paroles that Ethel and John Blemmer had pledged a lifetime home and care for Marion Lane.

It broke her heart, she says, when she had to sue John Blemmer to make good on the promise.

At the age of seventy-seven Marian went back to court. Her 1982 lawsuit charged that she had been kept as an indentured servant without formal wages, and feared revocation of her parole if she complained. As she explains it now, Dr. Blemmer told her to move out of the cottage, that he had another purpose for it. "I had to sue because I had nothing and Mother Nichols had promised me a home for life," she says.

A settlement was reached during the Christmas holidays of 1982: she was awarded a cash payment of $50,000 and a lifetime monthly income of $1,250.

The next year, the state of Arizona issued one Winnie Ruth Judd an "absolute discharge." That simple piece of paper meant she was no longer a parolee. It meant the state had ended all claims on her. She was a totally free woman.

She left the cottage she so loved and moved into a two-bedroom apartment in Stockton so she could be near her niece. "I can sleep seven people here," she told this writer in our first telephone interview in early 1990, noting how much she loved having company.

"Stockton does so much for the elderly," she went on. "You can ride the bus for ten cents. I've never gotten so much for a dime. Everyone is so courteous and kind."

When her niece's husband died, leaving the young woman with two small children, Aunt Marian helped finance her nurse's training so she could have a decent career. When the roof needed repair at the Free Methodist Church, Marian Lane gave a $500 contribution. "I've tried to do the good that I know how," she says. "I've helped quite a number of children financially in school, what I could spare."

She still has Skeeter, who she jokes is as old and decrepit as herself. "He's a good dog, a good companion," she adds. He is also a good watchdog—his growl and bared teeth warn visitors not to get too close to the mistress he loves.

Her apartment is filled with the lovely furniture that Mother Nichols gave her so long ago. It's upholstered in a flowered print that accents her favorite color—green. The same color covers the floors. Off the kitchen is a small patio where she grows the violets she still takes to her husband's grave.

She spends all her time these days being Marian Lane and forgetting a woman named Winnie Ruth Judd.

"I have never called anybody connected with my case," she says. "I just threw it all away, put it out of my life, and it was a new life. And I've talked to you more than I have to anybody in all these years.

"I try to get them off my mind as quick as possible, people that have ever done me wrong. I do know some that have done me terribly wrong. It destroys me if I think of it. I try to concentrate on the people that have been good, and the people that I want to be good to and just keep on—happy thoughts. I have to. You can't live in the past. That is completely walled off in my life. Completely. You can do that, like the men wall off the terrors of war, horrible things that they go through. You have to, to live.

"I've lived quietly in another world so long that when I read articles about my case, it doesn't even seem like me.

"To me, I'm Marian Lane. And to my friends, I'm Marian Lane."

Epilogue

It seems ironic that a train would play such a crucial role in the Winnie Ruth Judd case, considering how successfully Arizona railroaded her.

It seems amazing that so many could hide behind perverted "justice" so long, considering what a bald secret her case always was in Phoenix, Arizona.

It seems pitiful that the woman once known as Winnie Ruth Judd no longer sees any need for vindication, considering she hankered for it so long.

If the woman known today as Marian Lane had her way, this book would never have been written. She would prefer her given name were never spoken again. She would rather live out her last years anonymously, without anyone wondering anymore what happened so long ago.

There were many times in the last two years I thought she was right. That "stirring things up again," as she puts it, would do nothing but harm an old woman I had no stomach to harm. Even my parents wondered, "Why not just leave her alone?"

And just when I would decide that I should—that a few peaceful years were the least she was owed—I'd find another piece of this filthy puzzle and I'd get angry all over again.

When I first fixed on the Winnie Ruth Judd case, I hadn't expected any of this. I was a newspaper editor in Phoenix on the lookout for a good story, and it seemed interesting to explore "Whatever Happened to Winnie Ruth Judd?" If I could ever wrangle an interview from the woman who didn't give interviews, I could write about what she had done with her life since she left the state prison in the dead of night twenty years ago. Throw in a little background on her case, and it would be a good read.

Getting the interview, of course, was the key. For three years she refused. She has never explained to me why she finally agreed to talk, never explained to her last attorney, Larry Debus, either. One day, after all those rejected requests, she decided she should talk to someone. I spoke with her by phone for the first time in early January 1990, and set up a date for a personal interview for the first week in February.

She insisted I stay at her apartment in Stockton, worried that a motel would be too expensive. She was concerned that the plane fare would be costly and wondered if it wouldn't be cheaper for me to take the train to California—anyone who has ever been in a newspaper office can imagine the titters that provoked. She was very concerned that anybody would put out hard cash to visit her. Once I got there, I had to fight her over the bill at the grocery store for the salmon steaks for dinner. She insisted on paying for lunch in a restaurant. She treated me as a guest, played the role of the gracious hostess.

Originally I was to visit her on a Thursday and Friday. I wasn't staying the weekend because she had friends coming in Saturday afternoon. But Friday afternoon, she got violently ill; I took her to a doctor in the car I had rented. She was thankful for the transportation, since she usually travels by city bus. She had a bad case of the flu.

"I can't talk anymore," she pleaded when we got home. I assured her I wouldn't ask another question. But I also couldn't just leave her alone. I rearranged my flight to leave late Saturday, after her friends arrived.

Saturday morning, I woke up to find her so much better that she was fixing me breakfast. Eggs and bacon and toast and orange juice. She served on her good dishes—the Moss Rose pattern from Prince Albert China. She intends to leave the set to her niece, she told me.

And then she started talking again. There were stories she still wanted to tell. Like most of her stories, these were about her years in the state hospital. But now and then— just as she'd done for the last two days—she would throw out a sentence or two about "my tragedy," as she always calls her criminal case. Sometimes the sentences made sense from what I already knew. Sometimes they only became clear months later, when my research showed what she meant.

And then she pitched a story she wanted me to write. Not about the injustice done to Winnie Ruth Judd, but the injustice done to her friend, Mary—the woman who became her protector and friend in the state prison and was now a parolee living in California. It struck me that the entire visit might have been designed to get me to investigate *that* story of injustice. This woman who so values her privacy would risk it—knowing full well I was going to write about her— in the hope that exposing herself might bring some justice to a friend. If anything reveals the character of Marian Ruth Lane, it is that.

Investigative reporters each have their own system, but we all start with a basic premise: Something is wrong with this picture. That was what I had always heard about the Winnie Ruth Judd case—that the truth had never been revealed. If those rumors were accurate, then what really happened?

I always begin by making lists: all the possible sources of information, all the people who should be interviewed. My favorite list I call "spectacular possibilities." Letting my imagination run wild, I imagine the most shocking things I could hope to find. In this case, a major item on the list was the possibility of naming the accomplices who went unpunished. But the juiciest item was answering the question: Did she cut anybody up?

It doesn't take long to realize that the dismemberment of Sammy's body was the centerpiece of the crime. Without that, it would have been just another homicide in a backwater town that would have passed unnoticed by history. Like so many, I believed the press reports that Sammy's body had been "butchered" and "hacked to pieces." I believed that until months later, when I finally saw the autopsy pictures.

So the best I hoped to uncover was the truth about the most grisly aspect of this case.

Learning the real story of the dismemberment turned out to be the easiest part of the entire probe. The evidence was so overwhelming and so easy to get that I didn't feel I'd uncovered some long-lost truth. I felt I'd just looked up the dirty skirts of Phoenix, Arizona.

In between sessions poring over thousands of pages of historical documents on this case, I began searching for anyone who had been touched by it. One of the first people I found was Rita Grimm Esche, whose father was Ruth Judd's landlord. I interviewed her first over the phone. "None of us who knew her ever believed she did it," she told me.

I understood the comment to mean that nobody believed Ruth Judd had cut up Sammy. But then in a face-to-face interview weeks later, I realized that was not what she meant at all.

Rita Grimm Esche did not believe Winnie Ruth Judd killed anyone.

I had never really considered that. It certainly wasn't on my list of spectacular possibilities. I didn't seriously consider it then either, writing it off as Rita's sympathy for the kindly Ruth Judd who had helped her with her Spanish homework.

As in any investigation, one phone call often provides leads to other contacts, and that's how it was with this case. And the list of those who thought Ruth Judd a total innocent kept growing.

But she had confessed to shooting the women. Her argument was not that she hadn't pulled the trigger but that she had done it in self-defense.

The people telling me this fantastic possibility were now elderly women themselves, who remembered the case from their youth. In that day, they would clearly have been labeled "sob sisters."

But then I heard the same thing from ex-reporter Logan McKechnie, and from Hugh Ennis, an experienced police officer who could never be accused of sobbing over anything. Ennis is tough and blunt, and he wasn't a bystander at the time—he is an amateur historian who has studied the case. When he looks at evidence, it is through the eyes of a cop who has collected homicide evidence himself. "I think the jury is out whether she killed them or not," he told me in our first phone conversation—the first of dozens of interviews.

I started seeing things I hadn't seen before—a common experience in any complex investigation. A detail that means nothing one day becomes key as more and more information is amassed; evidence given short shrift because it doesn't fit one pattern looks quite different when the patchwork design is changed.

The day I first read about the two-bullet theory, I knew I had to start questioning everything about the Winnie Ruth Judd case.

History has forgotten that the original news stories said the autopsies show Anne and Sammy were killed with different guns—Sammy with a .25-caliber like the bullet in Ruth's hand, Anne—for whose death Ruth Judd was punished all those years—with a .32 caliber.

At first I dismissed this idea as being absurd. If there were two different bullets, there were two different guns. And if there were two guns, it was likely there were two killers. This was not a bit of information that could have fallen through the cracks.

I also gave no credence to the idea because one of the original police reports from Los Angeles included this notation on Anne's body: "One bullet hole in head. One .25 automatic bullet recovered from the body." It was only later that I wondered if the officer was talking about two separate wounds. Why didn't he say the .25-caliber bullet was recovered from her *head*? Even Ennis was left wondering.

So I started following the trail of this strange two-bullet theory, and at every step, my suspicions grew.

All the news reports were quite specific on this point.

Los Angeles Times, October 20, 1931: "The killer is believed to have used a .25 calibre automatic to murder Miss Samuelson, but a larger calibre weapon was used to kill Mrs. LeRoi."

Los Angeles Examiner, October 20, 1931: "Police found one of the death-dealing guns" in her hand luggage—a .25-calibre.

Phoenix Gazette, October 20, 1931: "Another gun is missing, for the autopsy disclosed that each of the women had been shot with a gun of different calibre."

Arizona Republic, October 20, 1931: "Two different calibre revolvers were used, autopsy surgeons said."

Phoenix Gazette, October 22, 1931: "Facts of the killings and butchery which point strongly to the theory that Mrs. Judd, a slight woman, could not possibly have completed the brutal task alone are: 1. The victims were shot with guns of different calibre, according to an autopsy performed in Los Angeles. 2. The weight of Mrs. LeRoi was greater than that of Mrs. Judd, indicating that the task of placing the victim in a trunk would have been too much for the one person."

And then the two-bullet theory disappears.

One day the *Gazette* enumerates two bullets as a major point in the investigation, and the next day—without a word of explanation—it simply stops mentioning it.

It should not be difficult to double-check a fact as significant as the caliber of fatal bullets. Instead, it turned out to be the most fascinating and frustrating issue left unanswered in this investigation.

I first went searching for the written autopsy reports that had been filed with the court. I found it strange that they didn't mention any caliber of bullet. The autopsies show the women sustained fatal shots to the head, with Sammy suffering other gunshot wounds as well. But the reports are silent on the caliber of bullet or bullets.

I next went to the record of the inquest hearing held in Los Angeles. Again there's discussion of the wounds, but no mention of what caliber bullet—or bullets—killed the girls.

I went to the trial testimony and found the same problem. Although there are pages of discussion of the bullet wounds, not once during the trial is the caliber of bullet addressed as an issue. Prosecutor Lloyd Andrews showed the jury the .25 caliber gun found inside the trunk. He showed them several bullets—all .25 caliber, and all still marked today with their identifying tags in the evidence box at the county records complex. He had the autopsy surgeons on the stand for a full day discussing the fatal wounds.

But the caliber of the deadly bullets is never mentioned.

There were two other places to double-check: the coroner's office in Los Angeles and the Los Angeles Police Department. But formal requests for files—some from me, some through Larry Debus—brought this news: Neither office any longer has a file on the Winnie Ruth Judd case.

The widely accepted explanation in the press for dropping the two-bullet theory was that it was simply a mistake. As the *Republic* reported, "Police here who had been basing a large part of their accomplice theory on the premise that two guns had been used in killing the two women were forced to discard that part when the Los Angeles autopsy surgeon's report showed that three bullets found in the bodies and trunks were all of the same calibre. Their earlier statement on two guns had been based on the fact discharged shells of two calibres were found in the trunks."

It seems like a plausible explanation. It just wasn't true.

Officers never found any .32 caliber bullets in the trunk. The only bullets or shell casings they found were .25 caliber. The files of the state archives include two original reports from the Los Angeles police detailing the contents of the trunks—one meticulously. Nowhere in those reports is there any mention of a .32 caliber bullet.

Besides, all the original stories said the two-gun theory came from the lips of the autopsy surgeons—not the contents of the trunks.

Suspicions are not satisfied when the explanation for an explosive piece of information is wrong.

Were the reporters just mistaken in the first place? Possibly. Not likely. As I've documented, the competition between the Los Angeles dailies was fierce and cutthroat. The cop shop reporters especially made their careers on outscooping their rivals. Here was the biggest scoop of all—a case so explosive it dominated the news for months in a city that was nothing but a destination point in the crime scenario. For the *Times* and *Examiner* reporters to make the same mistake, either they had to be sharing information—a ridiculous idea—or they both had to mishear the autopsy surgeons say there were two bullets. (The *Republic* and the *Gazette* initially got the information on the two bullets from wire service stories. The Associated Press was reporting the .25 caliber gun found in the luggage was the weapon used "to kill one of the women." So a *third* reporter heard wrong?) Those trained doctors could have been mistaken about the caliber of the bullets they removed from the victims. The caliber of a bullet refers to its width. Ennis says he can visually tell the difference between a .25 caliber and a .32 caliber, but that doesn't mean the surgeons could.

Wouldn't it seem, however, that if the surgeons had made such a mistake—especially one so widely reported and so crucial in the police investigation—they would have wanted to correct it? And wouldn't the simplest correction be to specify the caliber of the bullets in the written autopsy reports?

If this was really a mistake, it was an extremely strange and suspicious one. Considering the number of strange and suspicious twists I uncovered in this probe, I'm still left wondering if it was a mistake at all.

It wasn't until July of 1991 that I seriously doubted that Winnie Ruth Judd killed Anne LeRoi.

It has long been quite clear that she shot Hedvig Samuelson—exactly as she's always described it. The stab wound in Sammy's shoulder was the clincher. While she was in custody in Los Angeles, Ruth told how she had grabbed the flimsy bread knife. First of all, how could she have known about the wound? The press was focused on the fatal gunshots, not the superficial cuts and abrasions that had contributed nothing to the deaths. Second, if she'd shot Sammy in bed as she slept, there wouldn't have been an ineffectual stab wound at all.

Ruth Judd says the gun went off several times as the women struggled, just as the evidence shows. She says they were on the floor, rolling around, both of them clutching at the gun, when the final bullet ended the struggle—the bullet that went through Sammy's head.

Maricopa County coroner Heinz Karnitschnig twice reviewed the autopsy reports and trial testimony about the wounds. He was also supplied with Winnie Ruth Judd's explanation of the fight with Sammy. He concluded the fatal shot in Sammy's head "could have occurred" in such a fight.

But Anne's head wound could not have, Dr. K. said. She was shot with the gun up against her head, with the bullet traveling backward and downward. Ruth Judd said she shot as Anne was bending over her, "braining" her with the ironing board. If Ruth's version was right, that bullet should have been toward the front of Anne's head and certainly should have been traveling upward, not downward.

As Ruth Judd has always told the story, "I shot at Anne. When I woke up, I was lying between two bodies."

How is it possible that her story of the struggle can be so accurate for one victim and so inaccurate for the other? That is a question that has plagued me throughout this investigation.

It is a question that becomes even more intriguing with the suspicious news stories about two guns. Or when you start tracking the handgun found in the hatbox Ruth Judd carried on the train.

The .25-caliber gun belonged to Ruth Judd—a gift from her husband—but she always maintained she had left it at the girls' duplex when she moved to the Brill Street apartment. Prosecutors never contradicted that at her murder trial, nor did they ever explore the whereabouts of the gun during the fateful Friday night. Ruth told Sheriff McFadden that when she regained consciousness after the deadly fight, she fled the duplex, leaving the handgun behind. She said that when Halloran brought her back to the house later, she found the gun lying on the kitchen floor, picked it up, put it in her purse, and took it with her. Is it possible someone came into the house while Ruth Judd was back in her apartment, found Anne grazed but not dead, and put the gun to her head? Or is it possible Anne wasn't killed that night at all, but was only unconscious when she was put inside the trunk?

Some of these misgivings are underscored by the story the milkman told.

Milkman Wyman Owen of the Central Avenue Dairy told the *Republic* that he made his usual delivery at the duplex about 5 a.m. Saturday—hours after the killings. "I approached the service porch, as usual, on Saturday morning and heard someone stirring in the bedroom," he recounted. "So as not to frighten customers who stir when they hear me about their houses, I always rattle the milk bottles together. When I did so Saturday morning the noises subsided. It sounded like someone turning over in bed."

Owen said a fifty-cent piece had been left for him in payment for three quarts of milk. He put the milk in the icebox and left the thirteen cents' change on top of the cooler. On his usual rounds Sunday morning, he told the *Republic*, he saw that the thirteen cents was gone and someone had drunk about half a pint of the milk.

According to all the evidence, by Saturday morning Sammy's body had already been cut into pieces and Anne's body was still inside the big steamer trunk. So who was in the bedroom? Ruth Judd was in her own apartment by then, the evidence shows. The dirty deeds had been done and the house should have been deathly quiet. Yet the milkman distinctly heard someone.

He wasn't the only one who heard something strange that Saturday morning at the girls' duplex. So did neighbor Henri Behoteguy, a former secretary to the governor of Arizona. He later testified he heard what he thought were shots at the duplex about six-thirty Saturday morning, accompanied by the screams of a woman. Prosecutor Lloyd Andrews asked Behoteguy if it couldn't have been female laughter or revelry. He insisted it was not. It was a scream. Who was screaming in that house at that hour? The facts tell us there was no one alive to scream.

I have no pat answer for all these strange, puzzling questions.

I do know the evidence—the real evidence, not the fragments fraudulently presented to the jury—clearly shows:

Winnie Ruth Judd was not a cold-blooded killer.

This was not a premeditated murder.

She shot Sammy in a fight that left her wounded too.

She never took a scalpel to anyone.

She was a pawn in a ridiculous, cowardly disposal plan.

Yet her account of shooting Anne doesn't correlate with the fatal bullet that killed the young woman.

"I don't think Winnie Ruth Judd knows what happened," Hugh Ennis surmises. "She *thinks* she killed both those women, but did she, or was she led to believe she did?"

If she didn't kill Anne LeRoi, who did? And why?

Ennis maintains that the entire scenario of the crime smacks of something much more sinister than jealousy. He has long believed it possible the girls might have been killed to shut them up. "Blackmail certainly comes to mind," he says. Sheriff McFadden, from the start, advanced the idea that blackmail was involved. He told the press he thought the girls were killed because they knew too much about a narcotics organization. As he told the *Los Angeles Examiner*, "Without a shadow of a doubt the narcotics angle is plainly visible in this case. This isn't the first case we've had here where men and women have paid with their lives for knowing too much about the traffic in narcotics. I am convinced that the murder was bungled—that it was not carried out according to orders. When we find Mrs. Judd, I believe, if she isn't afraid to talk, we will learn the mysterious hold that someone had upon her. I am convinced that a man aided her in the sordid mess."

Virginia Fetterer, who was a young woman at the time of the crime, has always believed the girls were killed because they were blackmailing "powerful men in town" over an abortion ring. Indeed, news stories in the first days said authorities were investigating the possibility Sammy had died during an "illegal operation," with her body dismembered to camouflage the operation. In the 1930s, the phrase "illegal operation" was a nice way of saying "abortion." Anne Keim, the nursing aide from the state hospital, said Ruth Judd told her "one of those girls was pregnant." But there is no mention of pregnancy in the autopsy report on either victim.

Rumors about an abortion ring that was supposedly tied to the crime kept coming up during this investigation. But

I turned up no evidence to support the rumors. Ruth Judd's words back in 1932, however, raise an eerie possibility. She told the sheriff that on the night of the killings, Halloran immediately sought help from Dr. Brown and bragged he could count on Brown's assistance because he had enough on the doctor "to hang him." Could the doctor who "operated" on Sammy have been forced into it because he'd been part of an abortion ring? Unless Halloran was just swaggering, Dr. Brown had something so unsavory in his past that he would do anything to appease his friend, Jack. When Marian Lane is asked about all this now, she claims to know nothing.

Could either of those theories explain why Jack Halloran was "practically supporting" Anne and Sammy, as both Ruth Judd and Dr. Judd told officials? Was it just his generosity to the girls who entertained his friends that prompted him to give them money each month? If that was so, why wasn't he equally generous to the woman he was sleeping with regularly— Winnie Ruth Judd? There is no evidence that she was getting any financial help from Halloran before the killings. And the help she says he promised her afterward never came either.

There is no mistaking how the evidence stacked up against Jack Halloran. What is surprising is how *much* police and sheriff investigators discovered about his involvement in the crime—all of which has remained hidden until now. And if he had not been involved in something more, why would he have immersed himself in such a horrible mess instead of simply abandoning Ruth Judd that night?

Virginia Fetterer says she has known the truth for over fifty years.

"Winnie Ruth Judd wasn't even there when the girls were killed," she told me over the phone in early 1990, after my *New Times* series began. "I heard Halloran admit he'd done it."

Virginia's was one of nearly eighty phone calls I received in the aftermath of the articles. Most of them resulted in substantial information. Hers was a bombshell.

Virginia Fetterer was the daughter of Arizona pioneers. When she was a girl, her father had been a member of the Arizona legislature, and her favorite story is how she got him to sponsor a bill making the cactus wren the state bird.

She well remembers the New Year's Eve in the late 1930s when she encountered Jack Halloran, she told me. Virginia and her husband and a group of their friends had gone to downtown Phoenix to celebrate. After dinner, they went over to the "Adams Grill," the cover name for the well-oiled bar at the Adams Hotel. This hotel had long been the favorite gathering place in Phoenix. It was here that out-of-county lawmakers lived while the legislature was in session, and, as the folklore goes, more laws were made in the Adams Hotel bar than in the statehouse.

As Virginia described it, the streets of downtown Phoenix were blocked off to traffic on nights like New Year's Eve. There were street bands, and everyone wandered around drinking and dancing and visiting with friends in a town where everybody knew everybody. She told me as her party approached the Adams Grill, Halloran and his friends were coming out. "Somebody asked him a question, like if he could take care of a problem," she said. "And he was bragging that, sure, he could fix it. Then he said—I can't recall his exact words, but it was to the effect that if you knew the right people, you could fix anything in this town. He laughed and said that Winnie Ruth was out in the state hospital paying for what he'd done. He was bragging about it."

Then, she said, a drunk Jack Halloran staggered away.

"We weren't particularly shocked, because it was common knowledge he was involved," she added, noting she had never told any journalist the story before. "We were kind of shocked that he was admitting it in public."

Winnie Ruth Judd herself will not discuss any of this. I tried several times to bring up some of these revelations with her.

One day on the phone, I told her about my interview with McKechnie, relating that he wasn't convinced she was involved. "Well, I certainly was," she replied. "I certainly went to Los Angeles."

She quickly changed the subject before I could ask, "Are you trying to tell me that's *all* you did?"

Another time, I told her about Ennis's doubts that she was responsible for her friends' deaths. There was only silence on the other end. Finally she changed the subject and refused to go back to it.

I tried to tell her Virginia Fetterer's story, but the mention of Halloran's name turned her off and she made it clear she wasn't interested.

And then she begged me not to ask her any more questions about her case. "I can't talk about my case anymore," she said in a familiar refrain. "I just cry and cry and cry."

Eventually she broke off direct contact with me, communicating instead through a friend. Through this friend she sent me letters she'd received years ago from people who told her how happy they were she was finally free. "She wants you to know not everyone was against her," the friend explained.

By then I had an impressive list of people willing now—all these years later—to speak out on behalf of Winnie Ruth Judd.

"I have never regretted pardoning her," former governor Jack Williams told me.

"It doesn't appear she got a fair trial." Former Arizona Supreme Court chief justice Jack D. H. Hays was willing to state that it appeared she did not get a fair trial—not an easy admission for a judge with his conservative credentials.

"Can you tell her there were always a lot of people pulling for her," Virginia Fetterer requested.

"My grandfather—Dr. Jeremiah Metzger—was the superintendent of the state hospital when she was there and he thought she was sane as the day is long—he was very firm in his thoughts on that," Doug Turner told me.

"Tell her my father always thought she was a wonderful person and had gotten a raw deal," Renz Jennings, Jr., said on behalf of his deceased father, the county attorney who handled the preliminary hearing against Halloran.

Anne and Sammy got a raw deal too.

In tracking evidence and piecing together scenarios, it's easy to forget this story is also about two young women whose lives were tragically ended that Friday night in Phoenix, Arizona.

History well remembers the name of the woman accused of killing them; except for their families, nobody remembers the names of the victims. The last Phoenix news story about them makes you shudder: "Agnes Anne LeRoi and Hedvig Samuelson came home yesterday. They came as they went— as baggage."

Anne was cremated in Phoenix, and her ashes were sent to her family in Oregon. Sammy's body was eventually shipped to her elder brother, Samuel, who arranged for the funeral near their family's wheat farm in White Earth, North Dakota.

As the *Fargo Forum* reported at the time of her death: "The story of Miss Samuelson…was that of an average North Dakota girl who sought a normal school to complete her education, intending to enter the teachers' field. Until she contracted tuberculosis, she had taught regularly. Her life had been singularly without incident."

Sammy's death particularly affected her youngest brother, Arnold. He would go on to become the only acknowledged protégé of Ernest Hemingway. As Arnold's daughter, Diane Darby, later wrote in the foreword to his book, *With Hemingway*, the young man from North Dakota and the world-famous writer were drawn together by a most unusual circumstance. "At the age of nineteen," she wrote, "both men sustained a psychological shock that conditioned their view of life. With Hemingway, it was the near fatal wound he received in Italy during World War I. With my father, it was the brutal murder…of his favorite sister by Winnie Ruth Judd, which became infamous as the trunk murder case."

Were those mourning families ever satisfied that justice was done? In reading new stories on the unfolding murder trial in Phoenix—and all that came after—how often did they wonder what really happened that night? And how much more pain did their doubts cause?

Soon after my *New Times* series on Winnie Ruth Judd ran in early 1990, I called her in California. I held my breath as I asked her what she thought of the stories. "You said a lot of things that had to be said," she said. "I didn't know a lot of that. It was hard for me to read about it. Thank you for saying nice things about Mama and Father."

A month later, I called to tell her I was considering a book. "I guess that would be okay," she said timidly, although I wasn't sure she really meant it. I asked her if I could write out some questions for her to think about, and then come for another visit. She said she thought that would be all right.

But a few weeks after that, she changed her mind. "Don't you want the truth told?" I bluntly asked her. "What good would it do?" she responded, sounding so old and tired.

That was when she decided she didn't want to talk at all anymore.

Her friend who became my go-between later confided that she was afraid.

I am well aware how fearful Marian Lane still gets even after all these years.

I had just returned from our three-day visit in February 1990, when I got a frantic phone call. That day the *Republic* had run a "where is she now?" story about Ruth Judd. Reporter Randy Collier had found her unlisted number in California and called her for comments. She told him only that she was old and sick and liked living in Stockton, and then she hung up. The story included those few quotes and a recitation of the history of her case.

"I got a call from someone I knew at the prison," she told me in a frightened voice over the phone. "She said she saw the story and wanted to know what I was doing talking to a reporter. I told her I wasn't doing anything and she said, 'We saw what you told the reporter.' You know, my parole said I was never to tell my story. I don't want things stirred up again."

There was such pain in her voice. I understood instantly that she was terrified our interview would come back to haunt her. If a simple newspaper story with three quotes could bring a threatening call, she was convinced her talk with me was going to mean disaster.

I still remember my fury.

"Nobody has any right to do this to you," I raged. "Arizona has no jurisdiction over you anymore. It hasn't since 1983. And that clause that you couldn't tell your story was bogus in the first place. We have free speech in this country."

I tried to reassure her. I told her I'd write about the ridiculous call from the prison. I tried to soothe the fear she's known so long it's like a second skin.

She calmed down then, and our interviews continued for several months. But I know when she sits alone at night, that fear is still there.

I also know that the truth about this case had to be told.

It can't bring her justice.

It can't return those forty years of her life.

But I pray the truth can clear her name.

And bring her peace.

Acknowledgments

If Arizona didn't have such fine librarians and archivists, this book could never have been written. Over the years, these dedicated historians have carefully and aggressively compiled the records and files on the Winnie Ruth Judd case that comprise the foundation of this work. During the course of this investigation, they uncovered even more documents that opened long-closed doors. Their value to this book cannot be overstated.

Most sincere thanks go to Sharon Womack, director of the Arizona Department of Library, Archives, and Public Records. To state archivist David Hoober and his great staff, Jean Nudd, Carolyn Grote, and Steven P. Hoza. To Sarah McGarry, director of the Arts and Humanities Department at the Phoenix Public Library and to Burnice Armstrong, curator of the McClintock Collection in the library's Arizona Room. To Della Meadows at the Pinal Historical Society in Florence. To Ed Lambert, curator of education for the Arizona Historical Society in Tucson. To Barbara Judge at the Maricopa County Sheriff's Office. To Paul Diekelmann and Oscar Garcia at the Maricopa County Records Office. To Susie Sato at the Arizona Historical Foundation.

Out-of-state librarians also went out of their way to be helpful to this project. Most particularly, Ken Craven at the University of Texas at Austin; Dr. Bonnie Hardwick at the

University of California at Berkeley; Dacey Taube at the University of Southern California; and Andrea H. Halgrimson of the Fargo (ND) *Forum*.

Besides the historical documents these librarians provided, there were the invaluable insights of dozens of people who agreed to be interviewed to share their memories of the case. Many of them are quoted directly in the book, and I hope that will demonstrate their value and my appreciation. But a few need special mention. Retired Phoenix police captain Hugh Ennis could not have been more helpful or more dedicated to unraveling the truth. Private investigator Howard Sauter generously shared the voluminous files he compiled on the case. Maricopa County medical examiner Heinz Karnitschnig went far beyond the call of duty in studying the medical evidence. Attorney Larry Debus's persistence in getting me the interview with Winnie Ruth Judd was crucial, and then he went on to be helpful in so many ways I lost count.

The *New Times* of Phoenix deserves special thanks. I began research on this story for a two-part series I wrote for them in 1990. I want especially to thank executive editor Michael Lacey and president Jim Larkin. Extra thanks go to associate editor Ward Harkavy, who edited my original stories with skill, understanding, and honesty.

Then there are all the people whose names do not appear in this book, but whose help made it possible. These are friends, associates, and perfect strangers—all of whom shared the common goal of filling in the blanks so the whole picture of the Winnie Ruth Judd case could finally be seen. Some of them don't need to read the book—they've lived it with me for so long they already know all it has to say. To have friends like that—to keep friends like that through a project like this—is truly a gift I can never repay.

The very top of the list is shared by two precious friends, Mel Roman and Marge Injasoulian. Mel not only convinced me I could write this book but was passionate that I should write it. Then he opened up doors to help make it happen. I don't know which I appreciate more, his hand-holding or his pushing, but I'll never forget either. Marge proved herself such a good friend that she became a partner in the research of the book. She spent hours brainstorming on sources of information, then went on some interviews with me, read thousands of pages of documents and listened to hours of painstaking detail—all so she would be able to help me fit the pieces of the puzzle together. Without her, this would have been a lonely and painful project. With her, it was a joy.

Thank you, thank you, thank you to Linda Upton, Cynthia Hazeltine, Estelle MacDonald, Bruce MacDonald, Mary Margaret Sather, John Sather, John Douglas Cline, Joe Grassia, Linda Vachata, Cathy Eden, Scott Jacobson, Michael Burkett, Mary Bishop, Rory Hays, Cherrie Pennington, Jeb Rosebrook, Connie Koennen, Tommy Martinez, Georgia Alvarez, Barbara Hanson, Retha Williams, Larry Altherr, Sylvia Houle, Lois Boyles, Mike Arra, Athia Hardt, Kathy Busby, Charlotte Buchen, Mary Durand, John Jacquemart, Bill Hefter, Ree Cramer, Joy Casserly, J. J. Casserly, Budge Ruffner, Terry Greene, Monsignor Robert Donohue, Edward "Bud" Jacobson, Virginia Ullman, Nan and Dave Robb, Grace Goyette, Cookie Wascha, Rev. Tim Davern, Ted O'Malley, Paul Rubin, Joanne MacDonnell, Pete Corpstein, Sarah Wallace, Allan Stanton, Marvin J. Wolf, Pat and Jack Mason, Monsignor Ed Ryle, Heidi Ewart, Deborah Cox, Ann Kennedy, Pat Elliott, Tom Miller.

A special thanks to my agent, Barbara Lowenstein.

My deepest thanks goes to my demanding, relentless, "Mother Tiger" editor, Susanne Jaffe. And I was thrilled to have the expert copyediting of Jean Touroff.

My family was, as always, terrific. Their support and faith have always been an important component of my life, but now more than ever: my brother and sister-in-law, Gary and Trinity (who supplied the pencil); my sister, Judy; my brother, Duane; my nephews, Keith and Craig; my aunts and uncles and cousins.

In addition, several reference books were most helpful, especially in developing the historical perspective. They are: *Phoenix in Photographs, 1870–1970*, by Herb and Dorothy McLaughlin (Arizona Photographic Associates, Phoenix, 1970); *Phoenix—The History of a Southwestern Metropolis*, by Bradford Luckingham (University of Arizona Press, 1989); *Arizona*, by Odie B. Faulk (University of Oklahoma Press, 1970); and *All the Time a Newspaper—The First 100 years of The Arizona Republic*, by Earl Zarbin (Phoenix Newspapers Inc., 1990).

Most of all, I want to thank Marian Lane. If she hadn't found the strength to speak of Winnie Ruth Judd one last time, there would have been no reinvestigation, no discovery, no book. After hearing her stories of pain and suffering, I couldn't turn away. She is not only the subject but the inspiration of this investigation. And I will admit, she has touched my heart.

Remembering Winnie Ruth Judd

Reprinted with permission from *Phoenix Magazine*, February, 1999

It was the little things Miss Marian Lane of Stockton, California, did that express the true spirit of the woman once known as the Trunk Murderess of Phoenix.

She arrived in an upside down clown's outfit and all the children on my street came running. They were fascinated by two things: a costume so complex it came in two giant pieces, and the fact that it was worn by a tiny elderly woman with a shock of white hair.

"Wait 'til you see," she told the children (and me) as she put on all the pieces of the white suit covered with dots of purple and gold and red. All of a sudden, her face disappeared into the fabric and her entire appearance was transformed.

You'd have sworn she was a 6-foot-tall clown walking on her hands. Big gloves were sewn to the polka-dotted sleeves that covered her shoes. Giant shoes were attached to the soaring "legs" that rested under folds of cloth on her shoulders and went straight up into the air.

"Coooool," one of the kids said, and cool it was.

None of her adoring audience had any idea this was a remake of a costume the woman had first devised decades before, when her hair was still dark and there weren't any wrinkles on her pretty and famous face. They didn't know this was the costume the infamous "trunk murderess" Winnie Ruth Judd had worn for a party at the State Hospital for the Insane, where the state of Arizona kept her imprisoned from when she was 26 until she was 66. But even if they'd have known, I doubt they would have cared. To them, she was just an old lady with an incredibly cool costume who showed up at Jana's house the week of Halloween 1992.

I just kept smiling. "This is my friend, Marian," I told the children, using the name she'd started using some 30 years earlier when it was too dangerous and too painful to use her given name. As far as she wanted the world to know, Miss Marian Lane of Stockton, California, was paying a Halloween visit. In reality, Winnie Ruth Judd of Phoenix, Arizona, was coming to my home for the first time.

It was a pretty brazen thing to do, at that particular moment. Because the name Winnie Ruth Judd and all the grimy details of her life—were again on the lips of Phoenix that October, just as they had been in October of 1931 when this woman became a household name.

Just the month before, Simon & Schuster had published my book, a reinvestigation of her murder case, which remained, after all these years, one of the nation's most enduring crime mysteries. My probe concluded that history was wrong about Winnie Ruth Judd. Oh, she'd been involved in the deaths of her two girlfriends in a Phoenix duplex within an easy walk of my own home, but she wasn't the murderer, and certainly wasn't the "butcher" that history called her. Whatever crime she should have paid for, she paid 40 times over, first facing the gallows and then spending decade after decade in the "nut house" on 24th Street and Van Buren.

She'd been free since 1972, but had never talked to another reporter until I finally convinced her to talk with me in 1990. I apparently was the only exception in her blanket condemnation of the media, which had plagued her and dogged her and, in her worst nightmare, would find her again. I had promised I would never tell anyone where she was—and I never did.

I always found it intriguing that at this particular time, with so much attention being paid to her name and her history, that she'd choose to move back to Phoenix.

And now here she was in my front yard, in a most outrageous getup, and all I could do was smile. She'd told me on the phone that she'd read the book. Her only pronouncement was a short, "You did a good job." But being here at my home was proof that the book had not fulfilled her worst fears: that it would "just stir things up again" and accomplish nothing else. Already, the enormous media coverage had told her that people now were hearing her side of the story; were seeing the evidence that proved she wasn't the horrible monster she'd been labeled for six decades. While she'd once begged me not to write the book, she now was growing pleased that it had been written.

She greeted me warmly (if awkwardly), and we went inside for coffee.

She took off the costume and settled into a chair for a nice chat.

Finally, I cranked up my nerve enough to ask if she'd sign my copy of the book.

"What name shall I sign?" she asked. "Whatever name you're comfortable signing," I told her, knowing full well she hadn't signed her Christian name since the early 1960s.

I waited until she left to look at what she'd written.

And please forgive me if I still get a tear in my eye every time I open that book. Because after all those years, her own name was no longer so dangerous or so painful. She felt comfortable enough to sign "Winnie Ruth Judd."

Here's the way I'd usually answer the question, "Where is Winnie Ruth Judd these days?" I'd say, "She loves Stockton, California."

It wasn't a lie but it wasn't the truth. Yes, she did love Stockton, but she didn't live there anymore. (Still, I thought it was a most clever dodge.)

Sometimes the question was more direct and I couldn't squirrel out of it so easily. "I hear Winnie has moved back to Phoenix," a friend in the media said to me soon after she actually had. "No, she's in northern California," I lied. The friend didn't push it, and as far as I know, never tried to disprove it.

I can't count all the times I kept my promise never to tell. It wasn't hard, because once you knew Marian, you understood she feared nothing as much as the prospect that someday she'd open the door and a flashbulb would go off in her face as some crusty photographer said, "So Winnie, how's it goin' gal?" You can't dislodge fears buried at a time when photographers still used flashbulbs. All you can do is honor them.

But just because she was hiding out didn't mean she was hiding. Wherever she lived—alone at first, later at an elderly home, and, finally, with friends—she was outgoing, fun-loving and popular. Dozens of people came to her 80th birthday party. People who met her joined her army of protectors. Many who met her never realized who she was.

That was just the situation one day at the elderly home. I often visited her there, sometimes just stopping in to sit in her room; sometimes coming for lunch. She always loved to show off the nice grounds and introduce me to the friends she was making.

It was there that we experienced our funniest moment together.

One day we were walking to lunch—she was holding my arm as a secondary brace to her cane and a woman watching television in the day room rushed over and gushed that she'd read my book on Winnie Ruth Judd and she just loved it, and wasn't that some case and on and on.

Marian squeezed my arm as I smiled and demurred and thanked the woman for her kind words. As we walked away, Marian pulled me close and whispered, "She has no idea."

And then we giggled like school girls. If I close my eyes, I can still hear our glee.

Winnie Ruth Judd made me vote for Eddie Basha for governor.

She called me one day during his campaign against Fife Symington (who would win but lose the job when he became a convicted felon).

"Will you do me a favor?" she asked.

"Of course," I said.

"Vote for Eddie Basha."

"Marian, why would you care if I voted for Eddie or not?"

And then she told me a story drawn from 60 year-old memory banks.

Ruth Judd (she never was called "Winnie") was a 26-year-old medical secretary when she was arrested for the murder of her friends; one of them cut into pieces; both bodies stuffed into trunks taken as her baggage on the train from Phoenix to Los Angeles. Blood was leaking by the time they reached the station in downtown L.A.

She was returned to Phoenix to face trial. Her ailing, aging parents sold everything they had (which, as a Midwestern preacher, wasn't much) and came to Phoenix to be near their only daughter. They existed almost entirely on the generosity of Phoenix church people, who gave them shelter and food.

One of those people was Eddie Basha's father, who once gave her parents an entire turkey. "They'd never had a whole turkey in their lives," Marian told me. "So I want you to vote for Eddie to thank him back for what his father did for my parents."

And I did.

That little dog of hers made the cutest Santa puppy you ever saw.

That's how she dressed him when she brought him along to my annual Santa party. She came three times, and as I look over those pictures, it's amazing how fast she was aging.

But she loved this party, and, invariably, the children loved her.

There was something about Ruth Judd/Marian Lane that drew children to her. Maybe it was that her most unfulfilled dream was motherhood; maybe it was that she treated each child with such care.

Or máybe it was her spunk, because even as an elderly lady, she still had that spark of spunk that served her so well when she was young.

Some people in this town know more about Winnie Ruth Judd as an escapee of the State Hospital than they do as a convicted murderer. Phoenix kids now into their fifth and sixth decades remember shards of a rope-skipping song about her, with the erroneous line: "and she'll cut you to pieces."

Winnie Ruth Judd escaped from the State Hospital seven times, the last for more than six years.

The first time I met her, she shared the great secret of escapes that had so exasperated the Phoenix newspapers, they once suggested building a dungeon to hold her.

She took me into her bedroom in an apartment in Stockton and carefully removed a round black lacquer box from her bed stand. There's supposed to be a wooden knob on top, but it broke years ago and she held it in place with a piece of scotch tape. Inside this box was what she called her "survival kit."

It isn't much, but it went with her on each and every escape. The most important thing was a metal change purse imprinted with "Souvenir of Florida," which by now was all but worn off. Inside the purse (a gift from a nurse) were a few coins neatly slid into their slots. There was a clip on the lid to hold the bills. If you pried off the lid, there was just enough space to hide her most cherished possession: The key to the front door of the State Hospital.

The first time she told me she had the key I almost levitated off the couch in her small apartment. The key. To the front door. A present from some sympathetic soul whose identity she promised she'd never reveal and whose name went to the grave with her. She befuddled and confounded Phoenix for decades with escapes at will because she had the key to the front door of the crazy house.

I held that key in my hand that night so long ago and the two of us smiled and laughed and she had a sparkle in her eyes I saw only that one time.

As I wrote the book, that key—that simple piece of crafted metal—became a major triumph for this woman so badly abused and so excessively punished. I began to understand what it meant to her; I began to realize how it helped her survive and come out the other end, not all bitterness and bitchiness. Instead, there was a softness to her that reminded you of the word "grandmother."

Maybe that was what the children always saw as they hovered around her to show off their baubles.

The first year she came to my Christmas party, my friend Marge was the only one who knew who she was. Long after she'd left, the word slowly and quietly spread. I still have friends who won't forgive me for not alerting them.

But she was never invited to my home as a novelty. She was invited as my friend.

It was 1994 when she arrived with a tissue-wrapped present. "Put this under your tree," she told me, and I put the gift aside.

She'd already given me so many things I will always treasure: some of the beautiful crochet work she did so prolifically until her hands gave out (and bless the friend who gave me the handmade table runner she made for his family so many years ago). She gave me a beautiful table mirror she'd used for years to grace her dinner parties because she knows I like to entertain, too; and a dozen Christmas-tree-shaped molds she assured me were perfect for green Jell-O at the holidays.

Most of her gift-giving was spontaneous; given on a visit; handed over as she remembered. This was the first time for a present wrapped in tissue.

As I started to undo it, I began to suspect what it was. I had to stop and close my eyes just to catch my breath.

In my entire life, nobody had ever given me something so precious.

Winnie Ruth Judd felt safe enough.

Finally.

To give me her survival kit.

Winnie Ruth Judd died October 23, 1998, at the age of 92. She was buried somewhere secretly. There was no funeral. But that doesn't mean she wasn't mourned.

Final Thoughts for the Second Edition

Winnie Ruth Judd wouldn't have minded her front page obituary in *The Arizona Republic*, published on Saturday, October 24, 1998.

Ironically, the same Saturday 67 years earlier had her on the front page, too, but then it was because she'd just given herself up and was in custody in California for the grisly murder of her two best friends.

The Phoenix—and national—press back in 1931 didn't have much doubt about the guilt of this young beauty. Her claims of killing in self-defense were "absurd," and "inconceivable," the Phoenix papers reported on Saturday, Oct. 24, 1931.

Her obituary was far kinder. Most of the 32-inch story was devoted to quotes that debunked her reputation as the "trunk murderess."

Former Governor Rose Mofford said kind words about her; so did attorney Larry Debus. The story even quoted exonerating words from my book.

Ruth Judd, who went by the name "Marian Lane" would have been touched by those supporting words, although if she'd had her way, her passing would have passed without any notice in any newspaper.

To the very end, she feared the press would come after her and so she was buried in secret—even I don't know where.

I had to console myself with the last conversation I ever had with her, which happened about 10 days before her death.

I'd been sick and hadn't been appearing on the morning television show where I then worked. Marian called to be sure I was all right. I was lying on my couch when the call came and I was touched by her concern. She used her cheery voice, which I knew wasn't always indicative of how she felt, and her only complaint was that she was on oxygen all the time now and that really restricted her coming and going.

I suggested that once I was well, we should go out for Chinese food, which I knew was her favorite. I also knew she'd order Mongolian beef, because she always did. (She also loved the "awesome blossoms" at Chili's Grill & Bar.)

We never got a chance to have that dinner.

I found out she'd died when a California reporter called me. It was a sad way to get such sad news. I mourned for her privately, with close friends, and lit a candle for her at St. Mary's Basilica.

My mementos from her, of course, became all the more precious: The copy of my book that she'd signed, penning the name she'd tried to deny for six decades, "Winnie Ruth Judd"; the "survival kit" that had been her lifeline, including the infamous key that still fits the front door of the Arizona State Hospital; the lovely presentation mirror that is always on my dining table; the Christmas tree jello molds she knew I'd use.

After publication of the book, our relationship was primarily a private one, one of friends, one of looking forward, not backwards. In all the time I spent with her, we seldom went near her case or her pain—she had a lifetime to make up and was extremely good at marching forward.

But there was once, when I visited her along with another of her friends, that I dared broach the "tragedy" one more time. Her friend actually egged me on, since we both felt that given the right moment, Marian would reveal something we both felt certain was true.

Marian herself opened that door. She'd been sent a packet of old letters that she'd written from prison in the 1930s to a cousin back in the Midwest. She had one she specifically wanted me to read and it wasn't until I got into the second hand-written page that I realized why. Because it spoke directly to the most grisly part of the crime—the dismemberment of Sammy's body.

I remember holding my breath as I read the words she wrote in June of 1932. To paraphrase, she told her cousin that Dr. Charles W. Brown, who had done the dissection of Sammy's body, had died. She said he had a butcher knife in his hands and was apparently considering suicide when he died from a heart attack.

The words riveted through me, because those very words are quoted in my book, but not from the pen of Winnie Ruth Judd at the time, but from the pen of an Arizona historian who was writing the news to his friends at the *Los Angeles Times*.

Col. J.H. McClintock had sent that information to the editors at the *Times*, where he often wrote articles. After noting the heart attack and the butcher knife, McClintock said this: "This especially may be of interest to your men who took in the Ruth Judd trial. I understand that no evidence has been produced publicly, probably never will be produced, but I have heard a report that Brown was the individual who did the deft job of dissection."

Winnie Ruth Judd, of course, had no way of knowing Col. McClintock was telling a major newspaper the same things she was telling a cousin in Indiana.

After I read her letter, I mentioned how the information verified what Col. McClintock was writing, and she just nodded.

I felt I now had the opening I'd always wanted, and so I dared ask the question that most plagued me: "Marian, who killed Anne?"

"Well, I did," she answered immediately, perturbed at being asked.

"Are you sure," I ventured, quickly summarizing my findings of the second gun: initial news stories said Sammy was killed with a .25-calibre, while Anne, for whose death she had been punished all those years, was killed with a .32-caliber. (The press would later drop the two-gun theory like a hot potato and those that tried to explain it away, my investigation showed, made up their excuses.)

Besides, there's always been this vexing detail: If Jack Halloran came into this death scene after the killings, why wouldn't he just back out the door with a "see ya later, Toots." Why would he become so embroiled in all this?

I'll never forget the look in Winnie Ruth Judd's eyes as she listened to my words and seemed, for the first time in her life, to consider that something else had happened that night—something she had never known and never understood.

Our mutual friend offered more words to bolster my arguments, and Marian looked at her with the same astonished puzzlement.

And then she waved us off the subject as though the very thought of such things would destroy her.

I never brought it up again, and I'm betting her other friend never did either.

But I often wondered how many nights she lay awake trying to reconcile that revelation.

It told me something else. I had laid out all this information in my book. It was the dramatic ending of a book that I had always presumed Ruth Judd had read.

Her only critique had been "you did a good job,"—and you can imagine how inadequate that was to me when I had uncovered so much I hoped she'd now want to discuss.

She showed her approval of the book by purchasing dozens and dozens of copies that she sent to relatives and friends (often getting my signature before they went off.)

But I bet you she never read it. I bet she opened it up and tried to read it and found it all so painful that she couldn't go on. I'm betting she took her cues from friends who did read it and told her how it had revealed the truth about her case.

I'm betting that day in her living room when I told her about the two-gun theory was the first time she'd ever— ever, in all those 65 years—heard the idea.

I think of her often. Every time I entertain, I clean the presentation mirror and use it under my centerpiece. The picture on the cover of this book is in my office and I see it every day. Now and then I take out the survival kit and hold the key that had been her most precious possession.

I know that by the end, she had found some peace. I only hope I helped.

To receive a free catalog of other Poisoned Pen Press titles,
please contact us in one of the following ways:

Phone: 1-800-421-3976
Facsimile: 1-480-949-1707
Email: info@poisonedpenpress.com
Website: www.poisonedpenpress.com

Poisoned Pen Press
6962 E. First Ave. Ste 103
Scottsdale, AZ 85251